MONTREAL
MUSEUM OF
FINE ARTS

CONTINENTS

RIOPELLE

THE CALL OF NORT LAN

Edited by

ANDRÉANNE ROY
Art historian

JACQUES DES ROCHERS
Curator of Quebec and Canadian Art
(before 1945)
The Montreal Museum of Fine Arts

and

YSEULT RIOPELLE
Author and editor of the
Jean Paul Riopelle catalogue raisonné

AND IND CULTURES

HERN
DSCAPES

IGENOUS

1
Denise Colomb
Jean Paul Riopelle, Jacques Germain, Maria Elena Vieira da Silva, Pierre Loeb, Georges Mathieu and Zao Wou-ki
1953

In 1947, Riopelle met Pierre Loeb, who became his primary art dealer from 1952 to 1956. Loeb (shown here among artists of the Lyrical Abstraction circle) introduced the artist to Surrealists who collected non-Western art, in particular North American Indigenous art, including André Breton, Robert Lebel and Isabelle Waldberg.

2
Georges Duthuit in his University
Street studio in Paris with Riopelle's
Untitled (1954) and Northwest
Coast Indigenous objects in his
collection
N.d.

In 1948, Riopelle became friends
with Georges Duthuit, Henri
Matisse's son-in-law. The art
historian specializing in Byzantine
art and eritic of contemporary
art was also a collector of North
American Indigenous art.

3

3
Jean Paul Riopelle
Hochelaga
1947
Oil on canvas

THIS BOOK IS PUBLISHED
IN CONJUNCTION
WITH THE EXHIBITION

*RIOPELLE: THE CALL
OF NORTHERN LANDSCAPES
AND INDIGENOUS CULTURES*

INITIATED, ORGANIZED AND
TOURED BY THE MONTREAL
MUSEUM OF FINE ARTS.

THIS PUBLICATION IS DEDICATED TO THE RECENTLY
DEPARTED ART HISTORIAN FRANÇOIS-MARC GAGNON.

Exhibition Curators

ANDRÉANNE ROY
Art historian

JACQUES DES ROCHERS
Curator of Quebec and Canadian Art
(before 1945)
The Montreal Museum of Fine Arts

and

YSEULT RIOPELLE
Author and editor of the
Jean Paul Riopelle catalogue raisonné

Montreal
THE MONTREAL MUSEUM OF FINE ARTS
November 21, 2020–March 21, 2021

TOUR

Whistler
AUDAIN ART MUSEUM
May–September 2021

Calgary
GLENBOW MUSEUM
October 2021–March 2022

THE MONTREAL MUSEUM OF FINE ARTS

MICHEL DE LA CHENELIÈRE
President

DANIELLE CHAMPAGNE
Director General, Foundation

PASCALE CHASSÉ
Director, Communications

MARY-DAILEY DESMARAIS
Director, Curatorial Division

MÉLANIE DEVEAULT
Director, Education and Wellness

MATHIEU LAPERLE
Director, Administration

CAROLINA CALLE SANDOVAL
Acting Head, Exhibition Administration

SYLVIE OUELLET
Coordination

RICHARD GAGNIER
Head, Conservation

Exhibition Design
EXHIBITION PRODUCTION
in collaboration with TBA, Montreal

The exhibition *Riopelle: The Call of Northern Landscapes and Indigenous Cultures* is presented by Hydro-Québec, and was made possible by the generous contribution of the Audain Foundation. This project is funded by the Government of Canada, and benefits from the support of its partners Hatch, the Riopelle Foundation, Heffel Fine Art Auction House and Tourisme Montréal.

The Museum would like to acknowledge the invaluable contributions of its official sponsors, Air Canada and Denalt Paints, the Angel Circle of the Montreal Museum of Fine Arts and its media partners Bell, *La Presse* and *Montreal Gazette*.

The exhibition benefited from Heritage Canada's generous Canada Travelling Exhibition Indemnification Program. The Museum is grateful to the Ministère de la Culture et des Communications, to the Canada Council for the Arts and to the Conseil des arts de Montréal for their ongoing support. The Museum's International Exhibition Program receives funding from the Exhibition Fund of the Montreal Museum of Fine Arts Foundation and from the Paul G. Desmarais Fund.

The Museum would also like to thank its Volunteer Guides for their unflagging support, as well as the members and various individuals, corporations and foundations that magnanimously contribute, especially the Fondation de la Chenelière, headed by Michel de la Chenelière, and Arte Musica, headed by Pierre Bourgie.

The Museum sincerely thanks all those whose generous help, encouragement and support made this exhibition and scholarly publication possible.

MONTREAL MUSEUM OF FINE ARTS

PRESENTED BY

MAJOR PUBLIC PARTNER

MAJOR PATRON
THE | AUDAIN FOUNDATION

IN COLLABORATION WITH

HATCH
JEAN PAUL RIOPELLE FONDATION | FOUNDATION
Heffel
TOURISME / MONTREAL

OFFICIAL SPONSORS
AIR CANADA   DENALT

MEDIA PARTNERS
Bell   LA PRESSE   MONTREAL GAZETTE

PUBLIC PARTNERS
CONSEIL DES ARTS DE MONTRÉAL   Montréal
Canada Council for the Arts   Conseil des arts du Canada
Québec

4

4
Jean Paul Riopelle
La roue (Cold
Dog – Indian Summer)
1954–55
Oil on canvas

LENDERS

For making this exhibition possible with their loans, we thank the following institutions and people, including those who preferred to remain anonymous:

CANADA

BAIE-D'URFÉ

La Fédération des
coopératives du Nouveau-Québec
Richard Murdoch

CALGARY

Glenbow Museum
Donna Livingstone,
President and Chief Executive Officer
Allison Musial, Exhibits Coordinator
Melanie Kjorlien, Vice President,
Access, Collections and Exhibitions
Joanne Schmidt, Indigenous Studies Curator
Daryl Betenia, Manager, Collections
Katie Fisher, Registrar, Collections

CHURCHILL

Itsanitaq Museum
Lorraine Edna Brandson, O.M., Curator

GATINEAU

Canadian Museum of History
Mark O'Neill, President
and Chief Executive Officer
Christine Quinn, Acquisitions
and Loans Registrar
Benoit Thériault, Collections
Information Specialist – Archives
Vincent Lafond, Collections
Information Specialist – Photo Archives

JOLIETTE

Cécile Newashish

MONTREAL

Stephen Angers

Charles Dutoit

Galerie Eric Klinkhoff

Galerie Simon Blais

Louis Gill

Lune Rouge
Guy Laliberté, Founder
Robert Blain, Chief Executive Officer
Sylvie François, Director of Collections

McCord Stewart Museum
Suzanne Sauvage,
President and Chief Executive Officer
Guislaine Lemay,
Curator, Material Culture
Karine Rousseau, Assistant Head,
Collections Management

Power Corporation of Canada
Paul Maréchal, Curator

MONT-SAINT-HILAIRE

La Maison amérindienne
Chantal Millette, Executive Director
Audrey Renaud, Head of
Administration and Education

OTTAWA

Canada Council for the Arts
Amy Jenkins, Head, Canada Council Art Bank
Nancy Smith, Exhibitions and
Outreach Assistant, Canada Council Art Bank

Global Affairs Canada
Kerry Goodfellow, Manager and Curator
Leah Iselmoe, Assistant Curator

National Gallery of Canada
Alexandra Suda, Director
and Chief Executive Officer
Cayla Morency, Registrar,
Loans and Art Transit

QUEBEC CITY

Musée national des beaux-arts du Québec
Jean-Luc Murray, Director General
Phyllis Smith, Technician, Acquisitions
and Documentation Management

Yvon M. Tardif, MD

SAINTE-MARGUERITE-DU-LAC-MASSON

The Champlain Charest family

Huguette Vachon

CATALOGUE

This book is published by the Publishing Department of the Montreal Museum of Fine Arts in association with 5 Continents Editions, Milan, in conjunction with the exhibition *Riopelle: The Call of Northern Landscapes and Indigenous Cultures*.

Edited by
ANDRÉANNE ROY
Art historian

JACQUES DES ROCHERS
Curator of Quebec and Canadian Art (before 1945)
The Montreal Museum of Fine Arts

and

YSEULT RIOPELLE
Author and editor of the
Jean Paul Riopelle catalogue raisonné

MAIN PUBLISHER
The Montreal Museum of Fine Arts

PUBLISHING DEPARTMENT

PUBLISHER
Sébastien Hart
Department Head

EDITORIAL SUPERVISION, TRANSLATION AND REVISION—ENGLISH
Clara Gabriel
Translator-Reviser

EDITORIAL SUPERVISION, TRANSLATION AND REVISION—FRENCH
Juliette Hérivault
Translator-Reviser

COPYRIGHT
Linda-Anne D'Anjou

TRANSLATION
Judith Terry

REVISION
Donald Pistolesi
Kathleen Putnam

COORDINATION
Anna Ciociola

DOCUMENTATION
Manon Pagé

PROOFREADING
Jane Jackel

GRAPHIC DESIGN
Paprika, Montreal
Joanne Lefebvre, Louis Gagnon,
Daniel Robitaille

PHOTOENGRAVING
Photosynthèse, Montreal
with Yseult Riopelle

ASSOCIATE PUBLISHER
5 Continents Editions, Milan

EDITORIAL COORDINATION
Elena Carotti

PRODUCTION DIRECTION
Annarita De Sanctis

© 2020 The Montreal Museum of Fine Arts / 5 Continents Editions s.r.l., Milan for the present edition
ISBN The Montreal Museum of Fine Arts: 978-2-89192-427-6
ISBN 5 Continents Editions: 978-88-7439-943-7

Also published in French under the title:
Riopelle : à la rencontre des territoires nordiques et des cultures autochtones

ISBN Musée des beaux-arts de Montréal: 978-2-89192-428-3
ISBN 5 Continents Editions: 978-88-7439-942-0

Distribution in Italy and Canton Ticino: Messaggerie Libri S.p.A.
Distribution throughout the world, excluding Italy: ACC Art Books

Legal Deposit: 4th quarter 2020
Bibliothèque et Archives nationales du Québec
National Library of Canada

The Montreal Museum of Fine Arts
www.mbam.qc.ca

5 Continents Editions
www.fivecontinentseditions.com

Printed and bound in August 2020 by
Conti Tipocolor, Calenzano (Florence), Italy

MONTRÉAL
UNESCO CITY OF DESIGN

5
Jean Paul Riopelle
Un coin de pays
1962
Oil on canvas

AUTHORS

MICHAEL ARVAARLUK KUSUGAK (MAK)
Arvaarluk (Michael Kusugak) grew up in Repulse Bay, Northwest Territories (now Naujaat, Nunavut), living a traditional Inuit lifestyle. He first heard Inuit legends in his grandmother's igloo. He is the author of fifteen children's books, many of which have been nominated for various awards; his body of work in children's literature earned him the prestigious Vicky Metcalf Award in 2008. Arvaarluk recently moved to Manitoba. He continues to write and travel extensively throughout Canada and the world, telling stories.

NATHALIE BONDIL
Art historian Nathalie Bondil, head of the Montreal Museum of Fine Arts from 2007 to 2020, earned international recognition for her humanist vision of museums and her commitment in the fields of education, social and community action, and art therapy. In 2011, the Museum expanded by opening a fourth building, the Claire and Marc Bourgie Pavilion of Quebec and Canadian Art. Thanks to a gift of Old Master paintings from benefactors Michal and Renata Hornstein, Nathalie Bondil inaugurated the Pavilion for Peace in 2016, the fifth in the Museum complex, followed in 2019 by the Stéphan Crétier and Stéphany Maillery Wing for the Arts of One World. Under Bondil's leadership, the Museum exported its exhibitions to over forty cities. The recipient of numerous honours, she is Vice-Chair of the Canada Council for the Arts.

SERGE BOUCHARD
Serge Bouchard is an anthropologist, writer and broadcaster who takes every opportunity to share his passionate interest in the history of Indigenous peoples, nordicity and francophone America. He has conducted field studies in the Côte-Nord region, Labrador, Nunavik, James Bay and the Yukon. As well as publishing some twenty books, Bouchard has hosted several noteworthy programs aired on the Radio-Canada Ici Première radio network. An outstanding communicator, he has for the past three decades lectured across Quebec and Canada on subjects ranging from the Indigenous experience to various philosophical and topical issues affecting the contemporary world.

DANIEL CHARTIER
Daniel Chartier is a professor at the Université du Québec à Montréal, where he holds the Research Chair on Images of the North, Winter and the Arctic, and serves as Director of the International Laboratory for the Multidisciplinary Study of Representations of the North. In recent years, he has published about twenty books and close to a hundred articles on the representation of the North, the Arctic and winter, and also on Quebec, Inuit and northern cultures, cultural pluralism and the aesthetics of reception. They include *Le lieu du Nord* (2015), *Le froid* (2018) and the multilingual essay *What Is the Imagined North? Ethical Principles* (2019), published in French, English and fourteen northern and Arctic languages.

JACQUES DES ROCHERS (JDR)
Jacques Des Rochers has been Curator of Quebec and Canadian Art (before 1945) at the Montreal Museum of Fine Arts since 2002. He developed the exhibition concept for the collections under his care displayed in the new Claire and Marc Bourgie Pavilion, inaugurated in 2011, which incorporates a contemporary Indigenous perspective. He also edited the first catalogue devoted to this corpus, published for the opening. More recently, he co-curated (with Brian Foss) the exhibition *1920s Modernism in Montreal: The Beaver Hall Group* (2015–16), and co-edited the catalogue. Both projects have earned a number of awards.

FLORENCE DUCHEMIN-PELLETIER
Florence Duchemin-Pelletier holds a doctorate in contemporary art history. Her dissertation, defended in 2014, examines the reception of contemporary Inuit art in France from the 1950s to the present. From 2015 to 2018, she was a resident at the Institut national d'histoire de l'art in Paris, where she coordinated the project *Art global et périodiques culturels*. She has taught successively at the Université Paris Nanterre, the École des arts de la Sorbonne and the Université Lumière Lyon 2.

STACY A. ERNST
Stacy A. Ernst is a PhD candidate (ABD) in Cultural Mediations at the Institute of Comparative Studies in Literature, Art and Culture at Carleton University, Ottawa. Her current research examines intersections between modernisms, nationalisms, sovereignty and decolonization in the context of art made north of the 49th parallel by Indigenous and non-Indigenous artists. Her writing has appeared in the journals *World Art* (Spring 2016) and *RACAR* (Spring 2017).

LEENA EVIC
Leena Evic has been an essential voice in Nunavut, articulating a vision that is grounded in Inuit knowledge and wisdom passed along through the centuries. She is the Founder and President of the Pirurvik Centre, an Inuit-owned company dedicated to Inuit language, culture and well-being. In 2016, she was awarded the Meritorious Service Cross by Canada's Governor General in recognition of Pirurvik's transformative programs since 2003. Before launching Pirurvik, Evic was the Director of Social, Cultural and Educational Development with Nunavut Tunngavik, the Inuit organization that signed Canada's largest land claims agreement. She was also the Director of Policy for the Department of Justice in the Government of Nunavut, which was created in 1999 as part of the land claim. She holds a Bachelor's in Education from McGill University, where she also did graduate work on educational leadership and culture-based education.

FRANÇOIS-MARC GAGNON (FMG)
Dr. François-Marc Gagnon, a specialist in Canadian visual culture, was a teacher, scholar and lecturer. He taught at the Université de Montréal for thirty-five years before becoming Director of the Gail and Stephen A. Jarislowsky Institute for Studies in Canadian Art at Concordia University. He published numerous books, including *Paul-Émile Borduas: biographie critique et analyse de l'œuvre* (1978) and *Chronique du mouvement automatiste québécois, 1941-1954* (1998). His monograph *Jean Paul Riopelle and the Automatist Movement* (McGill-Queen's University Press) is being published posthumously.

LOUIS GAGNON
Louis Gagnon has organized over fifty exhibitions of Inuit art, using a visual semiotics approach. At the same time, he has dedicated himself to developing a form of museology adapted to the sociocultural environment of Nunavik. Since he joined the Avataq Cultural Institute as curator in 2003, he and his team have created a museology service and a museum reserve, the Qarmaq. He also served for ten years as the Director of Aumaaggiivik, the Nunavik Arts Secretariat. For close to twenty-five years, he has been participating in the scientific studies conducted at the petroglyph site at Qajartalik, which is featured on UNESCO's tentative list of world heritage sites in Canada.

SHAWN HUNT (SH)
Shawn Hunt is a Heiltsuk artist born in Waglisla (Bella Bella), British Columbia. Hunt's practice is directly informed by his Scottish, French and First Nations background and the visual culture and traditions that accompany them. He works with the traditional Northwest Coast design principle, known as formline, to create abstract, surreal and sculptural artworks based on ancestral Heiltsuk cosmology that often reference contemporary Indigenous life. After graduating from the University of British Columbia, Vancouver, Hunt apprenticed for five years with his father, Bradley Hunt, a prominent Heiltsuk artist. From 2012 to 2015, he apprenticed with Coast Salish painter Lawrence Paul Yuxweluptun. Hunt's work has been exhibited throughout Canada. In 2011, he was awarded the BC Creative Achievement Award for First Nations' Art. Hunt lives and works on the Sunshine Coast, British Columbia.

MARI KLEIST
Mari Kleist is Inuk, born and raised in Nuuk, Greenland, and has maintained a strong connection to her culture. She is an independent researcher, guest lecturer and external examiner at Ilisimatusarfik, the University of Greenland, Nuuk. She did her Bachelor's in cultural and social history at Ilisimatusarfik, and received her Master's degree in arctic archaeology from Memorial University of Newfoundland, in Saint John's. For her doctoral research at the University of Copenhagen, she examined various art carvings commonly found on sites across Canada and Greenland, investigating the social and historical importance of these carvings in Dorset society.

DUANE LINKLATER (DL)

Duane Linklater is Omaskêko Ininiwak from Moose Cree First Nation and he lives and works in North Bay, Ontario. His current practice explores the conceptual and theoretical structures of specific Indigenous architectures, namely the Mîkiwahp (teepee). These sculptural and architectural explorations are articulated in a careful selection of media and processes: lodge poles, linen, stone, large format printing, natural Indigenous plant dyes and drawing materials, which all produce unexpected outcomes within an installation context. He has presented solo exhibitions across the United States and Canada, and has taken part in international group exhibitions since 2012. Linklater was the 2013 Sobey Art Award winner.

CHUNA MCINTYRE (CM)

Chuna McIntyre is a Central Yup'ik elder, born and raised in Eek, Alaska, along the Kuskokwim River. He is the founder and Director of *Nunamta* ("of Our Land") Yup'ik Eskimo Dancers, which has travelled the world, sharing Alaska's native cultural heritage. McIntyre has spent more than three decades performing for Inuit and non-Inuit groups and working to restore Yup'ik cultural traditions and language; he has been declared a National Living Treasure by the Yup'ik people. He is a chief consultant on Yup'ik culture to the Smithsonian Institution, Washington, DC, and curator of the permanent Inuit installations at the de Young Museum, San Francisco.

SEAN MOONEY (SM)

Sean Mooney is Chief Curator for the Rock Foundation, one of the largest private collections of Indigenous arts in the world. He additionally holds the position of Curator of the Edmund Carpenter Collection of Arctic Art with the Menil Collection, Houston, Texas. He is the former Director of Exhibition Design with the Solomon R. Guggenheim Museum. Mooney has produced more than 200 exhibitions around the world over his museum career spanning some thirty years. He writes regularly on a variety of art-related topics, mostly emphasizing the Indigenous arts of the Arctic regions and other Native American groups.

RUTH B. PHILLIPS

Ruth B. Phillips is Canada Research Professor and Professor of Art History at Carleton University, Ottawa. Originally trained in African art history, she has taught and written primarily on Indigenous North American art history and critical museology. She served as Director of the UBC Museum of Anthropology and is a fellow of the Royal Society of Canada. Her recent publications include *Native North American Art* (2nd edition) with Janet Catherine Berlo; *Museum Pieces: Toward the Indigenization of Canadian Museums*; and *Mapping Modernisms: Art, Indigeneity, Colonialism*, co-edited with Elizabeth Harney.

YSEULT RIOPELLE

Educated during the 1960s in Montreal, Paris and New York, Yseult Riopelle possesses a multidisciplinary artistic background that encompasses dance, jewellery, sculpture, ceramics and art teaching. In 1988, her father, the painter and sculptor Jean Paul Riopelle, assigned her exclusive responsibility for the authentication of his works, and commissioned her to research and publish his catalogue raisonné. Since 1999, she has published the first five of the catalogue's nine volumes, along with a number of other books. She has been working as a consultant, expert and curator since the 1980s.

ANDRÉANNE ROY (AR)

Art historian and museologist Andréanne Roy has been working in the field of modern and contemporary art for the past fifteen years. She has occupied a variety of positions, both in the museum milieu and in the sphere of artist-run centres and private galleries. A PhD candidate in art history at the Université de Montréal, she is currently working as a curator and author on several independent projects. The notable exhibitions she has curated include *Riopelle à Saint-Fabien-sur-Mer, 1944-1945 : les années charnières* (2013), presented at the Musée régional de Rimouski.

BRUCE HUGH RUSSELL (BHR)

Born in Vancouver in 1952, Bruce Hugh Russell studied at the Vancouver School of Art and Concordia University in Montreal. An independent curator and art historian, he has written on contemporary art and art history for *Canadian Art, Studies in Visual Communications* and *Parachute*, as well as for the Canadian Centre for Architecture, the Belkin Gallery at the University of British Columbia, the Ottawa Art Gallery, the Montreal Museum of Fine Arts and the National Gallery of Canada. He recently retired as a sessional instructor for the University of Saskatchewan, teaching art history to Indigenous undergraduate students in the northern community of La Ronge.

MARC SÉGUIN

Marc Séguin, who graduated in fine arts from Concordia University, is a multidisciplinary artist active as a painter, writer and filmmaker. His paintings are represented in the collections of a number of major museums, including the Musée d'art contemporain de Montréal, the Montreal Museum of Fine Arts and the Musée national des beaux-arts du Québec. He has published four novels and a collection of poetry, as well as directed and writen the script for *Stealing Alice* (2016), his first full-length feature film. In 2017, he made the documentary *La ferme et son État*, a highly topical portrait of the forces driving Quebec agriculture and the aberrations it embodies.

GUY SIOUI DURAND

A Wendat (Huron) from Wendake, near Quebec City, Guy Sioui Durand is a sociologist (PhD), artist, art critic and independent curator who also teaches at the Kiuna Institution in Odanak and the Université du Québec à Montréal. His main fields of interest are contemporary and Indigenous art. He is a member of the Yanariskwa' clan (Wolf clan), participates in the gatherings and ceremonies of the Yanonchia' (the traditional Longhouse) and supports the Wendat language revitalization project.

JEAN TANGUAY (JT)

Jean Tanguay trained as an ethnohistorian. In fall 2012, he joined the team at the Musée de la civilisation in Quebec City, where he occupies the position of curator in the Collections Department. Previously, he worked as a heritage consultant for Parks Canada, specializing in the commemoration of places, figures and events associated with the history of Quebec's Indigenous peoples. Over the years, he has collaborated on the organization of a number of exhibitions, including the recent *Des images dans la pierre : l'art rupestre au Canada*, presented virtually by the Musée de la civilisation. Author of numerous articles and reports, he also co-edited *Voix, visages, paysages : les Premiers Peuples et le XXIᵉ siècle* (2016) and co-wrote *Les Wendats du Québec : territoire, économie et identité, 1650-1930* (2013), which was awarded the Prix de l'Assemblée nationale du Québec in 2014.

KRISTA ULUJUK ZAWADSKI

Krista Ulujuk Zawadski was raised in Igluligaarjuk (Chesterfield Inlet) and currently calls Rankin Inlet, Nunavut, her home. She completed a Master's degree in anthropology at the University of British Columbia in 2016, and has focused her education and career in the heritage sector in Nunavut and in the field of museology, with an emphasis on fostering accessibility to collections for Inuit. Zawadski is currently studying at Carleton University in an interdisciplinary PhD program.

AKNOWLEDGEMENTS

The Montreal Museum of Fine Arts is grateful to all those who, through their generous cooperation, encouragement and support, have helped make this exhibition and its catalogue a reality.

The Museum extends warm thanks to all the project's collaborators. First, its partners in circulating the exhibition: at the Audain Art Museum, Dr. Curtis Collins, Director and Chief Curator, and at the Glenbow Museum, Donna Livingstone, President and CEO, Melanie Kjorlien, Vice President, Access, Collections and Exhibitions, and Joanne Schmidt, Acting Curator, Native North America Collection.

The project has been made possible by generous support from the Audain Foundation, the exhibition's Major Patron, and we are most grateful to Michael J. Audain, Founder, and Chantal Shah, Executive Director. The Museum also thanks the Jean Paul Riopelle Foundation and Manon Gauthier, Executive Director, for their collaboration.

The Museum wishes to extend a very special thank you to Yseult Riopelle, whose outstanding work on the catalogue raisonné of her father's oeuvre and the numerous contacts she has established in seeking to identify the collectors of his works have greatly facilitated our research. For loans, research interviews and their support throughout the project, the Museum also warmly acknowledges Champlain Charest and Monique Nadeau, as well as Huguette Vachon.

We are also particularly grateful to the many lenders without whom the exhibition would not have been possible.

A number of loans have been the fruit of vital contributions from art dealers, auction houses and independent consultants, following rich and productive discussions. The Museum thanks, in Montreal, Simon Blais and Sylvie Cataford (Galerie Simon Blais), whose support has been unwavering; Eric Klinkhoff (Galerie Eric Klinkhoff); Stephen Angers (Galerie Angers); and Sophie Ouellet (Galerie Cosner). In Montreal and Vancouver, David K. J. Heffel, Robert C. S. Heffel, Patsy Heffel and Tania Poggione (Heffel Auction House). In Toronto, Miriam Shiell (Miriam Shiell Fine Art). In Paris, Morgan Gordon and Isabelle Maeght (Galerie Maeght); Frank Prazan (Applicat-Prazan); Julien Flak (Galerie Flak); Jessica Rémy (Tajan); Paul Nyzam (Christie's); and Olivier Fau (Sotheby's). In London, Cassi Young (Christie's). In New York, Michael Findlay, Eleanor Dejoux and Maeve Lawler (Acquavella Galleries); Caitlin Foreht (Christie's); Daniela Lazo-Cedré (Sotheby's); Donald Ellis (Donald Ellis Gallery); and Suzanne Modica (Modica Carr Art Advisory).

The exhibition curators also wish to acknowledge the many people who have enabled them to broaden their knowledge through fascinating discussions on the project's principal themes or aimed at discovering relevant written or iconographical sources: Elena Akpalialuk (Uqqurmiut Centre for Arts & Crafts, Pangnirtung); Madeleine Arbour; Pierre-Olivier Brault (Club L'Andalousie, Mont-Laurier); Janine Carreau; Danielle Charest; Andrew Coon; Pierre Desmarchais (Domaine Bazinet, Sainte-Émélie-de-l'Énergie); Karine Echaquan; Ray Ellenwood; René Gagnon and Claire-Hélène Hovington; Martin Gauvreau; René Gimpel (Galerie Gimpel & Müller, Paris); Roseline Granet; Mireille Gravel (Nibiischii Corporation, Mistissini); Rémi Labrusse; Gilles Lambert (Aviateurs Québec, Montreal); Jean-Jacques Lebel; Frédérique Lucien and Louis Gagnon (Avataq Cultural Institute, Montreal and Inukjuak); André Michel; David Moos; Jean-Jacques Nattiez; Cécile Newashish; Tanguy Riopelle; Marie Roberge; Marie Saint Pierre; Pamela Saunders (Microsoft Vancouver); Theo Waddington and Corinne Waldberg.

In their recommendations and the rewarding exchanges we have had with them, several of the guest authors have been of particular help: we gratefully acknowledge Florence Duchemin-Pelletier, François-Marc Gagnon, Ruth B. Phillips, Bruce H. Russell and Guy Sioui Durand. We offer thanks to the following individuals for having proposed potential authors for the catalogue: Christian Coocoo (Conseil de la Nation Atikamekw); Henri Dorion; Julie Edel Hardenberg; Anna V. Hudson (York University, Toronto); Heather Igloliorte (Concordia University, Montreal); and Andrew Kear and Darlene Coward Wight (Winnipeg Art Gallery). We also wish to salute the enthusiasm with which contemporary artists Alison Bremner, Shawn Hunt, Mattiusi Iyaituq and Duane Linklater agreed to take part in the project.

The Montreal Museum of Fine Arts extends gratitude to a number of other individuals and institutions who have enabled us to accomplish this project: Janne Sirén, Director, and Catherine Scrivo Baker (Albright-Knox Art Gallery, Buffalo); Shelley Falconer, Tobi Bruce and Christine Braun (Art Gallery of Hamilton); Shannon L. Parker (Art Gallery of Nova Scotia); Carolyn Brucken and Sarah Signorovitch (Autry Museum of the American West, Los Angeles); Tom Smart and Celine Gorham (Beaverbrook Art Gallery, Fredericton); Joanne Belzberg; Allison Andrachuk, Director and CEO (The Bill Reid Centre for Northwest Coast Studies, Vancouver); Kathryn Bunn-Marcuse (Burke Museum, Seattle); Philippe Bettinelli (Centre national des arts plastiques, Pôle collection – Cnap, Paris); Bernard Blistène, Director, Didier Schulmann, Raphaële Bianchi and Sennen Codjo (Centre Pompidou – Musée national d'art moderne – Centre de création industrielle, Paris); Mary-Dailey Desmarais; Anne Eschapasse; Brooke Perrin (Galerie de Bellefeuille, Montreal); Geneviève Goyer-Ouimette, Benoît Légaré and Isabelle Corriveau, who were involved in the project's initial stages; the Michael Hackett-Hale Collection (San Francisco); Jessica Phillips, Director (Hackett Mill, San Francisco); David Roche, Director, and Diana Pardue (Heard Museum, Phoenix); Erell Hubert; the Honourable Serge Joyal, P.C., O.C., O.Q.; Lisa Qiluqqi Koperqualuk; John Zeppetelli, Marie-Ève Beaupré, Anne-Marie Zeppetelli and Beatriz Leyva Calderon (Musée d'art contemporain de Montréal); Jean-François Bélisle, Nathalie Galego and Émilie Grandmont Bérubé (Musée d'art de Joliette); Nathalie Thibault (Musée national des beaux-arts du Québec, Quebec City); Stéphane Martin, President, Yves Le Fur, Paz Nuñez-Regueiro and Laurence Dubaut (Musée du quai Branly - Jacques Chirac, Paris); Philip Dombowsky (National Gallery of Canada, Ottawa); Natasha Johnson (Phoebe A. Hearst Museum of Anthropology, University of California, Berkeley); the Susanne and William E. Pritchard III Collection, Houston; Jessie Sentivan (Kay Sage catalogue raisonné); Marc Séguin, Gilles Gagné and Gina Vézina for the reception they gave us on Île-aux-Oies; Dale and Nick Tedeschi; and Jocelyne Faucher and Suzanne Pressé (Université de Sherbrooke, Galerie d'art du Centre culturel).

Thanks go too to all the teams at the Montreal Museum of Fine Arts who have worked on the production of this exhibition and its accompanying catalogue. The musical program was entrusted to Arte Musica, under the direction of Isolde Lagacé. As part of the project, the composer and violonist Alissa Cheung was commissioned to create a work premiering at Bourgie Hall, Montreal, on December 1, 2020, performed by the Quatuor Bozzini. Paprika is responsible for the splendid design of this catalogue, and 5 Continents Editions, Milan, has participated wholeheartedly with the Museum on the project.

6
Jean Paul Riopelle
Paysage d'autrefois
1977
Oil on canvas

Museums play a vital role in our communities. They allow us to discover the people and events that shaped our country's history while also showcasing our rich cultural heritage. That is why our government is committed to helping museums in their mission.

The exhibition *Riopelle: The Call of Northern Landscapes and Indigenous Cultures* provides a new perspective on the works of this renowned Canadian painter. The 150 works by Jean Paul Riopelle will allow visitors to learn more about his craft as well as the vast northern territories that are home to Indigenous cultures, which his paintings bring to life.

As Minister of Canadian Heritage, I would like to thank the Montreal Museum of Fine Arts as well as those who helped bring together this inspiring exhibition.

The Honourable Steven Guilbeault
Minister of Canadian Heritage

RIOPELLE'S NORTH:
A LAND OF TOTAL FREEDOM

It was not for nothing that the author André Breton dubbed Jean Paul Riopelle a "superior trapper." As the pope of French Surrealism had astutely observed, many of Riopelle's works are like vanishing points opening onto vast spaces, while others seem steeped in a nostalgia for untamed nature.

Riopelle was profoundly Québécois in the love, admiration and awe inspired in him by nordicity, from which he drew his essential coherence. Migratory birds in flight towards the pole, the artistic and cultural heritage of Indigenous peoples, boreal lands stretching to the horizon—all are symbols shared by those who see the North as a land of total freedom. This freedom, moreover, Riopelle never renounced, refusing to the end to be trapped by propriety or category, criticism or commerce.

The Ministère de la Culture et des Communications is pleased to be collaborating on this exhibition and this catalogue, which offer a foray into the breathtakingly beautiful nordicity of the one and only Jean Paul Riopelle.

Nathalie Roy
Ministre de la Culture et des Communications

Jean Paul Riopelle is the ultimate icon of freedom. His creative genius is inspired by his mythical love for nature in its many forms: the splendour of autumn foliage, the animals of the land, sea and sky and the ever-changing light above the Arctic snow.

As we make our way towards the centenary of his birth in 2023, the Jean Paul Riopelle Foundation is dedicated to broadening the appreciation of one of the greatest artists of the twentieth century, and to celebrating his contribution to the story of art.

We are honoured to support *Riopelle: The Call of Northern Landscapes and Indigenous Cultures* presented by the Montreal Museum of Fine Arts. Join us as we explore the landscapes, territories and cultures that inspired Riopelle and made such a profound impact on his oeuvre.

Riopelle once enigmatically remarked about his fascination with the Far North during a 1979 interview: "Icebergs are like ice cubes in a glass, they take on all the colours of everything around them." We embark on this remarkable journey across the northern landscapes and Indigenous cultures filled with that same wonder and awe.

Michael J. Audain, OC, OBC
Chair, Jean Paul Riopelle Foundation

Hydro-Québec is proud to present *Riopelle: The Call of Northern Landscapes and Indigenous Cultures* at the Montreal Museum of Fine Arts.

Hydro-Québec shares the Museum's vision of making the arts and culture accessible to citizens of all ages and from all walks of life. For this reason, Hydro-Québec is delighted to sponsor the Riopelle exhibition, which will give visitors a unique opportunity to discover a vast selection of his works and gain a better understanding of the influence that Indigenous art had on this remarkable artist.

Like Hydro-Québec, the Montreal Museum of Fine Arts is a Quebec jewel of international renown, so it was only natural for the company to contribute to the outreach of such a vibrant, accessible and forward-looking museum.

Julie Boucher
Vice President – Communications, Government Affairs and Indigenous Relations

7

8

I REMEMBER

SOME LARGER-THAN-LIFE ENCOUNTERS ON THE TRAIL OF JEAN PAUL RIOPELLE

Nathalie Bondil

1. *Riopelle* (Montreal: The Montreal Museum of Fine Arts / Connaissance des arts, 2002), p. 115.

2. The pan-Canadian exhibition *Riopelle: A Space of Freedom*, shown at the Centre d'exposition de Baie-Saint-Paul in 1998, consisting of works from the studio inventory, prefigured the exhibition at the Montreal Museum of Fine Arts. See *Riopelle* (Montreal: The Montreal Museum of Fine Arts / Connaissance des arts, 2002), p. 4.

3. *Riopelle*, 2002, back cover flap.

4. Eulogy given by Nathalie Bondil at the funeral of Bernard Lamarre, Mary Queen of the World Cathedral, April 15, 2016 (private archive).

5. Ibid.

6. Ibid.

7. Ibid.

8. Marie Pâris, "Laurentides : un resto dans le mythique bistro à Champlain," *Voir*, June 13, 2019: https://voir.ca/restos/2019/06/13/laurentides-un-nouveau-resto-dans-lancien-bistro-a-champlain/ (accessed July 15, 2020).

9. Champlain Charest to Nathalie Bondil, July 5, 2020.

10. According to Yseult Riopelle (July 5, 2020), Riopelle's plan dates to 1968, after the opening of the Fondation Maeght in 1964, but there are no documents of that time to this effect.

11. The exhibition *Riopelle* was held at the Montreal Museum of Fine Arts from November 26, 1991, to January 19, 1992.

12. Except for the magnificent painting *Autriche III*, acquired for the Montreal Museum of Fine Arts by Evan H. Turner in 1963.

13. Champlain Charest to Nathalie Bondil, July 5, 2020.

7
Éliane Excoffier
Paysage, Île-aux-Oies
2003

8
Marcel Masse, Riopelle, unknown, Clément Richard, and Bernard and Louise Lamarre at Château-Musée de Vallauris in France for the opening of the exhibition *Jean-Paul Riopelle : laves émaillées, terres, peintures* 1985

I REMEMBER JEAN PAUL RIOPELLE

It was cold and windy on the Saint Lawrence back in the fall of 2001. In my capacity as Chief Curator of the Montreal Museum of Fine Arts, I took a trip to the Isle-aux-Grues with my friends Stéphane Aquin, Curator of Contemporary Art, and his companion, the photographer Éliane Excoffier. We had been invited to the Manoir MacPherson, at the tip of the island, where Riopelle lived with his last companion, Huguette Vachon: "It's like being on a boat. I can hold out for a prolonged siege, spend the entire winter if necessary. An island is a sailing ship without a mast."[1] Huguette welcomed us. Later, we visited the studio, Le repaire, a little house suspended between the sky and the water that anchored Riopelle's connection with the land. The large, old-fashioned, pink cast-iron stove in the middle of the room was an amusing touch. A taxidermied goose frozen in flight hung from the ceiling. Through the windows, we could see the roiling river as it flowed seaward and, beyond the confines of the private hunting grounds, the public road of Île-aux-Oies. There was no smell of paint or turpentine—Riopelle no longer painted. The studio was a mausoleum. The artist had moved on. Éliane photographed the evening by candlelight—the state of the premises, the state of the god. It was all somewhat melancholy. We had come because we were planning a Riopelle exhibition at the Museum for June 19 to September 29, 2002.[2] We slept at the Manoir, where I was struck by the vitality of a paint-spattered wooden easel. We decided to borrow it. As it turned out, the exhibition was posthumous: Riopelle died not long after our visit, on March 12, 2002. He was given a state funeral. The easel, a symbolic absence, a monumental presence, was planted in an exhibition gallery like a cross: "Now my country is painting."[3]

I REMEMBER BERNARD LAMARRE

Art was not simply a diversion for this exceptional entrepreneur but, as he told me, "a source of inspiration for my life project, my professional project… It is artists I have taken as my model, it is they who inspired me… Meeting people with the ability to create stimulates me, encourages me to do the same in engineering and pushes me to try original things."[4] He considered his artist friends—Daudelin, Mousseau, Soulages, Riopelle—not "beneficiaries, but partners."[5] Impressed by *Refus global*, Bernard wanted, good-naturedly, to "thaw out our fellow citizens, make them enterprising, able to compete on the international scene, instill them with self-confidence and the desire to experiment."[6] His strength of entrepreneurial conviction always remained at the core of his strategy as a builder: "I owe my appetite for risk in part to artists."[7] He did not need to hope in order to undertake or to succeed in order to persevere. He was a pioneer, a giant in the vision of a modern Quebec and Montreal as a "cultural metropolis."

A jolly threesome saw each other often in Estérel; the Lamarre family's country retreat was in nearby Sainte-Adèle. They would gather for a fine meal at L'Eau à la bouche or at the restaurant Riopelle had christened Le Va-nu-pieds, in Sainte-Marguerite-du-Lac-Masson, near his studio. In 1974, the artist had alerted his friend Champlain Charest to the fact that the general store was for sale. Property developers wanted to demolish it and build a motel: "You have to buy it! This building cannot be demolished, it is too important to the village."[8] Famous for its wine cellar, a must for wine-lovers from here and abroad, the restaurant was later known as the Bistro à Champlain. Champlain recalls a witty remark made in the 1990s by Bernard—who was never at a loss for a pun—at a memorable feast in the studio, during which Riopelle was ruing the dearth of patrons in Quebec. "I'm no patron (*mécène*)," Mr. Lamarre said. "I watch my pennies (*me cennes*)."[9] In fact, he did a lot for the artist. With his friend Clément Richard, Quebec Minister of Cultural Affairs under René Lévesque, he supported the idea of a Jean Paul Riopelle Foundation, for which there were several attempts on paper as early as 1980.[10] In 1985, Bernard and Clément accompanied Riopelle to the Riviera for the opening of his exhibition of enamelled lava works at the Château-Musée de Vallauris. A major Riopelle retrospective[11] inaugurated the Jean-Noël Desmarais Pavilion of the Montreal Museum of Fine Arts, whose president at the time was Bernard Lamarre, the initiator of the largest cultural building project in Quebec. Although the artist was famous internationally for his lyrical abstraction, he was, alas, poorly represented in Quebec museums at the start of the twenty-first century.[12] For this reason, in 2001, Bernard Lamarre, still president of the Montreal Museum, convinced the Quebec government to grant it and the Musée national des beaux-arts du Québec funds for acquiring two large bodies of work from the artist's estate.

I REMEMBER CHAMPLAIN CHAREST

If ever there was a symbolic name, it is this instance of Champlain, evoking the figure behind the "grand design" for New France. The child was given the name by his grandmother in honour of the parish chaplain,[13] but to me it represents a kinship with the spirit of adventure. I met Champlain through the artist Marc Séguin and the chef Martin Picard, his hunting companions and gargantuan dinner companions. However, it is with Bernard Lamarre that, as a young museum director, I visited Champlain's collection—the Riopelles in particular—at Habitat 67 and, during an aesthetic and gastronomic outing, at his Sainte-Marguerite bistro. The two men enjoyed each other's company, and their easy conversation was a delight to their listener. In 2016, I informed Champlain that Bernard wished to say his farewell. It was an intense moment. Bernard died as he had lived, a winner. It is at such intense moments that the most binding promises are made, and I promised to organize an exhibition with Champlain. I set out on this project with Bernard's eldest son, Jean, an excellent man who died tragically in 2017. At the Museum's restaurant and at Champlain's bistro, presided over by the critical acumen of his taste buds, we listened to extraordinary accounts of the special friendship between Riopelle and his friend and patron. After the two men met in 1968, they hunted and fished together, which brought Riopelle back to this country more often. In 1974, their friendship grew stronger when the artist built a studio on the lot next to Champlain's in Estérel and they joined the Île-aux-Oies hunt club. A nomadic radiologist who owned a hydroplane, Champlain travelled in the North and the Far North of Quebec and Canada. To Riopelle it was an eye-opener that altered the form and iconography of his art. He expressed his admiration for the beauty of the North. Free in temperament and conviction, and united in their enthusiasm for the land and nature, hunting and fishing, food and wine, the two friends shared many an adventure, from the Laurentians to the Saint Lawrence, from the boreal forest to the Arctic Circle. Champlain played an indispensable role in Riopelle's aesthetic journey and his attachment to his native country, whose geography and fauna, with its bestiaries, anchor his work.

Through not only little-known works and unpublished documents, but also works from major collections, the exhibition *Riopelle: The Call of Northern Landscapes and Indigenous Cultures* reveals a facet of the artist's career—the influence of nordicity on his production—that has seldom been examined. On behalf of all our partners and teams, I thank the exhibition curators for applying themselves to this scholarly endeavour that renews our vision of Riopelle. After we asked Andréanne Roy to explore Champlain's archives and to broaden the subject, Jacques Des Rochers, our Curator of Quebec and Canadian Art (before 1945), joined the team along with Yseult Riopelle. The project thus grew in depth, in that since 2003, Mme Riopelle had herself been conducting in-depth research on nordicity in her father's oeuvre. At the invitation of the artist Marc Séguin, I returned to those islands in the Saint Lawrence with our three curators in 2018. I have known Marc, a mutual friend of Champlain, for a long time. He comes to the islands, where he occupies Riopelle's former studio, Le repaire. We were overcome with emotion on seeing Jean Paul's crushed paint tubes, preserved as relics. I have always been impressed by Marc's coherence, talent and development. He is an artist of immense territories, a hunter and a man of nature, an ecological entrepreneur, and his friend Champlain considers him the heir to Riopelle (whom Marc, too, is very fond of) but with one difference: Riopelle was a poor marksman and preferred to hunt images,[14] whereas Marc is a skilled hunter. In addition to Champlain, I wanted Marc to provide testimony here in writing. A page turns, and the story continues.

I WILL REMEMBER MICHAEL AUDAIN
This philanthropist collector, whom I first met in Vancouver in July 2017, has played an active role among the influential benefactors of the visual arts in Canada.[15] His family was from British Columbia, and he was nine years old when he arrived in Victoria with his parents in 1946, after living in Montreal. At seventeen, having visited the Royal BC Museum, he travelled by bus to Mexico to see the work of Diego Rivera and other radical Mexican mural painters. By turns a boxer, sailor, social worker, agricultural economist, property developer and activist, Michael led student anti-nuclear weapons protests at the University of British Columbia in the 1960s. An ardent defender of causes, culture[16] and grizzly bears, the businessman collects Mexican painting, Indigenous Northwest Coast art, contemporary Canadian art and Emily Carr,[17] as well as the Automatistes, Borduas and especially Riopelle, his great passion: "I have been fascinated by Jean Paul Riopelle since I was sixteen. That's a long time, for I am now eighty-two!… Today, I am happy to be among those who are seeing that Riopelle's work becomes more widely known and appreciated in Canada and elsewhere."[18]

That first meeting with Michael Audain was regarding plans for the exhibition *Riopelle: The Call of Northern Landscapes and Indigenous Cultures*. The Audain Foundation emphasizes, among other things, First Nations heritage, a project that coincides with our wish to intensify our activity involving Indigenous art. Retracing the travels that had fired Riopelle's imagination, and analyzing the various artistic and intellectual influences that had fuelled his interest in Canada's Indigenous cultures since the 1950s, this exhibition, in keeping with the intercultural perspective I consider vital, aims to create artistic links with Canada's northern areas and Indigenous cultures, in particular by including a selection of Inuit and Northwest Coast First Nations objects.

In 2018, Michael also established the Jean Paul Riopelle Foundation, of which he is the president, to further the status of the artist's work in Canada and abroad. "The foundation's objective is to promote the rediscovery of Riopelle's legacy as an iconic vision, a symbol of freedom, creativity and experimentation."[19] He has rallied two notable Riopelle collectors, André Desmarais and Pierre Lassonde, to his project, as well as the Honourable Serge Joyal, who has long supported the acquisition of works by Riopelle for the Power Corporation's outstanding collection; the art historian John R. Porter; and, of course, Riopelle's daughter, Yseult, co-founder of the Foundation directed by Manon Gauthier that makes a dream of Riopelle's a reality. Yseult has stated that she "always wanted to comply with Riopelle's wish, since 1968, to create a foundation along the lines of the Fondation Maeght, but with much greater breadth, encompassing artists' studios, exhibition areas, a large archive and an educational component."[20]

In discussing this exhibition with Michael in 2018, I learned that he was looking for a place to house his future Jean Paul Riopelle Foundation. I jumped at the chance and suggested the Montreal Museum of Fine Arts. An initial idea of installing the foundation in a nearby building on Du Musée Avenue was rejected, and I proposed instead to create Riopelle galleries at the top of the Jean-Noël Desmarais Pavilion. This idea was accepted by our new president, Michel de la Chenelière, and our two respective Boards of Trustees, and preliminary plans were quickly sketched out by Patkau Architects in concert with Provencher Roy. To pay glowing tribute to a giant of modern art, this transparent wing will be set opposite the wooded slopes of Mount Royal, in the heart of Riopelle's native city, immersed in dialogue with the nature and territory that so influenced him. Through tireless effort, a Quebec government subsidy supporting the project, with matching funds from the Jean Paul Riopelle Foundation, was secured on March 25, 2020, early on during the COVID-19 pandemic. Although the Museum's Riopelle collection has made spectacular gains in the past two decades—with more than four hundred works in all mediums—it is soon to be enriched in a most extraordinary fashion. Much remains to be done before this extension comes to be in 2023, the year of the Riopelle centennial and the 75th anniversary of the publication of the manifesto *Refus global*. What a wonderful gift to our visitors, to Quebec and to Canada!

I will remember Jean Paul, Bernard, Champlain, Michael and others. They embody the boldness of the pioneers, a creative pluck, a spirit of freedom, an uninhibited *joie de vivre*, pride in the land and the same willful affirmation that characterized the Quiet Revolution. The human heritage is immense. Today, our patrons continue to pave the way forward.

A chapter ends, but the story continues. And what wonderful memories!

14. See Guy Robert, *Riopelle, chasseur d'images* (Montreal: Éditions France-Amérique, 1981).

15. "Canada 150: Michael Audain among B.C.'s Most Influential Benefactors of Visual Art," *Vancouver Sun*, March 20, 2017: https://vancouversun.com/news/local-news/canada-150-michael-audain-among-b-c-s-most-influential-benefactors-of-visual-arts (accessed July 15, 2020).

16. He was Chair of the National Gallery of Canada (2009–2013), the Vancouver Art Gallery and the Vancouver Art Gallery Foundation, and a member of the British Columbia Arts Council.

17. His collection of works by Emily Carr and First Nations art has been given to the Audain Art Museum, in Whistler, and his collection of Mexican muralists, to the National Gallery of Canada.

18. Éric Clément, "Création de la fondation Riopelle : le rêve de Riopelle se concrétise," *La Presse* (Montreal), October 4, 2019: https://www.lapresse.ca/arts/arts-visuels/2019-10-04/creation-de-la-fondation-riopelle-le-reve-de-riopelle-se-concretise (accessed July 15, 2020).

19. Kevin Griffin, "Michael Audain heads Jean Paul Riopelle Foundation," *Vancouver Sun*, October 3, 2019: https://www.vancouversun.com/news/local-news/michael-audain-heads-jean-paul-riopelle-foundation/ (accessed July 15, 2020).

20. Clément, "Création de la fondation Riopelle."

9
Éliane Excoffier
Goose Hunting, Hiding in a Corn Field, Île-aux-Oies (from l. to r.: Marc Séguin, his son, Marc-Émile, and the hunting guide Gilles Gagné) 2003

10
Claude Duthuit photograph of Paul Rebeyrolle, Riopelle, Jacques Lamy and Champlain Charest on a fishing trip About 1975

9

10

11 | *Point de rencontre – Quintette* is the largest painting Riopelle ever made and the only one completed for an official commission. Executed in Paris for the Toronto Pearson Airport, it was given to France by the Canadian government to commemorate the bicentennial of the French Revolution. It was on display at the Opéra Bastille in Paris from 1989 to 2018. Its technique and composition are characteristic of the artist's production from the early 1960s, in which more clearly defined motifs stand out against a homogenous background. The title refers to Toronto and the history of the area's Indigenous occupants. The Huron word *toronto* can be translated as "place of meeting" (*point de rencontre* in French), pointing to the geographical importance of this crossroads by way of which Indigenous peoples made their way between Lakes Ontario and Huron. – AR

11
Jean Paul Riopelle
*Point de rencontre –
Quintette* (polyptych)
1963
Oil on canvas

11

12 I For a time, we lived at Nipissing First Nation, renting a house. Across the road lived our neighbour Doreen, and in her yard was a beautiful teepee. One summer, a storm toppled the teepee and damaged it. After the storm, she waved me over to help with taking her teepee down.

Unfurled on the ground, it bore signs of the many years of use by Doreen and her family. Discoloration of its mustard canvas from the sun and wind, smoke from countless fires imprinted in the fabric, the faded outlines of poles creating an incidental grid. We proceeded to fold the teepee into a neat bundle, after which she picked up the heavy canvas pack and unexpectedly said, "Here." Doreen's generous act precipitated an equal and reciprocative gesture. A long deliberate process ensued; for many years it lay silent in storage, the teepee cover resting in my mind.

Then, I proceeded to show it, put it up on the wall. Yet it called out for additional work and time. The proposition of showing this gift to point at an "uninterfered" exchange between Indigenous people seems particularly important and an idea that I have returned to time and time again. – DL

12
Duane Linklater
A Gift from Doreen
2016–19
Hand-dyed canvas,
teepee canvas, blueberry
extract, grommets, nails

13
Jean Paul Riopelle
Les masques (triptych)
1964
Oil on canvas

14

ᑕᑯᓚᐅᖅᓯᒪᓚᐅᙱᒃᑲᓗᐊᕋᒃᑯ Jean Paul Riopelle, ᐱᒃᑯᒋᕙᕋ ᖃᓂᒋᔭᖃᓚᐅᕐᓂᖓ ᑲᓇᑕᐅᑉ ᓄᓇᖃᖅᑳᖅᓯᒪᔪᖏᓐᓂᒃ, ᐅᕙᒍᑦ ᐃᓄᐃᑦ ᓄᓇᖓᓐᓅᖃᑦᑕᓚᐅᕐᓂᕐᒥᒍᑦ. ᐃᓅᓚᐅᖅᓯᒪᒐᒪ ᑕᐃᒪ ᓱᓕ ᐃᓄᐃᑦ ᓄᓇᒥᐅᑕᐅᑎᓪᓗᒋᑦ, ᐸᓐᓂᖅᑑᑉ ᓯᓚᑖᓂ. ᐸᓐᓂᖅᑑᖅ ᑕᐃᔅᓯᒪᓂ ᐃᓄᑭᑦᑐᑯᓘᑎᓪᓗᒍ ᐋᓐᓂᐊᕕᒃ, ᑐᔅᓯᐊᕐᕕᒃ, ᓂᐅᕕᖅᑎᒃᑯᑦ, ᐸᑖᓯᒃᑯᓪᓗ ᓄᓇᖅᑲᑎᒋᔭᐅᑎᓪᓗᒋᑦ ᐃᓄᓐᓄᑦ. ᓯᕗᓪᓕᖅᐹᒥᒃ ᐸᓐᓂᖅᑑᓕᐊᕋᒥ Riopelle ᑕᑯᒐᔭᓚᐅᖅᐹ ᐃᓄᐃᑦ ᐃᓕᖅᑯᓯᑐᖃᖓᑦ ᐊᓯᔾᔨᐸᓪᓕᐊᓂᖃᓕᖅᑎᓪᓗᒍ ᓄᑖᖑᓂᖅᓴᒧᑦ. ᐃᓄᐃᑦ ᐸᓐᓂᖅᑑᒧᑦ ᓅᑉᐸᓪᓕᐊᓕᓚᐅᕐᒪᑕ ᑕᐃᔅᓯᒪᓂ ᐅᑭᐊᓪᓕᕕᑐᖃᒥᓂᑦ. ᑕᑯᒐᔭᓚᐅᖅᐸᐃᓪᓗ ᓄᑖᑦ ᐃᓪᓗᑖᖅᑲᐅᑦ ᐃᓄᓐᓄᑦ ᐊᒻᒪᓗ ᓱᓕ ᐃᓚᖏᑦ ᖃᕐᒪᒥᐅᑕᐅᓯᖓᖅᑐᑦ.

ᐃᑉᐱᓇᖅᑰᔩᕗᕐᓗ ᖃᓄᖅ ᓂᕆᐅᓐᓂᖃᕐᓚᐅᕐᒪᖔᑦ ᑭᖑᓪᓕᕐᒥᒃ ᐸᓐᓂᖅᑑᓕᐊᓕᕐᒥᒐᒥ 1971-ᖑᑎᓪᓗᒍ. 1969-ᒥ ᑕᑯᒋᐅᓈᓚᐅᖅᑐᓂᐅᒃ ᐸᓐᓂᖅᑑᑉ ᑲᔅᓴᓇᕐᓂᐊᓗᐊ ᓲᕐᓗ ᓅᒪᔪᑦᑎᐊᒥᒃ ᓴᓇᔭᐅᓯᒪᒻᒪᑦ, ᖃᖅᑳᓗᖏᑦ ᐱᒃᑯᓇᖅᑐᐊᓗᐃᑦ, ᐊᐅᔪᐃᑦᑐᐊᓗᖏᑦ, ᑲᖏᖅᑐᖏᑦ ᓇᖅᓴᖏᓪᓗ ᑰᒐᓛᓛᑦ, ᐊᒻᒪ ᐱᖃᓗᔭᑦ. ᐊᖑᓇᓯᑦᑎᐅᒐᒥᓗ ᐃᓕᖅᑯᓯᕐᒥᒍᑦ, ᐊᑦᑐᖅᑕᐅᒪᔪᔅᓴᐅᓚᐅᖅᐳᖅ ᐅᒻᒪᔪᖃᕐᓂᖓᓄᑦ, ᐱᓗᐊᖅᑐᒥᓪᓗ ᐃᖃᓗᖏᑦ ᐸᓐᓂᖅᑑᑉ ᖃᐅᔨᒪᔭᐅᒻᒪᕆᓕᕐᓂᑰᔪᑦ ᑭᖑᓂᐊᒍᑦ. ᐃᒻᒪᖃᓗᖃᐃ ᓄᓯᐊᖅᑕᐅᔾᔪᑎᖏᑦ ᑕᒪᒃᑯᐊᖑᑎᓪᓗᒋᑦ, ᐃᒻᒪᖃ ᐸᓐᓂᖅᑑᑉ ᑲᔅᓴᓇᕐᓂᖓᓄᑦ ᓄᓯᑦᑕᐅᓕᖅᑭᑲᓐᓂᓚᐅᕐᒪᑦ 1977-ᖑᓕᕐᒥᑎᓗᒍ. ᐊᓪᓛᑦ ᐊᑦᑎᖅᑕᐅᒪᒻᒪᑦ ᐅᓪᓗᒥ ᐸᓐᓂᖅᑑᖅ ᓲᕐᓗᒎᖅ “Switzerland-ᒋᒻᒪᒍ” ᐅᑭᐅᖅᑕᖅᑑᑉ.

ᑕᐃᒫᔅᓴᐃᓐᓇᑖᓐᓇᕋᔭᓚᐅᖅᑐᖅ ᑕᑯᒥᓇᕐᓂᖓ ᐸᓐᓂᖅᑑᑉ – ᓄᓇᖓ ᓯᓚᖓᓗ ᓯᕐᕋᑦᑕᓗᐊᖅᑎᓐᓇᒋᑦ ᓱᓕ ᑕᐃᔅᓯᒪᓂ. ᑭᓯᐊᓂᓕ ᓲᒃᑲᓕᔪᒥᒃ ᐸᓐᓂᖅᑑᖅ ᐃᓕᖅᑯᓯᒃᑯᑦ ᐊᓯᔾᔨᓂᖅᑕᖃᓚᐅᖅᑐᖅ. ᓄᕕᖅᓴᕐᕕᒃ ᒪᑐᐃᖓᓕᖅᑐᓂ, ᐊᕙᓗᒥᐅᑕᑦᑎᐊᕚᓗᓐᓂᒃ ᓴᓇᕕᐅᕙᓕᖅᑐᓂ ᐃᓄᓐᓄᑦ, ᑎᑎᖅᑐᒐᕐᕕᒃ ᑕᑯᔭᔅᓴᓂᒃ ᐊᑐᐃᓐᓇᖃᓕᖅᑐᓂ, ᐊᒻᒪ ᐃᓄᐃᑦ ᓴᓇᐅᒐᖏᑦ ᐅᒃᑯᓯᔅᓴᑦ ᓴᖅᑭᔮᓪᓚᕆᓕᓚᐅᖅᑐᑦ.

ᑕᑯᓪᓗᒋᓪᓗ ᓴᓇᓯᒪᔭᖏᑦ Riopelle, ᐃᓚᐅᑎᑕᐅᖃᑦᑕᖅᑐᒥᓂᐅᕙᓗᑉᐳᖅ ᐃᓄᐃᑦ ᐊᖑᓇᓯᑦᑎᓪᓗᒋᑦ ᐊᕙᑕᐅᑉ ᐊᑐᖅᑕᐅᓂᖓ ᑕᑯᓯᒪᕙᓗᒻᒪᒍ. ᐃᒻᒪᖃᓗ ᐳᑖᕆᐊᖃᑦᑕᕐᓂᕋᒥ ᐃᓄᐃᑦ ᐊᖏᕐᕋᖏᓐᓄᑦ ᐊᔭᒫᖅᑐᓂᒃ ᐃᓚᐅᑎᑕᐅᕙᑦᑐᒥᓂᐅᕙᓗᑦᑐᖅ. ᐃᓄᐃᑦ ᐱᓐᓇᔭᓐᓂᖓᑦ ᐃᓅᓯᕐᒥᒍᑦ ᐊᑦᑐᐃᓂᖃᕐᕙᓗᔅᓯᒪᔪᖅ Riopelle ᓲᕐᓗᑦᑕᐅᖅ ᐱᓐᓇᔭᑦᑐᒥᒃ ᐃᓅᓯᖃᕐᕙᓗᓐᓂᑰᒻᒪᑦ. ᐃᒻᒪᖃ ᐃᓄᖕᒐᑕ ᓄᓇᐅᑉ ᐃᒪᐅᓪᓗ ᓴᐃᒻᒪᖅᑎᓚᐅᖅᑖ Riopelle ᐊᔪᙱᓐᓂᖓ.

ᓖᓇ ᐃᕕᒃ
ᐃᖃᓗᐃᑦ, ᓄᓇᕗᑦ

Although I never met Jean Paul Riopelle, I am intrigued by his enthusiasm and genuine connection to Canada's Indigenous cultures and people, in part through trips he made to our homeland, Inuit Nunangat.

I was born at a time when Inuit still lived on the land, in small permanent camps around Cumberland Sound. Pangnirtung was then a small post where Saint Luke's Mission Hospital, the Mission Church, the Hudson's Bay Company and the RCMP were based, along with some Inuit families. On his first visit in 1969, Riopelle would have witnessed the tail end of this era. The relocation of Inuit families from their traditional camps to town life in Pangnirtung was already underway. He would have seen newly constructed public housing units, while some families continued residing in *qarmat*, our traditional Inuit huts.

I can sense the anticipation he might have felt on his second trip to Pangnirtung in 1971. He had already seen the spectacular beauty of this place packaged in a grand design of majestic mountains, glaciers, icebergs, fiords and river valleys. As an avid hunter, the abundance of wildlife, Pangnirtung's famous Arctic char and a landscape that some have called the "Switzerland" of the Arctic would have spoken to him. He would return in 1977.

What he saw always remained as grand in great beauty—the land and climate were more stable then. However, changes in the small settlement were quickly transforming Pangnirtung. This included the opening of a weaving shop and the growing production of tapestries, prints and imaginative pieces of Inuit carving.

From his work, it is obvious that Riopelle saw the use of *avataq*, a float made of sealskin. Perhaps he enjoyed being taught *ajaraaq* (string games) while visiting Inuit families. The calming presence of Inuit left an equally calming influence on Riopelle. Perhaps, the spirit of the land and sea blessed his talent.

Leena Evic
Iqaluit, Nunavut

14
Claude Duthuit
photograph of Riopelle
in Pangnirtung, Nunavut
(detail)
July 1977

15

RIOPELLE AND THE CALL OF THE LAND: AN ADVENTURE BETWEEN TWO CONTINENTS

Andréanne Roy
Jacques Des Rochers
Yseult Riopelle

1. Marie-Charlotte de Koninck, "Territoire et construction identitaire," in *Territoires. Le Québec : habitat, ressource et imaginaire*, ed. M. C. de Koninck (Quebec City: Éditions Multimondes, 2007), p. I.

2. *Riopelle*, Rive Droite gallery, Paris, December 10, 1954–January 10, 1955. See the text herein by Florence Duchemin-Pelletier.

"Sculpture/totem = Creation/life"

– Jean Paul Riopelle, 1949

"A country opens up, reinvents itself, from a fragment to a whole, from canvas to canvas, like a broken sequence of indescribable events."

– Jacques Dupin, 1974

"For although Riopelle lives and works according to his own tellurism, the fact remains that his eye is able to feed off of fallen autumn leaves as much as off of the icebergs of Pangnirtung, and that, from the tales of Grey Owl, his imagination frolics between Monet's gardens at Giverny and the happy hunting ground, stopping on a whim before the emblematic figures of the Gitksan of Canada's Northwest Coast."

– Guy Robert, 1981

The exhibition *Riopelle: The Call of Northern Landscapes and Indigenous Cultures* spotlights two major influences that marked the artistic career of Jean Paul Riopelle. Driven by his empirical knowledge of Quebec and Canada's regions, nordicity and indigeneity translated poignantly into his work in the 1970s, at a time when he was in the country more often, mostly to hunt and fish. The two features appeared almost indistinguishably in Riopelle's work in relation to the notion of "territoire": "Space is physical; territory is space humanized."[1]

This northern imaginary that permeates Riopelle's output is now, for the first time, on display in a broad selection of key works and archival materials. To introduce a new perspective on the artist's approach, we go back over the trips that spurred his production, and examine the various artistic and intellectual influences that nourished his interest in North American Indigenous communities. Moreover, we have drawn unprecedented parallels by linking Riopelle's art with certain works that inspired him, principally through

a selection of Inuit masks and West Coast First Nations works. This method produces an alternative understanding of works that are quite different—in terms of formal or symbolic qualities—to better grasp what Riopelle envisioned and, at the same time, to honour the arts and material cultures of North American Indigenous peoples. It bears mentioning that Riopelle himself had thought of such a pairing in the context of an exhibition of his works held in Paris in 1954.[2]

Although the subjects of nordicity and indigeneity are highly topical these days, the origins of this exhibition project lie elsewhere. As early as 2016, the Montreal Museum of Fine Arts, looking to pay tribute to important local collectors and donors, conceived of an exhibition that would spotlight the role played by Dr. Champlain Charest in Riopelle's career, his important collection and his donations to the community. Great friends, the two men bonded while sharing their passion for hunting, fishing and flying, and together criss-crossed Quebec and made their way to the Far North, to today's Nunavik, as well as to the part of the Northwest Territories that is now Nunavut. In retracing their joint travels, our research further revealed the importance of the North and Indigenous cultures in Riopelle's process. Building on our initial observations, our project was then oriented around these two unifying subjects while, at the same time, situating the central role of Dr. Charest within the narrative we wanted to tell. It was

15
Basil Zarov
Jean Paul Riopelle outside of the Studio at Sainte-Marguerite-du-Lac-Masson with "La Défaite" in the Distance
About 1976

then that, having learned of plans for a major exhibition that Yseult Riopelle held dear and had been directing her research towards since 2003, we joined forces to come up with an exhibition of wider scope capable of shedding new light on the artist's approach. Following the 1991 and 2006 retrospectives of Jean Paul Riopelle's work held at the Montreal Museum of Fine Arts, the exhibition *Riopelle: The Call of Northern Landscapes and Indigenous Cultures* features a fresh look at two of the guiding themes that punctuated the output of one of Canada's greatest artists.

Looking into the sources of inspiration that could have sparked the artist's imagination with regards to our two themes, our discoveries revealed not only a nature-loving man—a well-known side of him—but also a cultured man who drew inspiration from the books he would devour and the exhibitions he took in, notably of First Nations and Inuit art. Besides enjoying the occasional company of Indigenous hunting and fishing guides, it was above all through books and exhibitions that Riopelle fuelled his interest in Indigenous communities and their lands and material culture. This intellectual and artistic pursuit had a particularly decisive impact on the artist in the 1950s and 1970s.

Also brought to light is the uncontestable sway of certain collectors from within the Surrealist milieu, especially the writer André Breton and the art historian Georges Duthuit. Not only was Riopelle able to become acquainted with their collections of non-Western objects, but he also maintained with them relationships that excited his interest in distinct cultures, especially those of North America. Many of the titles he gave to his abstract works speak to this. Yseult Riopelle's archival research has uncovered, among other things, new details regarding the intellectual connection between Riopelle and Georges Duthuit. They planned to co-publish a book inspired by the arts of the Pacific Northwest Coast, in collaboration with Marius Barbeau: Riopelle, who had met the Canadian anthropologist, was to have done the illustrations! We unearthed correspondence with the latter's son-in-law, the sociologist Marcel Rioux, that further testifies to this.

Furthermore, our research into the 1970s period has deepened what is known about the areas Riopelle visited in the North and produced a better sense of the fascination he had with them. A decade full of northern subjects— consider *Jeux de ficelles* (1971–72), *Rois de Thulé* (1973) and *Icebergs* (1977)—this period saw Riopelle take marked inspiration from Inuit culture and the northern landscapes. He was also influenced by the toponymy of the Indigenous peoples of Eastern Canada. As well, his attention continued to be turned towards the Pacific Northwest Coast during this decade, as seen especially in a series of silverpoint drawings incorporating the rich iconography inspired by several pieces in Duthuit's collection and borrowed from certain anthropological publications. We lift the veil on this little-known corpus by showing the sources that inspired them.

16 | As an active participant in the winter ceremonial life of his Kwakwaka'wakw community, contemporary carver Beau Dick brought to his work not only an initiate's understanding of the secret societies of his people, but also a wide knowledge of other coastal, as well as international and transhistorical, artistic traditions. Great artists are acutely aware of what they see, both within and outside their own cultures, and this is as true of Indigenous contemporary artists as it is of any others. Friends and critics, as well as Dick himself, have suggested influences as diverse as Japanese manga, the Italian baroque and neighbouring coastal traditions. From the perspective of his own mask-oriented material culture, Dick was attracted to the masks of the Alaskan Yup'ik. Closely based on a well-known prototype, Dick's "copy" introduces subtle touches to this work carved in his last years, like the carved hands that echo those used in his own culture's dances. – BHR

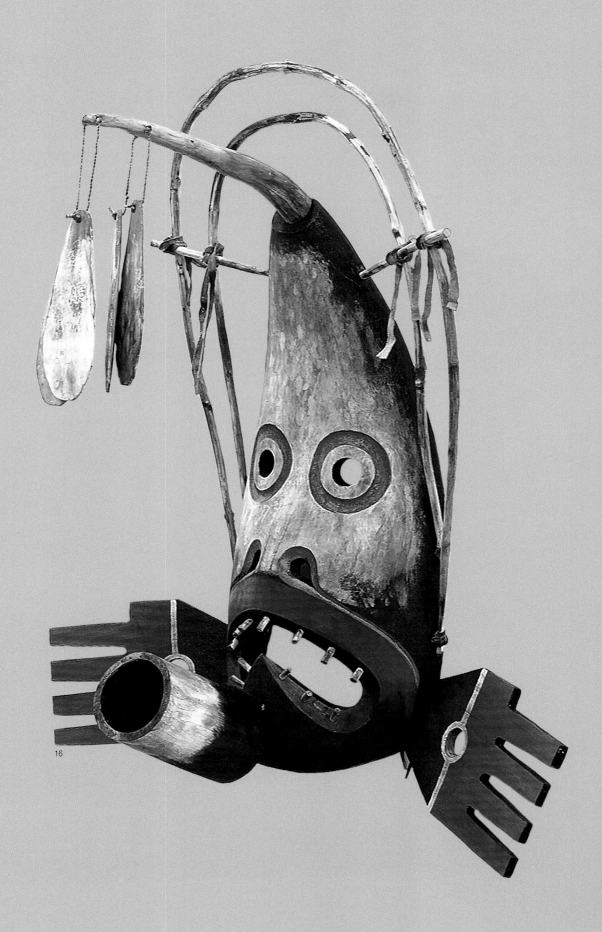

16

Beau Dick
Weather Spirit
N.d.
Wood, leather,
twigs, paint

Riopelle was a man of his time, a time that was not yet ready to question the dominant culture. Intercultural relations between Euro-Canadian and Indigenous peoples were not yet the subject of the postcolonial interrogations of today. Riopelle's production, with its borrowings of the arts and cultures of First Nations and Inuit and its titles referring to them, is today exposed to accusations of cultural appropriation, but, at the same time, it points to a rich body of little-known work to contemplate and elucidate. In fact, it may be more constructive and accurate now to showcase this production of another time by re-examining it critically, in order to give rise to an exploration of the divide and trajectory from the artist's early career in postwar Paris to today. We decided to revisit the work of this period from a new perspective informed by current approaches, through an interdisciplinary dialogue that links, in particular, art and anthropology. And to this end, we sought out the contributions of various authors from different fields of expertise, many of whom are members of the communities concerned.

Florence Duchemin-Pelletier, a specialist in the reception of contemporary Inuit art in France, looks at Riopelle's output of the 1950s executed in Paris, in particular the gouaches with titles making reference to "Eskimo"[3] and to "Gitxsan."[4] She describes the influence on the artist of works, including Yup'ik masks and Pacific Northwest Coast pieces, in the collections of various Surrealists and of the writings of the anthropologist Marius Barbeau. She also writes about the *Rois de Thulé* series (1973), which is, in part, influenced by the works Henri Matisse made for Georges Duthuit's book *Une fête en Cimmérie* (1963 and 1964). Moreover, she describes the connections between the artist and the Gimpels, who were London dealers exhibiting mainly Inuit art. Her essay provides insight into the French intellectual milieu in which Riopelle was to produce works inspired by Indigenous worlds.

Daniel Chartier, a specialist in cultural and literary history, examines Riopelle's "imagined north," a concept that contributes to the study of representations of the North. He shares his views on the artist's northern pictures by way of an examination of Riopelle's journey in conjunction with that of the geographer Louis-Edmond Hamelin, who came up with the neologism "nordicity." Featured in this essay is the unique connection of the artist to a nordicity deeply inscribed in his work, offering "a synthesis both personal and universal of the foundation and principles of winter and the North," whether in his figurative or his abstract work.

The Wendat (Huron) art sociologist and artist Guy Sioui Durand contemplates the closeness between Riopelle, the man and his work, and the Indigenous peoples of Quebec. He posits that Riopelle's vision is rooted in a "wild culture of the gaze," a way of being with nature characterized by "a keen sense of observation and a harmonious presence in the environment." This author offers an unparalleled reading of *La Joute* (1969–74) from an Indigenous viewpoint.

Inuit anthropologist Krista Ulujuk Zawadski looks at the series of acrylics on paper *Jeux de ficelles* (1971–72). Inspired by the Inuit tradition of *ajaraaq*—which entails making figures out of string, often to tell stories—the author contextualizes the series vis-à-vis the important cultural significance of string games among Inuit. She gives an overview of the presence of string figures in anthropological publications and underscores the influence of Guy Mary-Rousselière's book *Les jeux de ficelle des Arvilirgjuarmiut* (1969), which inspired the artist.

Greenlandic Inuk Arctic archeologist Mari Kleist turns her attention to the *Rois de Thulé* series. A specialist in Dorset culture, she posits a novel theory on the sources behind the series that looks like it could have drawn from the petroglyphs of Qajartalik, Nunavut, which were discovered in the early 1960s. She also traces the connections to other Dorset production, which Riopelle would have seen in exhibitions in Paris, and thus expands on the possible interpretations of this group of drawings.

Art historian and exhibition co-curator Andréanne Roy focuses on a group of oils on canvas dated to 1973. Executed after a long visit to James Bay, these works bear titles that connect to the areas visited and to nordicity. The author examines the role of these titles in the interpretation of the viewer and explores the artist's relationship to mimesis and to the landscape genre.

Anthropologist and great communicator Serge Bouchard takes a look at the use of Indigenous toponomy in Riopelle's production. He points out how various titles

3. "The word Eskimo is an offensive term that has been used historically to describe the Inuit throughout their homeland, Inuit Nunangat, in the arctic regions of Alaska, Greenland and Canada, as well as the Yupik of Alaska and northeastern Russia, and the Inupiat of Alaska. Now considered derogatory in Canada, the term was used extensively in popular culture and by researchers, writers and the general public throughout the world." Entry for "Eskimo" in *The Canadian Encyclopedia*, https://www.thecanadianencyclopedia.ca/en/article/eskimo (accessed June 8, 2020).

4. "Gitxsan (Gitksan), meaning 'People of the River Mist,' live along the Skeena River of north-western British Columbia in the communities of Hazelton, Kispiox and Glen Vowell (the Eastern Gitxsan bands) and Kitwanga, Kitwankool and Kitsegukla (the Western Gitxsan). In the 2016 census, 5,675 people claimed Gitxsan ancestry." Entry for "Gitxsan" in *The Canadian Encyclopedia*, https://www.thecanadianencyclopedia.ca/en/article/gitksan (accessed June 8, 2020).

5. Guy Viau, "Jean-Paul Riopelle," in *Jean-Paul Riopelle*, exh. cat. (Ottawa: National Gallery of Canada, 1963), n.p.

chosen by the artist, mostly in the mid-1970s, are evidence of his interest in the toponomy of the Indigenous peoples of Eastern Canada. Moreover, he examines this source of inspiration in the sociopolitical context of 1970s Quebec, where a newfound interest in the North and in indigeneity emerged.

Professor emeritus in art history François-Marc Gagnon, in an essay completed by Andréanne Roy, offers thoughts on the artist's relationship with mimesis by way of the seminal *Icebergs* series. He suggests that Riopelle's approach and connection to nature stems, rather, from *methexis* (participation), in the context of the artist's evolution (thanks to his trips to Pangnirtung) of an empirical knowledge of the Far North.

Art historians Stacy A. Ernst and Ruth B. Phillips examine a series of silverpoint drawings from 1977, the *Lied à Émile Nelligan* album (1977–79) and lithographs from 1979, which replicate Northwest Coast First Nations and Inuit works. They introduce us to a Riopelle inspired by the illustrations found in anthropological publications. In addition to tracing new sources of imagery, the two authors posit that the borrowings from Indigenous cultures made by Riopelle in his sociohistorical context are inscribed in an intercultural dialogic strategy.

Complementarily, Andréanne Roy also provides an interview with Champlain Charest, who was close friends with Riopelle and who accompanied him on several trips to Canada's boreal forest and Far North. It offers an introduction to a great, passionate collector of Riopelle's work and a donor who, through his gifts to the community, has played a part in the dissemination of his art. In addition, artist and author Marc Séguin proffers a personal view on Riopelle's career and on the importance, in his work and in his life, of the various regions of Quebec and Canada: the Far North, Estérel (where he built a studio in 1974) and Ile-aux-Oies (where he went hunting every year beginning in 1974). He highlights the role of Charest in helping the artist discover the Canadian territories that appealed to him.

The link between Riopelle and territory is obviously not new. It is also true that the artist's work was marked by the regions of France, where he had lived a long time, especially Île-de-France and southern France; many of his works and series are based on these. However, Riopelle, regardless of having lived in France or in Quebec, was strongly influenced by the regions of his native land, as the works presented herein make clear. We therefore found it relevant to recontextualize the indisputable importance of Canadianeity in the artist's approach: "Riopelle remains Canadian . . . Instinctively he retains a prodigious memory of his native country that leads us, through him to discover ourselves."[5] This exhibition, at the core dedicated to the 1970s, naturally goes back in time to explore how the artist had always maintained a certain rootedness in the land from which he came. This going back in time allows us to "get to know ourselves" and to probe and more fully grasp an era when the Quebec and Canadian North, in addition to the Indigenous communities living there, did not have the due interest directed at them today. It also helps us to appreciate, through the passing of time, the value and relevance of the work of Riopelle, a master of this, our time.

"SO, MY COME

FLORENCE
DUCHEMIN-PELLETIER

RIOPELLE INDIGENO

ESKIMOS FROM FRANCE":

AND THE US ARTS IN PARIS

"One day, I was in a restaurant. I saw a log by the fireplace. The pattern in the wood looked like the face of an Eskimo. I left with the log on my shoulder. I made imprints (**19, 20**). Later, there were manipulations, associations of images. . . So, my Eskimos come from France."[1]

Jean Paul Riopelle's work has often been interpreted in light of its Canadian origins. Certainly, the study of his paintings reveals a multitude of elements determined by the geography of his homeland, including a sense of space that reflects the vastness of the territory, a pictorial profusion that conjures its boreal forests and a thematic affinity with Indigenous knowledge and art. Yet the artist did not invariably approve this view, which, although it gave him distinction in the competitive postwar art world, failed to recognize the complexity of his singular path. When he first arrived in Paris, Riopelle the *coureur des bois* was no more familiar with Canada's northern reaches than he was sympathetic to the idea of taking root—for which he would later substitute the notion of "uprooting,"[2] in the sense not of a forced exile from which one hoped to return, but of a transcendence of national boundaries. It is really not surprising: Riopelle encountered his North in Paris through contact with the Surrealists and their associates, who since the 1920s had been casting a fascinated eye on the northernmost latitudes of America and the societies that lived there. In New York, during the war, Indigenous objects brought a welcome breath of fresh air: "We've plunged into the poetic atmosphere of Eskimo masks, we breathe Alaska and we dream Tlingit and we fall in love with Haida totem poles."[3] Back in France, they felt the impulse to transmit this knowledge. So it was in this intellectual and artistic context, driven by a profound belief in the regenerative power of Indigenous thought and in its corollary, the disintegration that results from deculturation, that Riopelle began exploring North America's Indigenous societies. The artists and theorists of Paris were not alone in shaping his vision, however. His meeting with the London dealer Charles Gimpel, a champion of contemporary Inuit art, would have the effect of broadening his perspectives.

Riopelle was already familiar with Surrealism when he arrived in Paris in 1947. In fact, he and his Montreal colleagues had for several years been practising a form of abstractionist visual automatism based on the Bretonian idea of the overturning of conventions and the liberation of creative forces. It was therefore natural that, once in France, the artist would seek to meet André Breton,

and it was the dealer Pierre Loeb (**1**) who arranged the introduction. Impressed by Riopelle's work, Breton invited him to take part in the *Exposition internationale du surréalisme*. Riopelle accepted, began frequenting the group and became a signatory of the collective declaration *Rupture inaugurale*. In 1949, he was given his first solo show at the La Dragonne gallery, run by Nina Dausset, where the Surrealists held weekly meetings. Breton substantiated his support for the young artist by providing a three-author foreword for the exhibition's catalogue (**23**), written jointly with Elisa Breton and Benjamin Péret. He also bestowed upon the artist the title of "superior trapper,"[4] a hugely and enduringly popular sobriquet that would be taken up in 1952 by the theorist Georges Duthuit (**2, 18**).[5] Full of poetic images, the foreword describes a North defined not only by Canada's landscapes but also by indigeneity: "If the Indians could come and see, they would be once more at home."[6] Interestingly, in a draft version Breton had included the word "finally" in the second clause—"the Indians . . . would be *finally* once more at home"[7]—offering a glimpse of the text's originally political thrust: the addition of the adverb alters the meaning by focusing on the restoration of a normality destroyed by Western colonialism, while simultaneously asserting the capacity of art to change the world—an idea dear to the Surrealists. Although the author ultimately dropped the term, the allusion to the encounter remained. This first association with Indigenous societies no doubt acted as a catalyst, encouraging Riopelle to begin exploring the extent of his affinity with them.

Wary of being tied to a dogma, however, the artist quit the Surrealist fold. But while rejecting the automatist doxa, he did not break with his Surrealist friends, notably the group of former New York exiles who had returned home with their suitcases full of masks and other objects. A few historical reminders will suffice here: it was from the dealer Julius Carlebach (**22**) that the group composed of André Breton (**53**), Enrico Donati, Georges Duthuit, Max Ernst, Robert Lebel, Claude Lévi-Strauss, Maria Martins, Roberto Matta, Bernard Reis, Yves Tanguy, Dolores Vanetti and Isabelle Waldberg made most of their purchases. In response to their obvious interest, Carlebach had come to an arrangement with the founder of the Museum of the American Indian, George G. Heye, who agreed to offer for sale pieces of less significance to him, among them objects of the Yup'ik and Northwest Coast peoples.[8] The fortunate enthusiasts, invited into the museum's annex in the Bronx, would point to the objects they wished to buy and then pick them up later from Carlebach's gallery. Although money was scarce, they were happy to impoverish themselves by spending it thus. The collection of images and the study of books on ethnography that were also part of their daily lives had an impact on their creative activity. For the Surrealists, animist beliefs corroborated their fascination with hermeticism, the supernatural and black humour. Duthuit saw the potlatch as an alternative to industrial capitalism, and the sculptor Isabelle Waldberg discerned in Yup'ik creations a fragility comparable to that embodied in her own *Constructions* (1942-48). Rather than diminishing their

1. Monique Brunet-Weinmann, "Riopelle, l'élan d'Amérique," *Colóqiuo Artes*, 2nd series, no. 56 (March 1983), p. 13. This brief anecdote concerns the *Rois de Thulé* series. But it should not be taken as an indication that Riopelle's experience in France was his only inspiration: he went beyond it by exhaustively exploring sources in the Canadian Arctic and Greenland. Since the goal of this essay is to describe the genesis of an interest, I have chosen not to delve into these developments and the multiple wellsprings of Riopelle's art. They are the object of study elsewhere in this catalogue.

2. Daniel Gagnon, *Riopelle, grandeur nature* (Montreal: Fides, 1988), p. 157.

3. Letter from Isabelle Waldberg to Patrick Waldberg, October 14, 1943, in Isabelle Waldberg and Patrick Waldberg, *Un amour acéphale, correspondance 1940-1949* (Paris: Éditions de la Différence, 1992), p. 105.

4. Elisa Breton, André Breton and Benjamin Péret, "Aparté," in *Riopelle à La Dragonne*, exh. cat. (Paris: Galerie Nina Dausset, 1949), n.p.

5. "Like a trapper fresh from the Canadian solitudes measuring his stride to our narrow pavements"; Georges Duthuit, "A Painter of Awakening: Jean-Paul Riopelle," trans. Samuel Beckett, in *Riopelle: First American Exhibition*, exh. cat. (New York: Pierre Matisse Gallery, 1954). See also Georges Duthuit, "A Painter of Awakening: Jean-Paul Riopelle," *Canadian Art*, vol. 10, no. 1 (Fall 1952), pp. 24-27; Georges Duthuit, "Les animateurs du silence," in Robert Lebel, ed., *Premier bilan de l'art actuel 1937-1953* (Paris: Soleil noir, 1953), p. 112.

6. E. Breton, A. Breton and Péret, "Aparté," n.p.

7. Elisa Breton, André Breton and Benjamin Péret, "Aparté," annotated handwritten and typewritten manuscript, February 1949. http://www.andre-breton.fr/work/56600100804240 (accessed June 13, 2020).

8. Like the Kalaallit of Greenland, the Yup'ik and Inupiat peoples of Alaska are part of the Inuit cultural continuum.

9. Riopelle saw this exhibition. Others that he may also have visited to which the Surrealists contributed through loans or texts include *Le surréalisme : sources – histoire – affinités*, curated by Patrick Waldberg and held at the Charpentier gallery (1964); *Art primitif: Amérique du Nord*, at the Jacques Kerchache gallery (1965); and *Chefs-d'œuvre du Musée de l'Homme* (1965) and *Arts primitifs dans les ateliers d'artistes* (1967), at the Musée de l'Homme. Paris also hosted *L'art indien aux États-Unis*, at the American Center for Art and Culture (1958), whose catalogue Breton is known to have possessed, and *Art esquimau du Canada*, at the Musée de l'Homme (1956), an exhibition devoted to contemporary Inuit sculpture that the group ignored.

17

17
Tlingit
Human-face mask
About 1900 (?)
Animal skull

To help Riopelle out financially about 1952,
Georges Duthuit tried to sell two Tlingit objects
in his collection—including this one—which
were produced primarily for the tourist market.
Neither found a taker, and Riopelle ended up
holding on to them his entire life. He made
a silverpoint drawing of one of the items (217),
an amulet (218), in 1977.

18
Georges Duthuit in his University
Street studio in Paris with Riopelle's
Untitled (1954–55) and a Northwest
Coast mask
N.d.

19

20

19
Jean Paul Riopelle
Le roi de Thulé
1973
Painted wood

20
Jean Paul Riopelle
Untitled (Bûche)
1973
Painted wood

10. The project was not realized.

11. Riopelle kept a number of these objects, including an amulet and a mask, both Tlingit, purchased from George G. Heye by the dealer Nasli Heeramaneck and likely resold to Julius Carlebach about 1943 (letter from Maria Galban to Yseult Riopelle, March 2017). It should be noted that Georges Duthuit was in better financial circumstances than the rest of the New York group. In 1944, Isabelle Waldberg wrote that he was "buying loads of primitive objects and other things, some of which must be very expensive" (letter from Isabelle Waldberg to Patrick Waldberg, October 16, 1944, in I. Waldberg and P. Waldberg, *Un amour acéphale*, p. 277). Claude Duthuit recalled that his father would stock up with birthday and Christmas presents purchased from Carlebach (Claude Duthuit, "Esquimaux ou des arts derniers," in *Les Esquimaux vus par Matisse. Georges Duthuit : Une fête en Cimmérie*, exh. cat. [Paris: Hazan; Le Cateau-Cambresis: Musée départemental Matisse, 2010], p. 14). It is not impossible that Riopelle himself had contact with Carlebach, although later and indirectly. Joan Mitchell, his companion from 1955 on, knew the dealer, for he had supported her in the early 1950s, when the galleries were showing little interest in her work.

12. Georges Duthuit, *Riopelle*, exh. cat. (Paris: Galerie Rive Droite, 1954), n.p.

13. Letter from Jean Paul Riopelle to Georges Duthuit, 1954, Georges Duthuit Fonds, archives of the Bibliothèque Kandinsky, DUTH 55-70.

14. The artist eventually gave up the idea since the temperature in the exhibition galleries could have had a damaging effect on the wood.

15. Michel Waldberg, "Ricpelle, l'écart absolu," in *Jean Paul Riopelle : catalogue raisonné, tome 1, 1939-1953*, ed. Yseult Riopelle (Montreal: Hibou Éditeurs, 1999), p. 23.

16. Another sketch by Kay Sage from 1941 features what appears to be a crane mask, identical to one the couple would acquire in 1945, which Sage bequeathed to Pierre Matisse upon her death.

21
Letter from Gabriel Illouz
to Yseult Riopelle
October 16, 1991

In this letter to Yseult Riopelle, Gabriel Illouz, Riopelle's friend, divulges his discovery of the object behind the *Rois de Thulé* series (and not, as he incorrectly states, the album of lithographs *Parler de corde*). What gave rise to the series teeming with northern references is a log that reminded Illouz of an Inuit face.

22
Advertisement for the Julius Carlebach gallery in New York In *VVV* (1943)

Many of the Surrealists living in New York during World War II visited the Carlebach gallery. This art dealer sold Northwest Coast objects to André Breton, Georges Duthuit, Robert Lebel and Isabelle Waldberg, who later became friends of Riopelle. He was introduced to their collections in Paris after the war.

interest, the return to France gave it new impetus. As collectors, they began lending their objects—one notable result being the exhibition *Le masque* (25), held at the Musée Guimet (1959-60)[9]—and publication projects were discussed. In 1947, Breton was making plans for a book devoted to the "great primitive arts of North America" that was to include essays by Lévi-Strauss, Lebel and Duthuit,[10] and Duthuit himself was considering a collection that would bring together non-Western art and poetry. Indigenous societies were centre stage.

In the years immediately following Riopelle's move to Paris, his paintings were not selling. Duthuit tried to help him raise money by putting a few of his Indigenous objects up for sale, but there were no takers.[11] It was finally Waldberg who, in 1951, gave Riopelle an unexpected chance by suggesting that he show paintings alongside her sculptures in an upcoming exhibition at the Henriette Niepce gallery. On the day of the opening, the previously cool Pierre Loeb declared he would buy everything. Riopelle had found his dealer, and his career took a decisive turn.

The actions taken by Breton, Duthuit and Waldberg on Riopelle's behalf should not be underestimated, for they reflect the nature of their friendship, which was of an intensity conducive to the sharing of enthusiasms: the transmission of passions is also a matter of intimacy. It was to Duthuit that the painter would become closest in the 1950s. The writer introduced Riopelle to his brother-in-law, Pierre Matisse, owner of a leading New York gallery, and became the regular commentator on his work. In 1954, Duthuit wrote an article for an exhibition held at the Rive Droite gallery (24) that takes the form of an open letter in which he expresses his affection for Riopelle and his admiration for the artist's commitment to the act of painting: "Do you, too, not turn yourself inside out like a glove, to pour yourself entirely, exposed and bloody, into your painting, giving to each picture the last minute of your life?"[12] Riopelle had always asserted his need to be in sympathy with his collaborators, whether dealers, critics or collectors. His relationship with Duthuit was one example, and it would be particularly enriched by the mutual regard and even fundamental similarity between the two men: "Sitting in the studio, I've just re-read your text, which I think is marvellous; marvellous in the sense of our relationship, for

it has the same effect on me as my painting does on you. It is at the moment so comforting . . . I think you can guess what I cannot express (27)."[13]

Another interesting passage in this letter of Riopelle's to the critic reveals that the exhibition at the Rive Droite gallery was originally supposed to include masks and other objects from British Columbia loaned by Duthuit (27).[14] It seems evident that this was intended to recreate the atmosphere of his study, which displayed a large painting by Riopelle flanked by several masks, including Kwakwaka'wakw and Inuit pieces (29-31).[15] Duthuit was skeptical of abstraction as an end in itself: for him, a successful work had to be present, very much of the world, closely connected to social life. Riopelle's art appealed to him because it reconciled opposites. He saw it as embodying the same active force as the one that enlivens Indigenous masks—objects that may well share an invisible lineage with Riopelle's creations.

This affinity was also recognized by Breton. Discovered among his collection was a watercolour by Riopelle from 1946 (44), the verso of which bears a copy of a preparatory sketch by the American artist Kay Sage for a set of tarot cards inspired by a Yup'ik mask. Yves Tanguy, Sage's husband, was among those who had been interested in Indigenous objects since the 1920s. Moreover, the writer and art critic José Pierre surmised that it was Tanguy who created the Surrealist map of the world from 1929 (32), which gives pride of place to the Arctic regions. In 1941, the couple, then living in New York, visited the exhibition *Indian Art of the United States*, organized by Frederic H. Douglas and René d'Harnoncourt and held at the Museum of Modern Art in New York. It included a mask featuring a fish that caught Sage's attention, identical to one purchased a few years later by Breton (49). This object, unusual in that it portrays only half a face, was copied and completed by Sage to produce an image rather like those resulting from the "exquisite corpse" game (45).[16] Breton's interest in the drawing is easy to understand, but it was the link to a watercolour by Riopelle that really intrigued. In making it, the poet was not suggesting that the Quebec painter had been directly influenced by Yup'ik art, but was rather pointing to a similarity of outlook between the Surrealists and Indigenous societies. It was via both physical

21

Julius Carlebach

AFRICA AMERICA OCEANIA
ANTIQUES AND ART OBJECTS

22

23
"Aparté," by Elisa Breton, André Breton and Benjamin Péret, in *Riopelle à La Dragonne*, exh. cat. (1949)

The catalogue of the exhibition *Riopelle à La Dragonne*, presented by the Nina Dausset gallery in 1949, included an "Aparté" (aside) by Elisa Breton, André Breton and Benjamin Péret in which André Breton dwelled on the artist's Canadian, untamed nature: "To me, it is the art of a superior trapper." He added, "If the Indians could come and see, they would be once more at home."

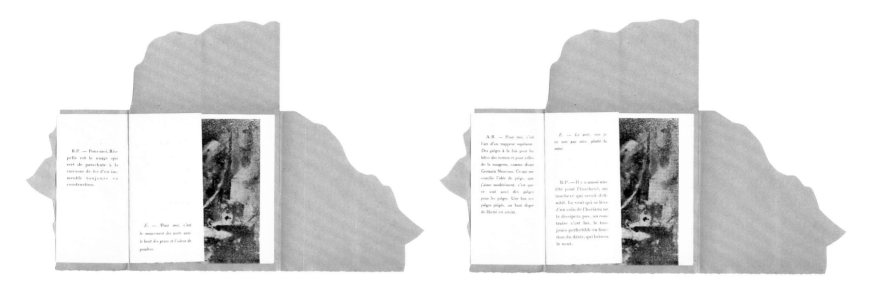

B.P. — Pour moi, Riopelle est le nuage qui sert de parachute à la carcasse de fer d'un immeuble toujours en construction.

E. — Pour moi, c'est le mouvement des ports avec le bruit des grues et l'odeur de goudron.

A.B. — Pour moi, c'est l'art d'un trappeur supérieur. Des pièges à la fois pour les bêtes des terriers et pour celles de la nougerie, comme disait Germain Nouveau. Ce qui me concilie l'idée de piège, que j'aime modérément, c'est que ce sont aussi des pièges pour les pièges. Une fois ces pièges piégés, un haut degré de liberté est atteint.

E. — Le port, non je ne suis pas sûre, plutôt la mine.

B.P. — Il y a aussi une fête pour l'inachevé, un inachevé qui serait définitif. Le vent qui se lève d'un coin de l'horizon ne le dissipera pas, au contraire c'est lui, le toujours perfectible en fonction du désir, qui brisera le vent.

A.B. — Les Indiens, s'ils pouvaient vous regarder, se raient de nouveau chez eux.

B.P. — Ils viendraient d'aussi loin que possible apportant leurs étoiles de deuils et leurs colliers arrachés aux plus somptueux oiseaux de la savane.

E. — L'ammanite phalloïde, gigantesque comme elle est là-bas, passe lentement parmi les feuilles d'automne.

B.P. — Tout chez Riopelle s'éclaire du soleil des grands bois où les feuilles tombent comme un biscuit de neige trempé dans le Xérès.

FÉVRIER 1949

DRAGONNE
GALERIE
NINA DAUSSET
Rue du Dragon - Paris 6ᵉ - Tél. : Litt. 24-19

and conceptual connections that Indigenous objects established a concrete place in Riopelle's works. Several gouaches on paper from 1955 and 1956 entitled *Masque esquimau* (or *Eskimo Mask*) (56-59) seem to echo Yup'ik masks in the protuberances around their outer edges and their expansive style. Many of the artist's so-called "Eskimo" works combine a fragmented composition with broad, powerfully contrasting dabs of pure colour—sometimes with the addition of drippings—and a nervous black stroke that creates a circular movement. The connection here is likely to pieces owned by Breton, Lebel and Waldberg rather than Duthuit, whose masks had fewer appendages and retained less of the original bright pigments. There is nothing random about these similarities: they reflect a lengthy period of familiarity with the objects and of meditation inspired by them. The impact was so powerful, indeed, that the objects would later become subjects.

The Surrealists were fascinated by the boldness of Yup'ik masks, their asymmetrical twists and grimacing faces (55). But even more than their purely aesthetic inventiveness, it was the emergence of these objects from an environment considered hostile that consummated, to Surrealist eyes, the poetic act. In the journal *Cahiers d'art*, the poet Paul Éluard ascribed to the masks of Alaska the power to "belie human frailty in the struggle against its climate."[17] Before 1935, these masks were known almost exclusively through photographs. In response to the group's interest, the collector and gallerist Charles Ratton borrowed a selection of pieces from George G. Heye and organized that same year the first exhibition devoted to the arts of Alaska and the Northwest Coast ever shown in France. Alongside Inuit masks and ivory carvings, it included Nisga'a, Tlingit, Kwakwaka'wakw, Haida and Nuu-chah-nulth pieces that the Surrealists found equally compelling. Breton was particularly fascinated by the masks with moving parts that could seem to come alive and change during rituals, and on his return from America he wrote enthusiastically of their evocative power: "In this respect, no static work, however acclaimed, can compare in terms of life (and anguish)."[18]

Missing from this panorama, though, is Gitksan art, to which a number of gouaches Riopelle executed between 1955 and 1959 refer in their titles (60-66). The ethnonym is strangely absent both from Parisian collections with which the artist was familiar and from exhibitions he could have seen.[19] The Gitksan were then often conflated with the Tsimshian, but ultimately the exact origin of the objects, of which the artist was unaware, mattered little. At a time when formal distinctions between related artistic productions were not necessarily acknowledged, it was for strictly aesthetic reasons that he invoked the most familiar name. The appearance of the term "Gitksan" in several titles nonetheless suggests that it took precedence over others in Riopelle's mind. The source of this interest is worth exploring.

A number of possibilities come to mind, and should be considered together: one, an encounter with the writings of the painter Kurt Seligmann (33), who had visited British Columbia in the late 1930s; another, a close familiarity with the work of the Canadian anthropologist Marius Barbeau (35). Riopelle must also have known the magazine *DYN*, founded in 1942 by the artist and former Surrealist Wolfgang Paalen; the issue combining numbers 4 and 5 was devoted to Indigenous America (26), but made virtually no mention of the Gitksan,[20] whose territory was subsumed on the map into that of the Tsimshian. Seligmann did not take the same shortcut, and the ethnographical accuracy of his research led to the publication of an article by him in the 1939 edition of the prestigious *Journal de la Société des américanistes*. In it, he made numerous references to observations recorded by Barbeau, with whom he was corresponding regularly at the time.[21] This intellectual connection is significant, since it casts light on the links between Surrealism and ethnography, but it is hardly surprising, given that Barbeau, an anthropologist working at the National Museum of Canada (now the Canadian Museum of History), was already well known in France by the 1930s. His books *The Downfall of Temlaham* (1928) (38) and *Totem Poles of the Gitksan, Upper Skeena River, British Columbia* (1929) (37), both devoted to the Gitksan, circulated among the cognoscenti, and his role in the acquisition of a Nisga'a totem pole by Paris' Musée de l'Homme had captured attention (34).[22]

17. Paul Éluard, "La nuit est à une dimension," *Cahiers d'art*, no. 5-6 (1935), pp. 99-101.

18. André Breton, "Notes sur les masques à transformation de la côte pacifique Nord-Ouest," *Neuf*, no. 1 (1950), p. 39.

19. Such as *L'art indien aux États-Unis*, for example, an exhibition presented at the American Center for Art and Culture in Paris in 1958, which was a condensed version of the one held at New York's Museum of Modern Art in 1941.

20. The only reference to them appeared in a footnote referencing Marius Barbeau's book *Totem Poles of the Gitksan, Upper Skeena River, British Columbia* (1929). For an in-depth study of Wolfgang Paalen and Kurt Seligmann's work in this field, see Marie Mauzé, "Odes à l'art de la côte Nord-Ouest. Surréalisme et ethnographie," *Gradhiva*, no. 26 (2017), pp. 180-209.

21. Ibid., pp. 187-198.

22. Marius Barbeau collaborated with the Musée de l'Homme on several occasions and helped Kurt Seligmann transport the "Kaiget" totem pole to the museum. He also met Wolfgang Paalen in Canada.

24
Cover of *Riopelle*, exh. cat. (1954)

25
"Pl. XIV. Masque de chaman à accessoires. Eskimo de l'Alaska" III. in *Le masque, Paris*, exh. cat. (1959)

In 1959 or 1960, Riopelle visited the exhibition *Le masque* at the Musée Guimet in Paris. It included Indigenous artworks from various collections, including those the artist's friends Georges Duthuit, André Breton, Robert Lebel and Isabelle Waldberg had amassed in New York during World War II. The mask in this illustration was loaned by Waldberg.

26
Cover of the "Amerindian Number" of *DYN* (1943)

DYN (1941–44) was a magazine put out by the Surrealist artist Wolfgang Paalen. The publication's content shows a general interest in North American Indigenous art— Paalen had visited British Columbia and Alaska in 1939— and the 1943 issue was largely devoted to it. Riopelle may have been familiar with *DYN* through his Surrealist friends.

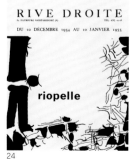

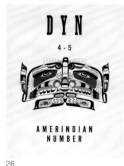

24　　　　　　25　　　　　　26

Paris 19 fév. 1954

Cher monsieur,

Il est malheureux que lors de votre retour à Paris nous n'ayons pu vous revoir et j'espère que votre retour au Canada s'est bien effectué. Mon ami Georges Duthuit en particulier aurait bien voulu vous rencontrer, (il s'agit du critique d'art dont je vous avais parlé comme ayant une collection importante d'objets Esquimaux et Indiens) Nous avons depuis beaucoup reparlé de la nécessité de faire mieux connaître en France cet art, et il s'y est déjà engagé.

Deux volumes sont en cours de préparation et bientôt achevés sur "Le Don Indien" et "la Fête Esquimau". Le Texte est de Georges Duthuit, les illustrations de Henri Matisse et Jacques Hérold, Les illustrations du Don Indien sont relatées à des légendes Tlingid, Haida, Kwakiutl, etc.

Deux éditions vont paraître, l'une illustrée de dessins, l'autre de gravures et de lithos. Trente photographies d'objets esquimaux et trente d'objets indiens (dont soixante en tout ou peut être un peu plus) complèteront l'ouvrage. Serait-il possible de nous faire parvenir des photos qui permettraient de compléter notre documentation (référence à la page dactylographiée ci-incluse)

Nous serions très désireux aussi d'avoir des légendes écrites, choisies parmi les plus caractéristiques, traduites en français s'il y en a, des Indiens de la côte Nord-Ouest. Si vous avez quelques essais susceptibles d'entrer dans cet ouvrage (de caractère plutôt poétique) nous serions heureux de les avoir, quant à la partie scientifique qui portera sur la description des objets reproduits, nous serions heureux d'avoir pour chacune des pièces photographiées, vos indications. Encore une fois, malgré la liste que nous vous donnons à titre de référence, votre propre choix surtout s'il porte sur des choses moins connues, nous sera des plus précieux.

Pour l'occasion de la parution de ces deux volumes, monsieur Duthuit envisage une exposition d'objets Indiens et esquimaux dans une des galeries importantes de Paris, comme chez Maght par exemple, mais ce point ne peut-être envisagé sans un envoi important d'objets venant ou de votre collection ou de celle du musée d'Ottawa, tout cela pourrait avoir lieu au début de l'automne.

J'attends donc de vos nouvelles avec impatience et espère que tout cela pourra se réaliser.

Mes meilleurs souvenirs à madame Barbeau, et amitiés aux Bioux que nous aimerions bien avoir à Paris.

Bien sympathiquement
Jean-Paul Riopelle

104 avenue de St-Mandé Paris XII

27
Letter from Riopelle to Georges
Duthuit
Vanves, 1954

This letter reveals that Riopelle had planned to include masks and other Indigenous objects from British Columbia that belonged to Duthuit in his upcoming exhibition at the Rive Droite gallery in Paris. However, Riopelle changed his mind out of concern for the conservation of the works.

28
Letter from Riopelle to Marius
Barbeau
February 19, 1954

This letter from a group of letters in the Canadian Museum of History (formerly the Museum of Man, Ottawa) reveals that Riopelle had met Marius Barbeau. It also shows that the artist had discussed the possibility of working together on the book project about Northwest Coast art that he was undertaking with Georges Duthuit. Seeing "the need to make this art better known in France," Duthuit and Riopelle envisaged an exhibition in Paris.

29

30   31

This map attributed to the poet
Paul Éluard, an important figure
in the Surrealist movement,
presents a skewed world in which
Alaska and the Arctic regions
are oversized. Subverting a
Eurocentric view of the world,
this document is evidence of
the Surrealists' interest in non-
Western societies.

Given the mandate to acquire
Indigenous works for the Musée
de l'Homme in Paris, the
Surrealist painter Kurt Seligmann
visited the Northwest Coast in
1938. He spent four months
with the Gitksan community in
Hazelton, having perhaps been
influenced by the work of Marius
Barbeau on the totems of this
northern British Columbia First
Nation. Riopelle may have read
Seligmann's travel writings,
which were published in various
magazines, including *Minotaure*.

23. Breton owned the first volume of Barbeau's *Totem Poles* (*Totem Poles: According to Crests and Topics*, bulletin no. 119, vol. 1 [Ottawa: National Museum of Canada, 1950]).

24. Georges Duthuit, *Une fête en Cimmérie* (Paris: Tériade, 1963). Another edition would be published by Mourlot in 1964.

25. A 26-page typed manuscript, found by Yseult Riopelle among documents the artist had left at Joan Mitchell's house, suggests that the project on the Northwest Coast was being reconceived in collaboration with Jean Paul Riopelle. Although the manuscript is neither dated nor signed, it can safely be attributed to Duthuit since it reflects both his writing style and his interest in Indigenous oral traditions. The subject of the text, moreover, recalls documents kept in the Georges Duthuit Fonds (Bibliothèque Kandinsky) —an alternative version of "Le don indien" (an article by Duthuit that first appeared in the journal *Labyrinthe* in 1946) and notes on the works of Marius Barbeau. The artist's participation in the project seems certain, since the text was inside a folder marked "Riopelle Copy," and the Duthuit Fonds includes a similar file labelled "Riopelle—for book (Indian stories)." The translations included in this folder of excerpts from Barbeau's book *Haida Myths Illustrated in Argillite Carvings*, published in 1953 (**36**), allow us to date the project to 1953-59.

26. Letter from Georges Duthuit to Paul-Émile Victor, December 29, 1950, Musée national d'histoire naturelle, Paris, Paul-Émile Victor archives.

27. Jean Paul Riopelle and Pierre Schneider, *Une fête en Cimmérie. Les Esquimaux vus par Matisse*, exhibition brochure (Paris: Canadian Cultural Centre, 1970).

28. Although Malaurie's book includes photographs and watercolours of Kalaaleq landscapes, objects and people, these images seem not to have had any formal impact on Riopelle's work. On the other hand, the documentary (with same title) the ethnologist made in 1969, which was broadcast on television, may have had a stimulating effect on his visual approach. For instance, Jean-Jacques Nattiez has identified in the *Rois de Thulé* series hints of the two-toned coats made of guillemot skin that appear in the film (email exchange of March 19, 2019, between Jean-Jacques Nattiez and this exhibition's curators, Andréanne Roy, Jacques Des Rochers and Yseult Riopelle).

So through his circle of Paris friends, Riopelle definitely had access to the publications of Paalen and Seligmann— both former Surrealists—as well as to those of his compatriot Barbeau.[23] It was undoubtedly the latter's studies of totem poles that were the principal inspiration for Riopelle's Gitksan series, for a number of the gouaches feature markedly vertical movements. Some years later the artist would make other works on paper that confirm this theory: part of an ensemble on the theme of British Columbia, they are titled *Du côté de chez Marius* (**221, 223**) This should not lead us to underestimate the extent of Riopelle's sources, however, since other Northwest Coast societies that absorbed Duthuit's interest and occupied a large place in the collections and publications of the time must also have penetrated his imagination and further shaped his conception of the Gitksan. In several works from the series, white areas are tightly hemmed in by tones of grey, as though forcing them into the kind of contraction that precedes an expansion. This generates a tension evocative of transformation masks, like the Kwakwaka'wakw piece lent to Riopelle by Duthuit (**31**).

Masks reappeared in Riopelle's work in 1973, with the *Rois de Thulé* series (**72-77, 126, 135, 137, 138**), but the approach had changed, for in the intervening years the painter had returned to figuration. His aesthetic panorama had also been enriched by new works whose simplicity contrasted with the exuberance of Yup'ik masks—the miniature Dorset and Thule masks he likely saw at the exhibitions *Masterpieces of Indian and Eskimo Art from Canada*, held at the Musée de l'Homme in 1969 (**39**), and *Sculpture of the Inuit: Masterworks of the Canadian Arctic*, shown at the Grand Palais in 1972 (**42**). Also part of his new artistic landscape were the Inuit-inspired portraits executed by Henri Matisse for the book by his son-in-law, Georges Duthuit, entitled *Une fête en Cimmérie* (**40, 127**).[24]

A few words must be said about this book focused on the Arctic, intended as the first in a series (a second on the Northwest Coast was under discussion) of remarkably ambitious scope.[25] Duthuit's initial goal was to assemble essays by himself, André Breton, Robert Lebel, Benjamin Péret, the composer Francis Poulenc and the ethnologist Paul-Émile Victor.[26] But the difficulties posed by obtaining the texts, finding a publisher and keeping Breton happy were ultimately too much for Duthuit, and nothing would be published but his own poetic wanderings through a once-more icebound New York. Duthuit's prose has the ring of conviction: the ludic celebration he pays tribute to is closely bound to the struggle against a militarist, missionarist and capitalist West. The text, full of references to Inuit spirits, betrays the author's fondness for legends but also his familiarity with the writings of the anthropologist Knud Rasmussen. The latter's best-known book, *Across Arctic America: Narrative of the Fifth Thule Expedition* (1927), would prove invaluable to Matisse, who when he agreed to take part in the project knew practically nothing about Inuit, aside, possibly, from a dim memory of Robert J. Flaherty's film *Nanook of the North* (1922). To nourish his visual repertoire, Matisse steeped himself in ethnographical studies. The photographs taken by Rasmussen and by Gontran de Poncins, author of *Kabloona* (1941), would become his models, and the film *Les quatre du Groenland* (1938), shot in Greenland by Fred Matter and Paul-Émile Victor—a friend of Duthuit—helped shape his imaginative vision. The result would be the thirty-one lithographs and twelve drawings that illustrate, respectively, the 1963 and 1964 editions of *Une fête en Cimmérie* (**127**).

Riopelle must have known almost from the outset about the project, which Duthuit first broached in 1947, but it was during preparations for the exhibition *Les Esquimaux vus par Matisse*, held in 1970-71 at the Canadian Cultural Centre in Paris, that he became thoroughly acquainted with the master's drawings and prints. For this event, Riopelle co-wrote an essay with the historian and author Pierre Schneider that describes the powerful impression Inuit masks had on Matisse when he saw them for the first time at Duthuit's.[27] By reducing the faces to a few basic strokes, the French artist was actually establishing a parallel with ritual masks, whose principal function is not to dissimulate but to invoke the invisible—a mediating role that appealed to Riopelle, at that time an avid reader of Jean Malaurie, author of *Les derniers rois de Thulé* (published in English as *The Last Kings of Thule*) (**41**).[28] According to Riopelle, his own *Rois de Thulé* series, which borrows from Malaurie's title, originated with the log anecdote recounted at the start of this essay. That said, we

32   33   34

35

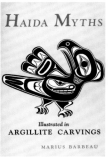 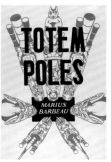 

36 37 38

35
Marius Barbeau standing by a mantel with a reduced totem pole. About 1940

On the wall is a painting by W. Langdon Kihn, an American artist who with other Canadian modern artists did the illustrations for *The Downfall of Temlaham* (1928).

36
Cover of Marius Barbeau, *Haida Myths Illustrated in Argillite Carvings* (1953)

Documents in the archives of the Joan Mitchell Foundation in New York reveal that between 1953 and 1959, Georges Duthuit and Riopelle entertained the idea of collaborating on a book dealing with Northwest Coast Indigenous arts and cultures. A file labelled *Riopelle / for book / Indian stories* in the Georges Duthuit archive at the Bibliothèque Kandinsky in Paris contains a collection of translated excerpts from Marius Barbeau's *Haida Myths Illustrated in Argillite Carvings* (1953), which points to the possibility that their co-publication would have been based on the anthropologist's work.

37
Cover of Marius Barbeau, *Totem Poles of the Gitksan: Upper Skeena River, British Columbia* (1929)

In the 1920s, the anthropologist Marius Barbeau devoted himself to studying the Tsimshian, in particular the Gitksan. Working in British Columbia for the Museum of Man (now the Canadian Museum of History, Gatineau) in Ottawa, he acquired a familiarity with, among other things, the totem poles of the Skeen River valley. He published his findings in *The Downfall of Temlaham* (1928) and *Totem Poles of the Gitksan, Upper Skeena River, British Columbia* (1929). Riopelle, who had met Barbeau, may have drawn inspiration from his work in coming up with the title for his series *Gitksan* (1955–59).

38
Cover of Marius Barbeau, *The Downfall of Temlaham*, ills. by A. Y. Jackson, Edwin H. Holgate, W. Langdon Kihn, Emily Carr and Annie D. Savage (1928)

39
Cover of Marcel Evrard, ed., *Chefs-d'oeuvre des arts indiens et esquimaux du Canada / Masterpieces of Indian and Eskimo Art from Canada* (1969)

In 1969, Riopelle visited the exhibition *Masterpieces of Indian and Eskimo Art from Canada* (Musée de l'Homme, Paris), at the time the most extensive exhibition of its kind ever presented in Europe. This may have been his first exposure to the wealth of forms of artistic expression from across Canada.

40
Cover of Georges Duthuit, *Une fête en Cimmérie* (1964)

Une fête en Cimmérie pairs a poetic text by Georges Duthuit with illustrations by Henri Matisse, his father-in-law. The thirty-one lithographs executed in 1948 and 1949 are based on Duthuit's collection of Inuit masks and photographic portraits reproduced in Knud Rasmussen's book *Across Arctic America: Narrative of the Fifth Thule Expedition* (1927).

41
Cover of Jean Malaurie, *Les derniers rois de Thulé. Une année parmi les Eskimos polaires du Groenland* (1955)

According to invaluable first-hand information from Yseult Riopelle, when the artist was working on his series *Rois de Thulé*, his bedtime reading was *Les derniers rois de Thulé*, which suggested the series' title. Written by the ethnologist and geographer Jean Malaurie, an Arctic specialist, and published in 1955, the book tells of the author's immersion in a Greenland Inuit community whose way of life and culture were being threatened by the establishment of an American military base in its territory.

42
Exhibition poster for *Sculpture / Inuit: chefs-d'œuvre de l'Arctique canadien (Sculpture of the Inuit: Masterworks of the Canadian Arctic)* held at Galeries nationales du Grand Palais, Paris, 1972

Riopelle visited this exhibition showcasing Inuit historical and contemporary artworks, and may have been inspired by it for his series *Rois de Thulé* (1973).

29. In 1774, Goethe wrote a poem entitled *Der König in Thule* [The King of Thule], which he used again in *Faust*; Riopelle owned a copy of the play. It should not be forgotten that "Ultima Thule" is a classical notion used to refer to the Far North that recurs frequently in literature. This idea of the farthest reaches of the world certainly resonated more with the painter than the fact that Malaurie used it to label Greenland, as a tribute to Knud Rasmussen and his Thule Expeditions.

30. For more on this subject, see Florence Duchemin-Pelletier, "Un silence éloquent. Du désintérêt des surréalistes pour l'art inuit contemporain," *Histoire de l'art*, no. 75 (2014), pp. 111–122.

31. Interview with Yseult Riopelle by Florence Duchemin-Pelletier, December 12, 2018.

32. There was no real contemporary Inuit art scene, with international visibility, until after James A. Houston arrived in the Arctic in 1948. Houston, with financial support from the Canadian Handicrafts Guild, encouraged artistic production among Inuit communities and facilitated its marketing.

33. Interview with René Gimpel by Florence Duchemin-Pelletier, February 18, 2019.

34. Letter from Charles Gimpel to Jean Paul Riopelle, January 6, 1961, Gimpel Fils archives.

35. *Sculpture of the Inuit: Masterworks of the Canadian Arctic* was a travelling exhibition organized by the Canadian Eskimo Arts Council with the support of the federal government. Between 1971 and 1973 it was shown in Vancouver, Paris, Copenhagen, Leningrad, Moscow, London, Philadelphia, Montreal and Ottawa. Inuit artists were invited to attend every opening. See Sharon Van Raalte, *Sculpture/Inuit: An Odyssey. Sculpture of the Inuit, Masterworks of the Canadian Arctic: Report* (Ottawa: Department of Indian and Northern Affairs, Social Development Division, [1975]), p. 43. While the exhibition was on view at the Grand Palais, Riopelle held a show at the Canadian Cultural Centre entitled *Strings and Other Games* (1972), featuring works inspired by Inuit practices. Films on the Canadian Arctic were screened at the Centre during the show's run.

36. Theo Waddington is a British art dealer whose Montreal, Toronto and New York galleries distributed contemporary Inuit art in the 1960s.

37. Emails from Theo Waddington to Florence Duchemin-Pelletier, April 2019.

38. Brunet-Weinmann, "Riopelle, l'élan d'Amérique," p. 13.

39. Riopelle and Schneider, *Une fête en Cimmérie*.

40. Gilbert Érouart, *Entretiens avec Jean-Paul Riopelle, suivis de Fernand Seguin rencontre Jean-Paul Riopelle* (Montreal: Liber, 1993), p. 39.

only see what we already know. The physical imprint of the wood on paper parallels the metaphorical impression of Indigenous cultures on the artist: occasional presences that dominate, emitting an aura that the technician reveals by "blowings," collages, broken strokes and tangled lines.

For his series, though, Riopelle rejected Malaurie's fatalism by shortening the title, making it almost identical to that of a poem by Goethe, *Der König in Thule* (1774).[29] The artist did not share the rather disdainful lack of interest shown by the Surrealists and their allies towards contemporary Inuit art.[30] On the contrary, although he did not collect this art and it had no detectable influence on his work, he admired it greatly.[31] It was through Charles Gimpel, the French-born London dealer, who with his brother Peter had founded the modern art gallery Gimpel Fils, that Riopelle first came into contact with contemporary Inuit art, of which the gallerist was a fervent defender.[32] It was Gimpel who built the European market for this work and ensured its presence in leading galleries. In 1956, Riopelle began showing his work at Gimpel Fils: Peter became his dealer, and Charles his friend. The latter's son, René Gimpel, recalls that his father "liked Riopelle very much, as a man."[33] They were both keen sports fans, and their relationship went beyond the professional. In a 1961 letter to Riopelle, the gallerist mentions a recent trip to the Arctic: "I'm just back from the Far North, where I spent a month with the Eskimos, and I also spent several days in Montreal, where I visited a few galleries, but in fact I was more interested in the North than in my visit to Montreal."[34] Gimpel brought back many photographs and artworks from his various expeditions, which Riopelle must have seen. Clearly interested, the artist attended the 1972 Paris opening of the travelling exhibition *Sculpture of the Inuit: Masterworks of the Canadian Arctic*, largely in the hope of meeting Inuit artists. There, he likely encountered carvers Michael Amarook and John Kaunak, who were both present at the event.[35] Finally, it was also due indirectly to Gimpel that Riopelle made his first trip to the Arctic. In the early 1960s, the dealer had taken the young Theo Waddington on one of his expeditions,[36] and it was the latter, by that time an habitué, who would accompany Riopelle to Pangnirtung (Panniqtuuq), on Baffin Island, in 1969 and 1971; Riopelle

returned in 1977 and spent time with Georges Duthuit's son Claude (**161**).[37] These trips, although aimed principally at fishing Arctic char and hunting caribou, gave Waddington and Claude Duthuit the opportunity to purchase artworks from local cooperatives. Thus are enthusiasms inherited and passed on.

Ultimately, Riopelle's vision was oriented by two influences. It was his Paris friends who first led him to understand the power of Indigenous arts and societies, but they valued only what corresponded to their idea of "authenticity." Their search for traces of a past apparently gone forever would prompt the artist to question aspects of a culture—in this case the culture of the Arctic peoples—kept alive artificially.[38] But after encountering his English contacts, Gimpel and Waddington, he wrote that "once away from the factory and the supermarket, [Inuit] easily rediscover the path of the gods."[39] These apparently contradictory positions are not an indication that the artist's development was passive: his approach was based on a rejection of certitudes, on constant intellectual questioning. Moreover, it was to test the ideas that had shaped his perception of Indigenous art to that point that he chose to travel to the Arctic, where empirical experience would enable him to assess the validity of external discourses. As soon as things became comfortable, Riopelle was eager to upset the routine. It was an intellectual process: theories had to be undermined, contradictions accommodated. When asked about the high and low points of his oeuvre, and the significance of Inuit string games in particular, Riopelle's response is unsurprising: "A hierarchy? I don't know. No. Nothing is important. Everything is important."[40]

39 40 41 42

43

44

45

43
Jean Paul Riopelle
Untitled
1947
Watercolour and ink on paper

44
Kay Sage
Copy of a design for a tarot card
(verso of **46**)
About 1946
Ink on paper

45
Kay Sage
Design for a tarot card
1941
Gouache, brush, pen and India
ink on paper

46
Jean Paul Riopelle
Untitled (recto of **44**)
1946
Watercolour and ink on paper

Riopelle discovered Yup'ik art
through his connections with the
Surrealists. On the back of this
watercolour that once belonged
to André Breton is a drawing by
the American artist Kay Sage,
which was largely inspired by the
Fish Mask in Breton's collection.
Two different artistic expressions
and traditions that enable the
"re-enchantment of the world"
are blended together here,
marking the link between them:
the exploration of automatism
in painting, and the vision quest
in Indigenous production. The
latter was a tremendous source
of inspiration for the Surrealists,
including Sage.

46

47

48-49 | Historically, the creation of a traditional Yup'ik dance mask began with the vision of the village *angalkuq*, the shaman who would either create the mask directly, or would commission its creation from skilled carvers. The vision of the *angalkuq* would be manifested in a song, forming the basis of the dance narrative to be performed. The design of a mask was often a complex compilation of the various verses and activities being described in the dance. Usually, Yup'ik masks were created in pairs or groups, each mask reflecting the particularities of the verses and dance structure. There are many terms in the Yup'ik language to describe the multiplicity of forms these paired masks can take.

Yup'ik dance masks follow centuries of traditional vocabularies, and numerous symbols immediately understood by the audience are included. Items such as the *ellanguaq* (pretend universe or consciousness) are found in the form of a hoop or ring, made from bent spruce roots and adorned with feathers, surrounding the top crown of the mask. The *ellanguaq* represents the threshold between planes of consciousness, through which the spirits (and the *angalkuq*) must pass.

Perhaps the most important and central feature of the mask is the *yua* (personal spirit), which is often represented as a human face emerging from the centre of the mask's animal body. In the Yup'ik cosmological system, all beings are expected to possess a *yua*, and every object (visible and invisible) has the potential to be alive and have a spiritual essence. For this reason, among many others, great respect is paid to every living creature, upon which life in the Arctic depends for survival. – SM

48

47
Film still from *L'invention du monde: les surréalistes et le cinéma* (1952)

48
Southwest Alaska, Yup'ik
Mask
About 1910
Driftwood, baleen, feathers, paint, cotton twine

49
Southern shores of Kuskokwim Bay, Goodnews Bay, Yup'ik
Mask representing a fish
Early 20th c.
Painted wood, feathers

49

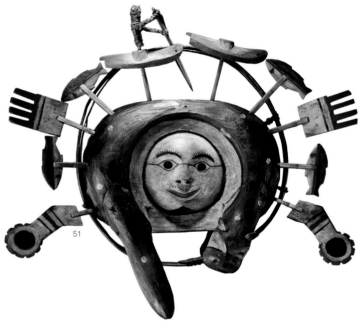

50-52 | Masks cover, protect and hide our faces from the spirit world. At the same time, they reach out to the essence of mystery that is out there in the cosmos. Our Yup'ik masks are our spiritual skin wrought from wood, feathers and sinew.

Employing them in dance and ceremony helps us to connect to the spiritual realm. Yup'ik masks evoke dreams and visions, and bring them into our collective consciousness. They give us a glimpse into the celestial universe that is within us and beyond.

That is the nature of Yup'ik masks. – CM

50
Lower Yukon, Alaska, Yup'ik
Mask
Early 20th c.
Wood, driftwood, spruce
root, pigment, watercolour,
nails, cotton thread, rattan (?)

51
Lower Yukon, Alaska, Yup'ik
Mask
Early 20th c.
Wood, driftwood, spruce
root, rattan (?), feathers,
pigment, watercolour,
cotton thread, nails, glue

52
Hooper Bay region of
southwest Alaska, Yup'ik
Mask
Early 20th c.
Wood, driftwood, spruce
root, pigment, watercolour,
nails, cotton thread

52

53
Sabine Weiss
André Breton at Home in France with His Art Collection
About 1960

André Breton is shown standing in his home in front of five Yup'ik masks of paramount importance. Most, if not all, of these masks were acquired in New York from the art dealer Julius Carlebach during World War II. Riopelle, who circulated among Breton's circle in the late 1940s, probably had the opportunity to see this Surrealist's exceptional collection.

54
Attributed to Ikamrailnguq
Dance mask representing *Tunutellgem Yua* (Arctic loon spirit), formerly in the collection of Georges Duthuit
About 1900
Wood, feathers, pigment and vegetable fibres

54

55
Set of pages from Robert Lebel's
sketchbook of drawings of
Yup'ik masks
Ill. in *Collection Robert Lebel:
vente* (2006)
1942–46
Ink, graphite and coloured pencil
drawings on paper in a
cardboard-bound sketchbook

Robert Lebel, a writer in
the Surrealist milieu, built up a
significant collection of North
American Indigenous art when
he lived in New York during
World War II. His sketchbook
contains renderings of the
Yup'ik masks he and his friends
André Breton, Georges Duthuit
and Isabelle Waldberg—all
future acquaintances of Riopelle
—acquired.

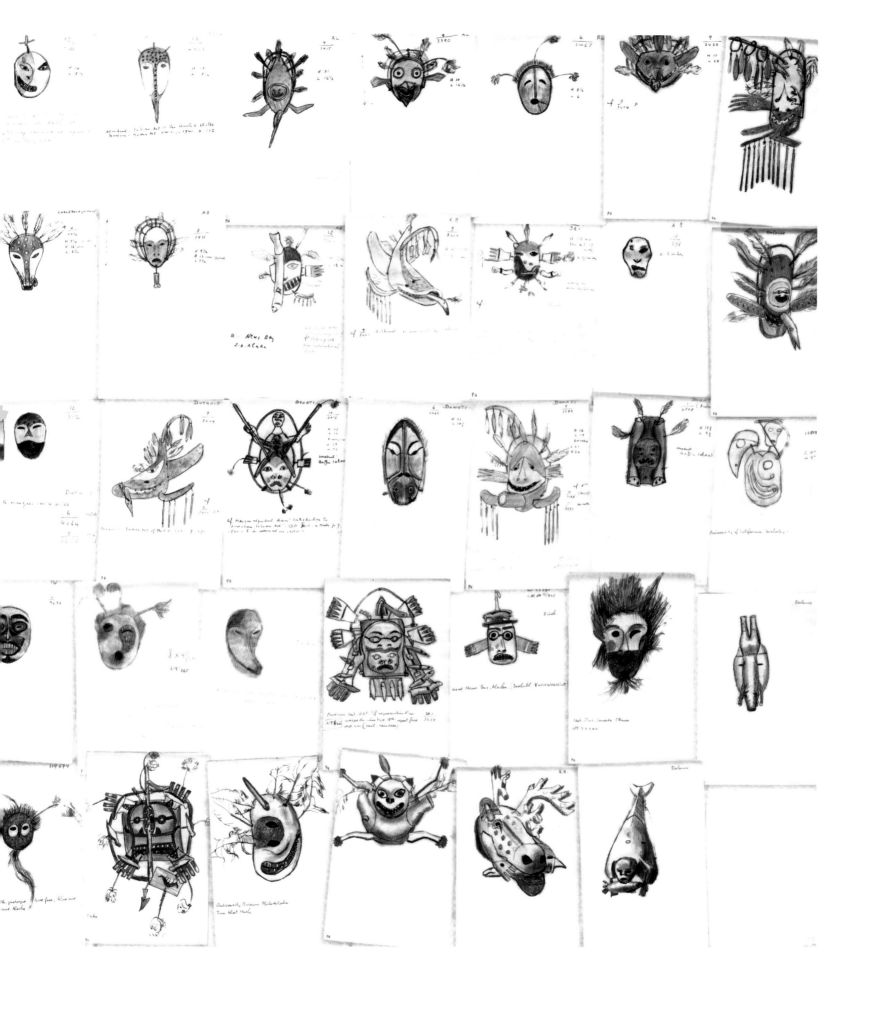

56

56
Jean Paul Riopelle
Masque esquimau
1955
Gouache on paper

57
Jean Paul Riopelle
Masque eskimo
1955
Gouache on paper

57

58

58
Jean Paul Riopelle
Eskimo Mask
1955
Gouache on paper

59
Jean Paul Riopelle
Masque esquimau
1955
Gouache on paper

59

60

61

60
Jean Paul Riopelle
*Sous le mythe
de Gitksan n° 4*
1956
Gouache on paper

61
Jean Paul Riopelle
*Sous le mythe
de Gitksan n° 3*
1956
Gouache on paper

62
Jean Paul Riopelle
*Sous le mythe
de Gitksan n° 2*
1956
Gouache on paper

63

64

66

66
Jean Paul Riopelle
Un autre Gitksan
1957
Gouache on paper

67
British Columbia,
unidentified origin
Human-face
mask with clan
crest markings
About 1800–50
Painted wood

67

68 | The master carvers of the Northwest Coast have been making three types of masks: vividly realistic portraits of chiefs and high-ranking ancestors, fantastic mythological beings present on ceremonial occasions, and portrayals of the spirit-beings invoked by shamans in their healing. Their wonderfully sculptural and dramatically polychromed masks are arguably among the most magnificent ever made, as one would expect in a culture where both visual art and dramatic performance are so highly esteemed. They have also been eagerly sought after by collectors, from first contact in the eighteenth century to today. Mask-making remains a lively genre on the contemporary art scene of the region. Still rooted in the winter ceremonial life of these communities, masks are never static sculpture. Mask-carving has always been an evolving practice dependent on traditional dramaturgy, but continually challenged by the need to keep captivating audiences. Tragically, many masks in museum collections have been separated from any memory of their origins. Their lost context through the collecting process at times embodies the full weight of colonial repression, but their power to mesmerize remains intact. Increasingly, these masterworks are finding their way back to their communities of origin, where they can be reinterpreted by elders, play a part in reviving performance traditions and inspire new generations of artists.

Northwest Coast masks have fascinated several generations of non-Indigenous Canadian artists, from Paul Kane to Arthur Lismer. Edwin Holgate, who was encouraged to paint in the Gitksan Nation in the 1920s by Canadian anthropologist Marius Barbeau, built a collection of Indigenous objects during his travels. These include this mask in the collection of the McCord Museum in Montreal. Holgate was among the artists Barbeau presented in his pioneering *Exhibition of Canadian West Coast Art*, which displayed traditional Indigenous objects alongside paintings by artists of settler origin who had been inspired by them. – **BHR**

68
Gitksan (?)
Mask
1920–25
Wood, paint, metal

68

69-71 | The cultures of the Northwest Coast are stratified
societies. Their house communities are led by hereditary
elites who are charged with preserving the clan's privileges,
oral history, origin stories and related crests. The status of
this nobility, confirmed by their role in public events, was
a source of pride to the entire clan. Precious objects that
were worn or used by the nobility displayed the clan's
crests and demonstrated their wealth. Such prestige luxury
objects were later eagerly sought after by collectors and
museums. These particular works—a feast ladle, a shaman's
spirit catcher and a sun or moon crest frontlet of Tsimshian
origin—housed in the Montreal Museum of Fine Arts, were
acquired from the same dealers, including Julius Carlebach
(from whom this ladle was acquired), who were patronized
by the French exiles living in New York during World War II.
– BHR

69
Northwest Coast,
Alaska, Tlingit
Ladle
About 1870
Mountain-sheep
horn, abalone shell,
copper

70
Northwest Coast,
British Columbia,
Tsimshian or Gitksan
Soul catcher
Early 19th c.
Bone, abalone shell,
paint

71
Northwest Coast,
British Columbia,
Tsimshian
Amhalayt (frontlet)
About 1880
Painted wood,
abalone shell

71

72

73

72
Jean Paul Riopelle
Les rois de Thulé
1973
Mixed media on paper

73
Jean Paul Riopelle
Untitled
From the series
Rois de Thulé
1973
Acrylic, gouache and
charcoal on paper

74
Jean Paul Riopelle
Les rois de Thulé
1973
Mixed media on paper

75

75
Jean Paul Riopelle
Les rois de Thulé
N.d.
Mixed media on paper

76
Jean Paul Riopelle
Les rois de Thulé
1973
Mixed media on paper

77
Jean Paul Riopelle
Les rois de Thulé VII
1973
Gouache on paper

76

77

75-77 | The series *Rois de Thulé*, which consists of seventy works painted in Paris, was created by Riopelle using a log as a matrix (**19, 20**). Although the term "Thule" has more than one meaning—does it refer to Greenland's Thule, to Thule culture or to the mythical Thule of antiquity described by Pytheas?—it points us in the direction of the Inuit world. The central motif recurs in different compositions. Some works are of a striking sobriety, and others are far more complex. The artist employed a variety of mediums: pastel, gouache, charcoal, watercolour, acrylic sprayed through a pipette. Some works in the series, like these, appear to conjure a face encircled by the fur on a traditional parka. Others, with their black dabs, may recall the guillemot skin clothing worn by Inuit. – AR

RIOPELLE

DANIEL
CHARTIER

AND THE

IMAGINED NORTH

This translation was supplied by the author, and not the Publishing Department of the Montreal Museum of Fine Arts.

For millennia, artists and writers have been imagining and representing the cold world, which we sometimes indiscriminately call "North," "Far North," "Arctic" and, by extension, "winter" and "high mountains."[1] Taken together, such representations form a pluralistic system of signs, an organic whole sustained by new works that often challenge what came before. This mix is based on a consistency—a simplification of forms and colours—and includes elements such as ice, snow, darkness, remoteness and cold. For the sake of convenience, I have called this system of signs the "imagined North."[2] This northern imagery is the result of a double perspective, looking out and looking in. As of late, this mainly European invention has been called into question by the people who live in the North and who, until recently, have been overlooked. Presented as empty, immense, white, remote, extreme, harsh and powerful, this vast area allows the West to project itself into an absolute that is in accord with deep values. These representations are not without moral, ethical, political and environmental overtones or lingering stereotypes that can be irritating to the people of the cultures firmly rooted there.

Part of Jean Paul Riopelle's work arises on the one hand from a unique construction of an imagined North, coloured by his exposure to art collections, readings, time spent in the area and winter activities he engaged in as a youth in a northern region (**79-82**); and on the other hand from the universal contribution of a long series of representations of the North, winter and the Arctic passed down in recent centuries. Unlike Riopelle, few artists and writers have known the North and the Arctic other than through cultural representations. Their "North" is built more on discourse reprised and rearticulated over time than from first-hand experience of the area. Some artists have skilfully drawn from this system of signs to create their own imagery; others have confronted their perceptions with actual experience of the territory, highlighting the tension between the external and internal dimensions of such representations. This is true of Riopelle, who created unsettling works that shifted notions of the "North," "nordicity" and "imagined North" through an approach that was at once individual and universal.

A PATH PARALLEL TO THAT OF LOUIS-EDMOND HAMELIN

When geographer and linguist Louis-Edmond Hamelin coined the word "nordicity" in his Québec City laboratory in the 1960s, he prepared the groundwork for a major critical field. This new word denotes the entire circumpolar area and expands the notion of the "North" by providing it with a multidisciplinary scope.[3] According to Hamelin, the North involves not only climate and geography, but also populations, perceptions, social practices and cultural representations. The concept of nordicity is central to grasping the important role played by the "North" in the Western imagination.

The term "nordicity" quickly entered common parlance, where it was amalgamated with its corollaries North, Arctic winter, "Far North," cold country, Inuit cultures, ice and snow. For Hamelin, the concept of nordicity can be broken down into three aspects: winter, high mountains and the Arctic. These three facets were part of Jean Paul Riopelle's biographical and artistic journey, each marking an evolution in his handling of the imagined North.

Hamelin and Riopelle, two pioneers of the Quiet Revolution, arrived at nordicity by way of an uncommon journey. As brilliantly demonstrated by Copenhagen's Louisiana Museum of Modern Art's *Arctic* exhibition in 2013–14, most of the Arctic's first visitors, explorers and scientists had developed an initial idea of the North based on European discursive and visual knowledge before venturing into the region with this imaginary concept already etched in their minds. Riopelle and Hamelin were first exposed to cold country in the Saint Lawrence Valley, which has one of the harshest winters of all inhabited territory, and then left for Europe, to the "high mountains" of the Alps (to Grenoble, in the case of Hamelin in 1948, and Austria[4] for Riopelle in 1954). This introduction to "mountainness" was decisive for their ideas of the North. And finally, in a third phase, they visited the Arctic: Hamelin went to Svalbard in 1960, then Nunavik in 1961; Riopelle travelled around the eastern shore of Hudson Bay, Quebec, in 1972 and went to Pangnirtung, Nunavut, in 1969, 1971 and 1977. The parallel paths of these two men—starting from winter, passing through mountains and arriving at the Arctic—gave rise to novel impressions of the cold world: Hamelin, through his ideas, and Riopelle, through his works, contributed to altering the collective relationship with nordicity.[5]

Up until now, the critical discourse around Riopelle has made hardly any mention of the imagined North; although the omission is regrettable, it does point to how connection to place, territory and, indeed, reality is never straightforward when it comes to interpreting a complex body of work. Without the right tools to grasp the idea of place and the North, the study of the relation to nordicity is likely to be limited to figurative works. With Riopelle, even his abstract works, by putting forward the "mental space of his reference points" (or his signs), reveal—without necessarily involving mimesis—a synthesis both personal and universal of the foundations and principles of winter and the North.

1. I wish to thank Charlotte Coutu and Yannick Legault, who, through their previous research, have made the writing of this essay possible. I'm also grateful to Luba Markovskaia for having reviewed it.

2. I have proposed the following definition of "imagined North": "All of the discourses stated about the North, the winter, and the Arctic, which can be retraced both synchronically—for a given period—or diachronically—for a specific culture—, derived from different cultures and forms, accumulated over the centuries according to a dual principle of synthesis and competition, form what could be called the 'imagined North.' It is a plural and shifting sign system, which functions in a variable manner according to the contexts of enunciation and reception." See Daniel Chartier, *Qu'est-ce que l'imaginaire du Nord ? Principes éthiques* (Montreal: Imaginaire I Nord; Harstad, Norway: Arctic Arts Summit, 2018), p. 12. This definition, resulting from many exchanges throughout the circumpolar regions, has been translated into fourteen northern and Arctic languages.

3. Before Hamelin's work, the French word *nord* referred solely to Scandinavia.

4. Riopelle returned to mountainous country in late 1964 and early 1965, staying at the Luchon-Superbagnères resort in France for a ski vacation (**82**). A knee injury kept him off his feet the entire trip, and he executed a series of small works on paper inspired by his view of the Pyrenees.

5. Contrary to most of the Arctic's first visitors, artists and researchers, Riopelle and Hamelin were familiar with cold country first through their experiencing winter, then altitude and finally travelling to the Arctic. This sequence allowed them to make connections between these three cold realms and thus to renew the vision of the Arctic, which until then had been understood as a world apart, a vision built through an approach that began with the abstract (the imagination and knowledge of the Arctic) and was later compared against the experience of time spent in this land.

78
Jean Paul Riopelle
Blizzard sylvestre
1953
Oil on board

78

78 | Executed in Paris, the canvas *Blizzard sylvestre* exemplifies an imaginative world marked by nordicity. This theme would dominate Riopelle's output of the 1970s through more direct representations of northern attributes, including cold, snow, ice and white. When *Blizzard sylvestre* was painted, the influence of the North was initially seen in titles, several of which evoke the fury of the elements in a hostile climate. The artist's spontaneous gesture is evident in the energetic movement of the handling and the composition. With its vibrant palette, all-over composition of superimposed dabs applied with a spatula and network of lines produced by paint flung onto the surface, *Blizzard sylvestre* is one of Riopelle's finest works of this period. – **AR**

79

80

6. Esther Trépanier, "Le froid, le peintre et le tableau. Quand l'hiver s'installe en ville," in Jan Borm and Daniel Chartier, eds., *Le froid. Adaptation, production, effets, représentations* (Quebec City: Presses de l'Université du Québec, 2018), pp. 265–293.

7. This is also observed in other forms of non-figurative art, namely poetry and instrumental music, which employ a language of the imagined North that does not rely on description.

8. In *Esthétique du pôle Nord* (Paris: Grasset, 2002), the French philosopher Michel Onfray observes the prevalence of stone in the Arctic landscape, including in the cultural forms (for example, sculptures and inukshuks) produced there. It can thus be posited that, in its twofold function as semaphore and trace, the inukshuk aptly symbolizes the inseparability of the land, material, gesture and form particular to the Inuit concept of *nuna*.

9. Quoted in *Jean-Paul Riopelle. Peinture, 1946-1977*, exh. cat., ed. Pierre Schneider (Paris: Musée national d'art moderne, Centre Georges Pompidou; Quebec City: Musée du Québec; Montreal: Musée d'art contemporain, 1981), p. 12.

10. Barry Lopez, *Rêves arctiques : imagination et désir dans le paysage arctique* (Paris: Albin Michel, 1987), pp. 257–258.

11. Guy Robert, *Riopelle, chasseur d'images* (Montreal: Éditions France-Amérique, 1981), p. 77.

12. The multidisciplinary artist René Derouin, born in Montreal in 1936, has created works inspired by the Laurentians and the Arctic as much as by Mexico.

13. Schneider, *Jean-Paul Riopelle*, p. 12.

14. Claudine Caron and Caroline Traube, "L'imaginaire du Nord et du froid en musique. Esthétique d'une musique nordique," *Les Cahiers de la société québécoise de recherche en musique*, vol. 14, no. 1 (May 2013).

79
Riopelle photograph of *Apparition – Triceratos automatique* (1947–48, H. 24 cm)
N. d.

Jean Paul Riopelle said: "I modelled some clay sculptures in 1947, but very few survive because I used a very fragile, breakable clay. But before that, from when I was small—and still today when I get a chance—I made snow sculpture. I've sculpted snow far more than I've modelled clay."

80
Riopelle photograph of *Hommage à Sade* (1947–48, H. 34 cm)
1947–48
N. d.

81
Jean Lespérance (?) photograph of Françoise and Riopelle on a ski trip
About 1946

82
Sylvie Riopelle photograph of Riopelle at Superbagnères, Pyrenees
December 1964

NATURE-INSPIRED ABSTRACTION

The art historian Esther Trépanier observed that, with the arrival of winter, the appearance of the landscape undergoes a sweeping change and that, although this season is at times simply "subject matter" for a painting, it is primarily a chromatic, formal and visual idiom.[6] It is also seen in non-figurative works,[7] for example, in the use of shades of black and a restricted palette, a simplification and mineralisation[8] of forms, indeed a gestural abstraction wholly its own.

As a young adult, Riopelle grew aware of the possibilities nature offers to create new approaches to abstraction, developing a method that he returned to during various periods of his career, whether in his evocations of the Alps, the Laurentians or Nunavut. Based on his observations of the changing tides at Saint-Fabien-sur-Mer, in the Lower Saint Lawrence, the young artist executed a painting that his friends called "non-figurative," to which he replied, "I painted exactly what I saw."[9] What he "saw" should be understood as a construction at once formal and imagined, as well as singular and elaborated through a complex process in relation to reality.

On January 1, 1954, Riopelle flew over the Atlantic: the flight gave him a view of the world from up high that predated his large paintings presenting abstract perspectives of territory and its topography. Seen from the sky, the Earth's surface becomes a medium favourable to compositions that are both spare and violent. The flights over the Laurentians (and beyond) in Champlain Charest's seaplane in the 1970s gave the painter a unique perspective of the North. Barry Lopez has pointed out how important the aircraft's role was in creating a unique and abstract vision of the North and the Arctic that both distorted and synthesized the landscape.[10]

In Austria, contemplating the mountains and snow, Riopelle developed a unique relationship with colour and whiteness. Far from home, he became reacquainted with the formal qualities of the light, form and colour of cold country. Like others before him, it was by taking distance that he awoke to an awareness of the imagined north, which was as good a way as any to arrive at the "outsider's view" that best highlights the characteristics of a place. An initial semantics of visual nordicity appears in the paintings *Autriche* (**84**) and *Avalanche* (**90**), among others, in which, according to Guy Robert, "the spatula builds up large white patches that flashes of colour besiege or encroach upon."[11] Riopelle returned to the high mountains in late 1964 and early 1965, staying at the Luchon-Superbagnères resort in

France for a ski vacation. A knee injury kept him off his feet the entire trip, and he executed a series of small works on paper inspired by his view of the Pyrenees.

Riopelle's time abroad heightened his interest in the North and Inuit art. Rather than projecting his own exoticizing gaze onto the northern landscape, he developed, through distancing, a healthy relationship of discovery with the territory. Riopelle and, later, René Derouin[12] were pioneers in the representation of Québec's North. Foreign lands—France for the former and Mexico for the latter—led both to grasp from a broadened perspective what is inherently interesting about winter and northern landscapes.

Riopelle made it to the "Far North" for the first time in 1969, visiting Pangnirtung on Baffin Island: he could at last explore the territory and see for himself how far it really was from the imagined North. This trip provoked a radical shift in his visual treatment of the North: the sky becomes black and now hangs over nothing but the stylized forms of icebergs interlocked on the painting's surface. The painter incorporated his experience into his personal understanding of the North, transforming the real experience of the land into an abstract gesture.

Riopelle often gave his abstract works titles referring to real places in the North, such as *Iceland* (1973), *Ungava* (1974), *Mistassini* (1975), *Labrador* (1977). He made the following striking statement in 1981: "Perhaps we travel to find titles for the works we make."[13] The use of titles to evoke places in abstract works is not unique to painting. In the issue "L'imaginaire du Nord et du froid en musique. Esthétique d'une musique nordique" of *Les Cahiers de la Société québécoise de recherche en musique*,[14] Claudine Caron demonstrates that instrumental musical works—which can be considered non-figurative—most often fall under a northern register simply by their title, which dictates the interpretation of the piece. Riopelle later adopted this

81   82

method, opting for Inuit-specific words as titles not only for abstract works but also for paintings inspired by the practices of this people, in both cases referring back to an Inuit register.

In his later years, with the series featuring snow geese (261), he once again shifted his gaze towards the North, thus baffling the critics. Gone were the radical use of black and white and the forms that evoked nature's raw power: instead, birds (such as are found on the Saint Lawrence) were given centre stage. The symbol of the goose—which on rising skyward sees the land as a matrix—stands for the eternal movement between the Arctic and the rest of the world, as well as the beginning and end of winter. This figure, present in various northern cultures,[15] refers to the cycle of seasonal migrations and displacements between the North and the rest of the world. It is one of the most comprehensive signs of the imagined North and winter.

MEDIATING AN INDIGENOUS INSPIRATION

Meeting the legendary figure Grey Owl in 1936 left a mark on Jean Paul Riopelle, who went on to identify with the owl. The man hiding behind the nickname was either a trickster or a fraud: the well-known "Native" was a persona invented by Archibald Stansfeld Belaney, whose parents were English. His ruse was brilliant: the man built from scratch a fake identity for himself based on a smattering of imagined materials (the North, nature and Indigenous peoples), and changed views on land conservation for the better.

Spending time with the Surrealists gave Riopelle access to Inuit and Indigenous art, which was then seen as a raw form of expression capable of inspiring the art of the day. This discovery was important to the construction of Riopelle's unique North. The collection built by the writer and art critic Georges Duthuit in New York[16] attributed to the artist's northern imagery a moral view of Indigenous art, understood as a return to fundamental values. Duthuit's thinking was thus in line with the idea of the North as a potential source of renewal for European influence and inventiveness.[17]

For his *Rois de Thulé* series (72-77, 126, 135, 137, 138), Riopelle drew inspiration from Henri Matisse's illustrations in Duthuit's book *Une fête en Cimmérie* (1956) (40), which in turn were inspired by the author's ethnographic collection. Nothing better demonstrates the fundamental principle of fabricating an imagery than this overlap of aesthetic choices, which—here with little experience of Inuit Nunangat, as the Inuit territorial homeland is now known, and no relationship at all with Inuit creators—makes it possible to mediate influences into an original whole. Duthuit's ideological choice, Matisse's aesthetic project and, finally, Riopelle's creative gesture in turn form fascinating layers of meaning that construct the imagined North from knowledge that essentially disregards the real North. Riopelle was aware of these layers of meaning and of the West as a mediating agent that first gave him access to Inuit art, opening the way for his original and distanced approach: "My Eskimos come from France,"[18] he joked.

The artist's Inuit inspiration thus did not fundamentally stem from first-hand experience. For example, the idea for the *Jeux de ficelles series* (111, 119, 121, 122, 125) came from the title of a book by the anthropologist Guy Mary-Rousselière (113).[19] Riopelle was fascinated by the simplicity of forms, the striking contrast of black against white, the gesture that creates the image—in short, the Inuit semiological and symbolic system. In his *Jeux* and *Rois de Thulé*, Riopelle drew inspiration from the imagined Arctic and Inuit practices, rather than their corresponding territories, and honed in on the interplay that adapts and shifts the parts of an imaginary landscape already largely coded, mediated and overloaded.

Riopelle's approach to Inuit art is not devoid of stereotyping, but it would be unfair to fail to consider the context of his time. By turning to such art, the artist acted as a pioneer. After him, steps were taken to promote Indigenous art, followed by the raising of Native voices, which have led to a more ethical relationship between the Western gaze and Indigenous production. Riopelle's actions were a necessary step towards these subsequent developments.

Inspired by art reconstrued through a colonial lens, Riopelle's work shows borrowings from Inuit and First Nations cultures. But by setting out to encounter the North, by hunting, by visiting countless northern lakes, he added an experience of the land to his cultural awareness of it. Through this concrete understanding of the realities of the land, he earned the respect of Indigenous peoples,[20] approaching a way of being that led him to discover a powerful force, close to nature.

15. For example, Selma Lagerlöf's Swedish epic of 1907, *The Wonderful Adventures of Nils* (London: J. M. Dent and Sons, 1950).

16. Rémi Labrusse, Claude Duthuit et al., *Autour de Georges Duthuit*, exh. cat. (Arles: Actes Sud, 2003).

17. At a talk given November 20, 2018, as part of the colloquium *L'avantage du froid*, held at North-Eastern Federal University, Yakutsk, the philosopher Olga Lavrenova defended the idea that Europe, having run out of new knowledge, has had to turn towards the East, South and North for ideas in order to ensure its survival and that of its influence. This would in fact explain part of the interest in the imagined North and, along with it, Indigenous cultures. The French translation of the proceedings was published in the group essay *Géocultures. Méthodologies russes sur l'Arctique* (Montreal: Imaginaire | Nord, 2020).

18. Monique Brunet-Weinmann, "Riopelle, l'élan d'Amérique," *Colóqiuo Artes*, 2nd series, no. 56 (March 1983), pp. 5–15.

19. Guy Mary-Rousselière, *Les jeux de ficelle des Arviligjuarmiut*, Bulletin 233 (Ottawa: Musées nationaux du Canada, 1969).

20. At least that of Guy Sioui Durand, who devoted two texts to him: *Jean-Paul Riopelle : l'art d'un trappeur supérieur. Indianité* (Sainte-Foy: Les Éditions GID, 2003) and *Les très riches heures de Jean-Paul Riopelle* (Trois-Rivières: Éditions d'art Le Sabord, 2000).

21. Robert, *Riopelle, chasseur d'images*, p. 181.

22. Gilles Daigneault, "Quelques notes furtives sur Jean Paul Riopelle," in *Riopelle. Mémoires d'ateliers*, eds. Yseult Riopelle and Gilles Daigneault (Montreal: Catalogue raisonné de Jean Paul Riopelle, 2010), p. 30.

A PERSONAL AND UNIVERSAL IMAGINED NORTH

Although Jean Paul Riopelle refused to see his work limited to landscape or abstraction, his geographical itineraries suggest a certain influence of northern territories on his production. The connection lies in the mediation made possible by the construction of a personal imagery: "Landscapes, if one absolutely insists, but then only a mental landscape!" declared the artist.[21] Some of nordicity's materials, such as snow, which can be used for sculpting, had captured his interest from childhood, and he acknowledged going back to it often in "fantastic improvisations to which [his] bronze sculptures are greatly indebted" (**83**).[22]

The power of Riopelle's paintings of the North lies in the impossibility of defining his production as figurative or abstract, or of reducing his approach to a desire to reproduce the North and the Arctic's particular "nature" in visual form. This unsettling discomfort remains constant before his abstract glacier figures, the multiple references condensed into the *Rois de Thulé* series, the simplified abstract games inspired by the practice of string games, his memories of flying over wintry landscapes, his observations of the raw brutality of hunting, animals and nature, and even his stylized geese that guide the eye upwards, between the seasons and territories of the "Far North" and the rest of the world.

His work assimilates multiple traces and influences into an organic whole that deploys its own use of forms and meaning, opening the path to an imagery entirely unique to the artist, yet having forever changed our ideas of the North and the Arctic.

83
Basil Zarov
Bernard Morisset, Riopelle and Madeleine Arbour outside the Studio at Sainte-Marguerite-du-Lac-Masson
About 1977

In this photograph taken in 1977, Riopelle appears in the company of his dear friend Madeleine Arbour and Bernard Morisset. The artist draws a parallel between a clay sculpture and a snow "sculpture," both of which he made. He once said, "Starting with the traditional children's snowman, I would create fantastic improvisations to which my bronzes owe a good deal."

83

84

84
Jean Paul Riopelle
Autriche
1954
Oil on canvas

85
Jean Paul Riopelle
Autriche III
1954
Oil on canvas

85

86

86
Jean Paul Riopelle
Blizzard
1954
Oil on canvas

87
Jean Paul Riopelle
Blizzard
1954
Oil on canvas

88

89

88
Jean Paul Riopelle
Regel
1957
Oil on canvas

89
Jean Paul Riopelle
Lumière du Nord
1957
Oil on canvas

90
Jean Paul Riopelle
Avalanche
1957
Oil on canvas

90

RIOPELLE

GUY SIOUI DURAND

ONKWE

AMONG THE

HONWE

TSIE8EI
8ENHO8EN

1. I am writing this essay as a Wendat. Who are we? Generally, we, the Indigenous peoples, name ourselves in our own languages. In Kebeq, aside from the Wendat (Huron), there are nine other First Nations: the Eeyou (Cree), the Innu (Montagnais), the Naskapi, the Mi'gmaq (Micmacs), the Wolastoqiyik (Maliseet), the Anishinabeg (Algonquin), the Waban-Aki (Abenaki), the Kanien'kehá:ka (Mohawk) and the Atikamekw, as well as Inuit of Nunavik. As a present-day sociologist and writer in pursuit of an Indigenous history of Indigenous art, I am also faced with a plethora of moralizingly "correct" appellations that are exogenous to our identities. Labels like "Savages," "Indians," "American Indians," "Aboriginals" and "Indigenous" can be traced back to the Indian Act (1876), still in force in Canada, and to the changing designations produced by the colonial languages of Spanish, French and English and transmitted via the broad field of social sciences and other languages spoken since 1492. In this essay I shall use all these appellations interchangeably, with explanations where necessary. In his time, Riopelle spoke of the "Indian." As far as the generic concept of "Indigenous" is concerned, I understand it in a geopolitical sense to include the members of the First Nations, the Métis and Inuit of Nunavut and Nunavik. There are also scholarly concepts such as *Amérindien* and *autochtonie*, used exclusively in the francophone social sciences, or equivalents from anglophone cultural studies like "Native," "Indian," "Aboriginal," "Indigenous" and "indigeneity." From a literary and activist point of view, the labels "American Indians" and "Savages" appeal to me for the sense they convey of people untamed, wild, unconquered and unassimilated, along with the idea of unceded territories.

2. There are certain expressions in our languages that clarify and expand on the status of "real" people, those women and men who still inhabit the territories, travel through them and set up camp in them, who practise traditional ways there and are steeped in knowledge of a way of life they are keeping alive. An expression like Onkwehonwe harks back to the ancient era of mythological cohabitation with the animist world of spirits and the fabulous realm inhabited by animals and other forms of life.

3. Georges E. Sioui, "The Discovery of Americity," in *Indigena: Contemporary Canadian Perspectives*, exh. cat., eds. Gerald McMaster and Lee-Ann Marin (Hull: Canadian Museum of Civilization, 1992), pp. 59–70.

4. The original reads: "If the Indians could come and see, they would be once more at home." See Elisa Breton, André Breton and Benjamin Péret, "Aparté," in *Riopelle à La Dragonne*, exh. cat. (Paris: Galerie Nina Dausset, 1949), [n.p.].

5. Gilles Havard, *Histoire des coureurs de bois: Amérique du Nord, 1600-1840* (Paris: Les Indes savantes, 2016), p. 610.

6. E. Breton, A. Breton and Péret, "Aparté."

7. Gilbert Érouart, *Entretiens avec Jean-Paul Riopelle, suivis de Fernand Seguin rencontre Jean-Paul Riopelle* (Montreal: Liber, 1993), pp. 25-26.

8. Gilbert Érouart and Michel Noël, *Signes premiers: Riopelle, Kijno, Chu Teh-Chun*, exh. cat. (Quebec City: Le Loup de Gouttière, 1988), pp. 38-39.

91
Jean Paul Riopelle
L'Indien
1969–70,
cast about 1971
Bronze

For the Wendat,[1] there are dreams, amplified by art and literature, that lead us towards a wild, untamed nordicity. These imaginary territories teem with mythological figures, legends, fabulous stories and visual forms rooted deep in the past. Furthermore, they correspond to actual topographies. The boreal forests and tundras of North America, with their rich flora and fauna, are still inhabited by First Nations, Métis and Inuit people. These regions were a source of inspiration for the Quebec artist Jean Paul Riopelle: first at a distance, from his home in Paris and during trips to New York, and later, after his return to Quebec, through his sojourns among the "real" Onkwehonwe,[2] the women and men born on the back of Yandiawish, the Big Turtle, who have lived and travelled daily through our lands since time immemorial.

Adopting a viewpoint indissociable from the Wendat concept of *ohtehra*, which articulates the indivisibility of the circular vision of time and the animist relations between the life of ideas (the sacred, culture, knowledge, historicity, art) and all living things, this essay explores two comprehensive strains of a shared nordicity in Kebeq (Quebec) and Kanata' (Canada), expressive and symbolic evidence of which can be found in the works of this talented artist.

For Riopelle travelled to the frontiers of "Americity," a concept introduced by the Wendat historian Georges E. Sioui to point to an understanding distinct from that of the established appellation of "America."[3] For the same reason I paraphrase here in the present tense the comment made by André Breton, the "pope" of Surrealism, when speaking of Riopelle's abstract works: "If the Indians can come and see, they will be once more at home (**48, 49**)."[4] This is true in at least two ways: first, rather than merely framing landscapes, the pictorial eye shaping these paintings is as watchful as the Indigenous peoples moving through their territories; and second, the works express a joie de vivre, a blend of the geniality and the orality of the storyteller, that calls to mind the mythical figure of the trickster.

A WILD CULTURE OF THE GAZE

In my view, an aspect of Riopelle's extraordinarily rich work reflects an affinity, even a homology with the Indigenous mindset, a way of observing and interpreting *in situ*, in nature. In short, a wild culture of the gaze. This culture, vital to survival on the land, is characterized by a keen sense of observation and a harmonious presence in the environment.

During their travels, as the historian Gilles Havard tells us, the *coureurs des bois* of days gone by observed, learned and assimilated this "permanent need to scan the horizon to spot impending dangers, to observe nature in order to detect evidence and information . . . Like sailors, these men undoubtedly possessed a greater sense of visual acuity than most other Europeans of the period."[5] This kinship between the wild gaze shared by Indigenous people and

the one acquired through mimetism by fur traders venturing into First Nations territories suggests that Riopelle brought a similar visual acuity to bear in the realm of contemporary art.

It seems to me that Riopelle transposed visually into his work that vital honing of senses constantly on the alert— but also the gaze of someone enthralled by nature, someone pursuing the same freedom sought by the early *coureurs des bois* who adopted traditional Indigenous ways. Riopelle's status as an heir to this lineage was captured beautifully by André Breton in his famous description of the artist as a "superior trapper."[6]

Riopelle's art is based in part on this capacity to "see," decode and memorize each significant fragment, each one of a territory's human or animal traces in order to integrate them into his creations. This state of alert is the source of empirical Indigenous knowledge of a territory's topography, its waterways, valleys and mountains. Riopelle, a fishing enthusiast from earliest youth, practised silence and patience, and was used to observing and listening to animals.[7] It is no surprise that when he spoke of travelling by water, or of goose or moose hunting, he displayed an Indigenous attitude towards animals, which involves thinking like them, talking to them, honouring them, engaging with them.

For the moose, it's even more difficult [than to imitate the call of the goose]. You have to call every half hour. You can't see him, but he can hear you. As you sense him getting closer, you have to convince him that you're a moose as well. You become an animal, an animal with antlers that breaks branches as it moves around. This is the crux: the branches we're supposed to have broken must fall from the correct height. The length of the drop, the time the branch takes to hit the ground: this is what's required for the moose. If he "believes" it, then he also believes there's another male around, a potential rival . . . Jealous, furious, he shows himself . . . You want to hunt moose? You have to be a moose. Not everyone is! I've drawn all this, the print called Champlain à la chasse à l'orignal (**119c**). *It also includes string games . . . String games are fundamental. The knowledge possessed in this realm by the Indians, the Eskimos, is fundamental.*[8]

This code is the basis for the sacred Aboriginal ritual of hunting bear during hibernation, a killing that is required for the holding of a *makusham*, or feast (*maku* means "bear" in the Cree language). It is why Riopelle, although a devotee of hunting and fishing in remote territories (in lands occupied by "Indians," as we were called in those days), by making these practices part of his art set himself apart from the reigning "sportsmen" culture through his ability to assume, like Indigenous hunters, the behaviour and habits of animals, and to consider Indigenous hunters as more than mere guides, to see animals and fish as more than mere hunting and fishing trophies.[9]

In fact, the many conversations people report having had with the artist about his passion for speed and the sports and activities he practised, which included hockey, automobile racing, sailing and flying expeditions, offer ample evidence of this wild culture of the gaze: for all depend on accurate visual observation and precise gestures, none allow any margin for error.

This explains in part why his pictorial and sculptural works, however modern and urban they may be, so easily integrate gestures and movements of nature that non-Indigenous analysts, concerned with constructing an official history of art, have seen simply as the "accidents" and "coincidences" of Automatisme or Surrealism.

THE ICONOCLASTIC VITALITY OF THE TRICKSTER

The second strain of wildness associated with Riopelle's wanderings through nordicity seems to me to be his artistic persona, some features of which recall the well-known Aboriginal figure of the trickster, whose incredible stories are rooted in subterfuge, traps and ambiguities. As the Quebec art historian François-Marc Gagnon has shown, if we look at Riopelle's large abstract paintings, we can interpret them as enigmas of formal creativity. But we can also discern in the figurative works, such as those featuring greater snow geese, the silhouettes of indeterminate forms. With his gleeful and wily talent as a raconteur and his reflections on the art of Indigenous people, Riopelle assumed the enigmatic and mischievous mantle of this constantly metamorphosizing teller of fabulous tales.[10]

On the one hand, Gagnon offers a stylistic key to Riopelle's approach by pointing to the tension that results from the dialectical interplay in his works between the invisible and the visible. Right across the pictorial output—decalcomanias, lithographs, pastels, Automatiste experiments and, particularly, the large paintings executed in oil or spray paint—Gagnon detects what he describes as recurring artistic "instants" of invisibility: muddled tracks, absence/presence, empty forms and negative impressions that trigger the spectator's imagination.[11] This analysis explains both the wild nordicity that runs throughout Riopelle's oeuvre and the joyful spirit of continual reinvention so akin to that of the Indigenous trickster.[12]

But the artist, who was a superb and comical storyteller—as evidenced by, for example, his acting out of the story of L'Indien qui se trompe (92)[13]—always refused in his interviews to be identified with any particular movement or avant-garde trend, or even to be classified as either abstract or figurative.

ARTISTIC NOMADISM

Taking as a starting point the impact of northern regions on Riopelle's visual sensibility and the suggested kinship with the figure of the trickster, I decided to explore these notions in relation to five types of work representing different facets of the artist's brilliant career. They encompass the "impenetrable forests"[14] of the monumental abstract works, which simultaneously conceal and conjure up the Indigenous territories surrounding the Hudson and James bays; the artist's love of sailing and of the Atikamekw canoe, which recalls his hospitality and his interest in Indigenous ingenuity; the icebergs, kings of Thule and string games that drifted south from Inuit territories into works that, aside from evoking the destinations of his major hunting and fishing expeditions, express a form of ecological humanism; the playful urban ambush of La Joute in Tiöhtià:ke (Montreal) (100, 101); and the migratory cycles of the greater snow geese centring on the great river—an artistic flight and an ultimate geography.

THE IMPENETRABLE FORESTS

If we adopt the Aboriginal view of a circular temporality to understand the nature/culture paradigm through art—a temporality quite distinct from the chronological linearity of Western historicity—it could be maintained that the abstract work produced by Riopelle between the 1940s and the 1970s already offered "wild" hints of nordicity and indigeneity. A number of his large gestural abstractions resemble "impenetrable forests" that seem to conceal the vitality of untamed nature and of the world inhabited by those who were known then as "American Indians," and who are actually referred to in several titles.[15] In my view, the multicoloured "mosaic" paintings, executed with a palette knife, contain early covert signs of the seasonal cycles and of a wild bestiary composed of owls and greater snow geese, moose and bears, fish and hunting dogs. They have been shaped by that formal process of invisibility identified by François-Marc Gagnon, but from an exogenous, distant perspective, for they were produced in Paris, one of the great European capitals of modernity, where there was considerable interest in anthropological studies of Native peoples, where many collectors were drawn to the subject and where exhibitions called "human zoos" were held.[16]

9. Industrial and urban modernity, and the railway it gave rise to (which became the symbol of the formation of Canada), but also the development of agriculture and the ascension of the logging companies, has been reflected in a reduction and transformation of ancestral Indigenous territories into recreation areas (national parks, private sporting clubs), along with changes in traditional ways of hunting and fishing. With the advent of what I call the age of "sportsmen," many Atikamekw, Innu, Anishinabeg, Eeyou and Wendat people in the province of Quebec became seasonal guides. Moreover, this approach underpins the government regulations that control today's recreational hunting and fishing "industry." Valuable light is shed on this question by the small and little-known book by Sylvain Gingras, Sonia Lirette and Claude Gilbert entitled Le Club Triton : l'histoire du plus prestigieux club de chasse et pêche au Québec (Georges E. Sioui, ed. [Quebec City: Les Éditions Rapides Blancs, 1989]). Also, the devastating documentary Une tente sur Mars (2008), by artist Martin Bureau and his associate Luc Renaud, shot in the Nitassinan region, near Matimekosh, home to the Innu, reveals only too clearly the techniques adopted in the raids conducted in Quebec by American hunters in search of caribou.

10. Rémi Savard, Carcajou à l'aurore du monde : fragments écrits d'une encyclopédie orale innue (Montreal: Recherches amérindiennes au Québec, 2016). See also François-Xavier Michaud, ed., Terres de Trickster : contes des Premières Nations (Montreal: Possibles Éditions, 2014).

11. François-Marc Gagnon, "Riopelle: Visibility and Invisibility," in Jean Paul Riopelle : catalogue raisonné, tome 4, 1966-1971, eds. Yseult Riopelle and Tanguy Riopelle (Montreal: Hibou Éditeurs, 2014), pp. 42-43.

12. Louise Vigneault, Espace artistique et modèle pionnier : Tom Thomson et Jean-Paul Riopelle (Montreal: Hurtubise, 2011), p. 382.

13. Guy Sioui Durand, Jean-Paul Riopelle : l'art d'un trappeur supérieur. Indianité (Sainte-Foy: Les Éditions GID, 2003), pp. 25-29.

14. This idea is evoked in Claude Bouyeure, "Entretien avec Jean-Paul Riopelle," Les Lettres françaises, no. 1236 (June 12-18, 1968), p. 28.

15. Titles, for example, such as Hochelaga (1947) (3); Ontario (1945 and 1947-48); Entre les quatre murs du vent, j'écoute – Nadaka (1947); Forêt (1953); Sous le mythe de Gitksan (1956) and simply Gitksan (1955-59) (60-66); Avatac (1971) (111); Point de rencontre – Quintette (1963) (11).

16. The exhibition Human Zoos: The Invention of the Savage, its catalogue and a series of related conferences organized in 2011-12 by the Musée du quai Branly - Jacques Chirac, in Paris, focused specifically on this phenomenon.

92

92
Jean Paul Riopelle
(photo Bruno Massenet, 1955)
Ill. in Huguette Vachon et al.,
Jean Paul Riopelle : les traces
de l'envol (2003)

In three photographs taken by Bruno Massenet, Riopelle strikes stereotypical poses of the "fictitious Indian," as the artist put it. In a reductive, non-Indigenous construction of Indigenous identity, he mimics, among other things, an Indigenous person wearing a headdress in the form of an animal's head.

93-94 | In 1974, Riopelle had a house/studio built in the Laurentians on a property next to that of Champlain Charest's home. The shape of the building was inspired by old barns, which the artist took an interest in, as demonstrated by the inclusion of various books on the subject in his library. The wood for the building's exterior siding came from the barn belonging to Champlain Charest's father. Riopelle took his inspiration from a project of Barney Rosset (the former husband of Joan Mitchell) at Three Mile Harbour, Long Island. In 1960, Rosset had four barns moved to the site and hired an architect to convert them into residences for artists and writers. Riopelle saw this group of buildings during a months-long stay on Long Island in 1960 and 1961. According to the artist's biographer Hélène de Billy, the house/studio was the culmination of his end-of-study project at the École du Meuble, which consisted of plans for a "painter's house in the country." The interior of this three-storey house overlooking Lac Masson was decorated by Madeleine Arbour. – AR

93
Basil Zarov
Jean Paul Riopelle outside of the Studio at Sainte-Marguerite-du-Lac-Masson
About 1976

94
Basil Zarov
Jean Paul Riopelle with "Hibou-pelle" (1969–70) outside of the Studio at Sainte-Marguerite-du-Lac-Masson
About 1976

95

96

97

95-97 | The Atikamekw Nehirowisiw canoe maker César Newashish (1902–1994) came from Manawan in the Haute-Mauricie. Over the years, his bark canoes became an emblem of the nation's culture. A documentary film made by Bernard Gosselin in 1971 showcases the artisan's talents and know-how. Today, his canoes are found in various museum collections around the world and with private collectors. Steeped in his Nation's oral tradition, Newashish was an ardent defender of the environment and territorial rights of his people. At the end of his life, at the age of ninety-one, he left a message for his kin: "Tell them that we never ceded our land, that we never sold it, that we never traded it, and that we never decided otherwise with regards to our land." – JT

17. Gilles Daigneault, "Some Furtive Notes on Jean Paul Riopelle," in *Riopelle: Studio Memories*, eds. Yseult Riopelle and Gilles Daigneault (Montreal: Catalogue raisonné de Jean Paul Riopelle, 2010), p. 41; Monique Brunet-Weinmann, "Les anés dionysiaques," in *Jean Paul Riopelle : catalogue raisonné, tome 2, 1954-1959*, ed. Yseult Riopelle (Montreal: Hibou Éditeurs, 2004), pp. 56-60.

18. Pierre Gauvreau, "Réflexions sur l'art indien," *Journal musical canadien* (December 1954), p. 6.

19. François-Marc Gagnon, *Chronique du mouvement automatiste québécois, 1941-1954* (Montréal: Lanctôt Éditeur, 1999), pp. 574–576 and 581.

20. The collaboration of Karine Echaquan Newashish, César Newashish's granddaughter, on the exhibition of contemporary Indigenous art entitled *Of Tobacco and Sweetgrass: Where Our Dreams Are*, which was presented at the Musée d'art de Joliette in the winter of 2019 and which I curated, gave me an opportunity to talk to them about this friendship and even to discover a photograph that shows Riopelle with the canoe made by César Newashish.

21. The book edited by Yseult Riopelle and entitled *Riopelle. Les migrations du bestiaire* (Montreal: Kétoupa Édition, 2014) focuses on the various animal images in the artist's work. From an Indigenous perspective, the important animal figures are the bear (*L'ours*, 1969-70; *Avatac*, 1971, which pictures the polar bear, the lynx and the walrus); the eagle (*Grand Aigle*, 1968); the fox (*Les deux renards*, 1971); the Canada goose and other species of goose; large members of the deer family, such as the moose (*L'Élan*, 1968; *Orignal*, 1973; *Orignal rouge*, 1981), the caribou and the wapiti (*Famine wapiti*, 1970); and also the hare (*Le lièvre au collet*, 1971). Ever the keen fisherman, Riopelle also portrayed fish, including trout. Significantly, Akiawenrahk, the Wendat name for the Saint-Charles River between Wendake and Quebec City, means "trout river." As art critic René Viau has pointed out, "from the bestiary [that Riopelle] was exploring at the time, the goose and the owl would emerge as principal totems" ("Quand passent les oies blanches," in Yseult Riopelle, ed., *Riopelle au Cap Tourmente : de la nature à l'atelier*, exh. cat. [Montreal: Kétoupa Édition, 2016], p. 5).

22. This series was presented in the exhibition *Riopelle: Strings and Other Games*, held at the Canadian Cultural Centre in Paris and the Musée d'art moderne de la Ville de Paris in 1972.

23. Denis Vaugeois, Louise Tardivel and Louise Côté, *L'Indien généreux : ce que le monde doit aux Amériques* (Montreal: Boréal, 1992).

95
Riopelle and Cécile Newashish
About 1992

In the 1970s, Riopelle acquired a bark canoe made by Atikamekw César Newashish from Manawan. These two photographs show the restoration of the canoe by Roger Echaquan and Claude Kistabish.

96
Claude Kistabish, Roger Echaquan, Riopelle and Cécile Newashish
About 1992

97
César Newashish working on a bark canoe with a child watching on
N.d.

Like his contemporary Jackson Pollock, Riopelle was attracted by the aesthetics of the carved totems and masks produced by First Nations artists of the Pacific Coast.[17] This interest was reinforced in Paris by his friendship with collectors of ethnographic objects, including masks, and in Montreal during visits to the home of fellow Automatiste Pierre Gauvreau, who was a supporter of West Coast Native arts[18] and of the political activism of the Wendat Jules Sioui.[19]

THE CANOE

During the 1970s, when the gradual process of the artist's return to Quebec had begun, he set up a studio (**93, 94**) in the *pays d'en haut* on the frontier of Nitaskinan, land of the Atikamekw. There, he became close to the well-known maker of birch canoes César Newashish and his family, even inviting them to his home in Estérel (**95, 96**).[20] Although Riopelle, a keen sailor, no doubt found in the canoe a sublimation of his artistic and nomadic fascination with hunting and fishing—one thinks immediately of his *Canot à glace*, painted in 1992 (**98**)—he also discovered in Newashish a consummate storyteller.

It was during this period too that the artist began making major hunting and fishing expeditions further north. He flew over, camped, navigated, hunted and fished extensively in the Anishinabeg and Eeyou Istchee territories around the Hudson and James bays. He visited the Abitibiwinni near Barrière Lake, the Innu and Naskapi in Nitassinan and Inuit of Baffin Island—where icebergs are continental in scale—even venturing close to the Métis lands of the Prairies. As time went on, his Native references, his titles evoking northern regions and his bestiary multiplied and became progressively more explicit.[21]

THE SOUTHWARD DRIFT OF ICEBERGS AND STRING GAMES

From the mid-1960s to the mid-1970s, in a significant and evolving creative sequence marked by a gradual shift from abstraction to representation, Riopelle drew on his northern expeditions to introduce new works into the field of international art. Reconsidered today, the aesthetic approach taken to their themes reveals an ethical dimension that could scarcely be more pertinent.

There are the *Icebergs* (1977) (**178-181, 185**), for example, a group of black and white paintings that presage the erosion and peril threatening the Arctic. These followed the magnificently colourful series inspired by Inuit string games, the *Jeux de ficelles* (1971–72) (**111, 119, 121, 122, 125**).[22] And between the two the artist created the *Rois de Thulé* (1973) (**72-77, 126, 135, 137, 138**) series, based on the legend of those who inhabit the most northerly reaches of present-day Inuit territories. The ecological innovation of these works is more evident now than ever.

THE PLAYFUL URBAN AMBUSH OF *LA JOUTE*

The sculptural installation *La Joute* (**100, 101**) does justice to the marvellous title of the book *L'Indien généreux : ce que le monde doit aux Amériques*, for it evokes the Indigenous invention of team games—not just the game known as "Capture the Flag," but also lacrosse and hockey.[23]

For a "Wendat in search of art,"[24] Riopelle's only public outdoor sculpture brings to mind the great gatherings and feasts that in different Indigenous languages are called *uduron'*, *makusham* or potlatch. In fact, through art, *La Joute* confronts us with a total social fact of Americity,[25] since in its execution and elements it combines the principal components of the Indigenous imagination. It embodies a circular vision that is spectacularly enhanced by the circle of fire around the centre of the pool; the arrangement of the elements reflects their division into teams; it transforms the Indigenous war strategy of ambush into a game; by presenting as leader a chief wearing the ceremonial headdress of the Plains tribes (**91**), it highlights the noble responsibility borne by chiefs; and, finally, a sense of respect for the spirits of animals envelops the sculpture. To the Aboriginal gaze, then, it embodies no fewer than six Indigenous expressive and symbolic components.

Although an urban pool, *La Joute* also resembles a lake— an effect reinforced by the circle of fire. This is compatible with the animist concept of the indivisibility of all forms of life on Mother Earth, whose primary source is water, as expressed by the Wendat term *ohtehra*.[26] From this viewpoint, Riopelle's fountain-sculpture can no longer be seen as belonging exclusively to a Eurocentric world.

The impression we have of *La Joute* as an inclusive camp that encourages different forms of transmission is strengthened by the presence of bas-relief motifs derived from Inuit string games, which represent non-verbal forms of socialization.

La Joute is a mythological gathering enriched by all its human-looking animal figures, which are like marvellous "Hunters-Shamans-Warriors"[27] (as I call contemporary Indigenous artists), because they are imbued with the spirit of animals. Rather than the owls or the dog, it is the bear, with its haughty pose, that occupies the central, key place. It is the bear that knows the territory and its nurturing plants best. It is the indefatigable bear that hibernates and conjures up the spirit of the *makusham*.

98

98 | Once a means of transportation for the inhabitants of the shores and islands of the Saint Lawrence Estuary, the canoe is also at the heart of the popular winter sport of ice-canoe racing. Riopelle acquired one from his friend and goose-hunting guide Gilles Gagné, a former captain of the Île-aux-Oies ice-canoeing team. By depicting snow geese on the hull, the artist suggests that, with a little help from the Devil, the canoe might take to the air, as in the Canadian legend of the "Chasse-galerie" (Bewitched Canoe). This canoe was hung from the ceiling when it was exhibited for the first time at the Centre d'exposition de Baie-Saint-Paul (now the Musée d'art contemporain de Baie-Saint-Paul) in 1998. It was with this in mind that it has been displayed suspended in the Montreal Museum of Fine Arts' Pavilion of Quebec and Canadian Art since 2011. The canoe, which is painted inside and out, only lets us see one side on the condition that the other remain hidden. – **FMG** and **AR**

98
Jean Paul Riopelle
Le canot à glace
1992
Mixed media on wood

99
César Newashish
Bark canoe

99

99 | This bark canoe built by César Newashish once belonged to Jean Paul Riopelle. Its dimensions indicate it could have accommodated one or two people for hunting or fishing near camps in the spring and summer. This variety of canoe is called *à pince* in French because of the characteristic pinched-in shape of the stern and bow. Its five thwarts, many ribs and gunwale form the craft's pegged structure. The hull is covered in birchbark. After everything was stitched and lashed together with spruce roots, the seams were sealed with a resinous spruce gum. The only tools the canoe maker used were a carving knife, a jackknife, an awl and a wooden mallet. A wave motif scratched under the gunwale creates an illusion intended to help keep the hunter from being detected when stealthily approaching an animal. A moose, the animal that supplied the Atikamekw Nehirowisiwok with necessities like food, clothing and materials for making tools, is depicted on either end of the canoe. – JT

La Joute is an ambush of players who seem like warriors. There is the bear, the three owls (**105, 106**), the fish and the dog, along with the pole that is essential to the flag game but that could also be the shaft of one of the sticks used to play lacrosse and ice hockey, Canada's two national sports. The sculpture's composition is a playful reflection of the spirit of team sports, brought to the world by Aboriginals. This approach did not exist in Europe before contact with the three Americas, where ball games were invented by the Incas and the Mayas, and the game of lacrosse by Indigenous peoples of the north.[28]

La Joute, as Riopelle confided to his great friend Madeleine Arbour, is a team awaiting its fantastical adversary.[29] This is just a thought, but it strikes me that this adversary team, maybe echoing his friend Samuel Beckett's famous play Waiting for Godot (1948), could have consisted of a team led by the great Ojibwe artist Norval "Copper Thunderbird" Morrisseau and made up of the ten artists whose works adorned the Indians of Canada Pavilion at Expo 67. The notion is prompted by the nobility of the sculpture's leading figure, the bust of an Indian, and the fact that Quebec and Canadian art history is now in a revisionist mode, having for too long excluded Indigenous people from its official narrative. Although the two artists were contemporaries, there was no direct contact between Morrisseau—who the Europeans would name "the Picasso of the north" when he took part in the famous Magiciens de la terre exhibition, held in Paris in 1989[30]—and Riopelle, the "superior trapper," who should have been part of that event, as he was of Man and His World.

THE MIGRATORY CYCLES OF SNOW GEESE

The 1980s and 1990s were, for Riopelle, the years of the Magtogoek, "the great path that walks," the Saint Lawrence River—navigated from the Baie des Chaleurs and the Gulf by the Mi'gmaq, the Wolastoqiyik, the Waban-Aki, the Wendat and the Kanien'kehá:ka, all the way to the Great Lakes and the territories of the Haudenosaunee (Iroquois)

Confederacy. The artist would set up his last artistic camp on Île-aux-Oies, between Cap Tourmente on the north shore and the river's southern bank.

A number of events and exhibitions would feature the owls and geese that soon became signature components of the Riopelle legend. After the flocks of owls marking the 1970s, the 1980s would be shaped by the cyclical movements of the greater snow and Canada geese (**261**). Although they started appearing in 1981, it was with the exhibition Riopelle. Les oies sauvages, held at the Pierre Matisse gallery in New York in 1985, that flights of these great migratory birds would begin making significant landings in his works, up to and including the moving Hommage à Rosa Luxemburg (1992).

ART SPEAKS TO ART
"What would we do without Indians?"[31]

In relation to our territories, but also to new interpretations of our intercultural relations, it is interesting to note the inclusion of a selection of eighteen works by Riopelle in the major exhibition Signes premiers : Riopelle, Kijno, Chu Teh-Chun, presented in 1994 at the Musée amérindien de Mashteuiatsh,[32] and to reconsider his large painting entitled L'étang – Hommage à Grey Owl (**110**). Grey Owl, the famous usurper of Indigenous identity, described in the 1930s as "Canada's most famous Indian," had been an idol of the young Riopelle since 1936, when he attended one of his lectures on animal conservation. In today's period of heated controversy on the question of cultural appropriation, new readings are taking shape.[33]

Ultimately, though, art speaks to art. Jean Paul Riopelle has bequeathed a great oeuvre that we can share, and to my Wendat gaze his style and many of his themes encourage a renewal of relations through rewilding.[34] This is a conversation we are having: a dialogue based on friendship and solidarity, ventures that will be pursued. Thus can we follow the mythical Riopelle in his nordicity, walking together in the footsteps of the ancients.

Onenh.
Salutations.

24. Guy Sioui Durand, "Un Wendat à la recherche de l'art, ou le souffle activiste d'un Tsie8ei," in Wendat et Wyandot d'hier et d'aujourd'hui / Wendat and Wyandot Then and Now / Eonywa'ndiynonhratehkwih chia' ekwää'tatehkwih : actes du premier Congrès d'études wendat et wyandot, Wendake, Québec, 13 au 16 juin 2012, eds. Louis-Jacques Dorais and Jonathan Lainey (Wendake: Éditions Hannenorak, 2013), pp. 51–63.

25. The potlatch, in the Indigenous languages of the Pacific Coast, has its eastern equivalent in the Innu makusham and the Wendat uduron'. They are gatherings, feasts, ceremonies, rituals and art practices that bring together all aspects of an Indigenous community, observed by European and American anthropologists and clearly conceptualized by the sociologist Marcel Mauss as a "total social fact" in Essai sur le don. Forme et raison de l'échange dans les sociétés archaïques (1925; first published in English in 1954 under the title The Gift: Forms and Functions of Exchange in Archaic Societies), in which the author draws fascinating parallels between the Kwakwaka'wakw and the Tlingit of the North American West Coast, the Indigenous people of Scandinavia, the Sami, and the Māoris of Oceania. For Mauss, the total social fact encompasses the spheres of war, shamanism and mythology, along with feasts and celebrations, the visual and performing arts, masks, totems, ceremonies, games and rituals, with a focus on the giving and receiving of gifts, disputes and rivalries. By harking back to its Indigenous origins and transposing it into art, the notion of "the total social fact of Americity" can be applied particularly aptly to Riopelle's fountain-sculpture La Joute. See Guy Sioui Durand, "Le ré-ensauvagement par l'art. Le vieil Indien, les pommes rouges et les Chasseurs-Chamanes-Guerriers," Captures, vol. 3, no. 1 (May 2018). http://revuecaptures.org/node/1277 (accessed May 13, 2020).

26. Guy Sioui Durand, "L'onderha," Inter Art Actuel, no. 122 (winter 2016), p. 3.

27. Sioui Durand, "Le ré-ensauvagement par l'art. Le vieil Indien, les pommes rouges et les Chasseurs-Chamanes-Guerriers."

28. Vaugeois, Tardivel and Côté, L'Indien généreux, pp. 112, 128–129 and 146–147.

29. "Riopelle": Femme d'aujourd'hui, VHS, directed by Jeannette Tardif (Montreal: Société Radio-Canada, 1972).

30. The unusual and innovative exhibition Magiciens de la terre, curated by Jean-Hubert Martin and presented in 1989 at the Centre Pompidou and the Grande halle de la Villette, in Paris, aimed to show that contemporary artistic creation was not exclusive to the West by assembling works by some one hundred artists from every part of the world.

31. Érouart, Entretiens avec Jean-Paul Riopelle, p. 78.

32. Of the eighteen works by Riopelle in the exhibition, which was also presented at three other Quebec venues, all were untitled except Wou-Ki salut! (1990).

33. Such as the re-examination of the use made of the traditional headdress of warrior chiefs, which was integral to the performance and video featuring the marriage between Miss Chief Eagle Testickle, alter ego of the artist Kent Monkman, and the fashion designer Jean Paul Gaultier, presented on the occasion of the exhibition Love Is Love: Wedding Bliss for All, held at the Montreal Museum of Fine Arts in 2017.

34. Sioui Durand, Jean-Paul Riopelle, pp. 25–29 and 71.

100

101

100
La Joute (plaster
model) exhibited
at the Musée d'art
moderne de la Ville
de Paris
1972

101
La Joute on display
outside of the Olympic
Stadium, Montreal
After 1976

102
Jean Paul Riopelle
Grand duc
1970
Oil on canvas

102

103

104

103
Jean Paul Riopelle
Hibou-masque
1973
Bronze

104
Jean Paul Riopelle
Hibou-totem
1973, cast 1986
Bronze, 3/8

105
Jean Paul Riopelle
Femme hibou
1969–70,
cast about 1971
Bronze

106
Jean Paul Riopelle
Hibou A
1969–70, cast 1976
Bronze

105

106

107

108

109

110 | Archibald Stansfeld Belaney, later known as Grey Owl, was born in Hastings, England, in 1888. He immigrated to Canada in 1906, became a fur trapper and invented an Indigenous identity for himself. In 1925, his wife, Anahareo, of Algonquin and Mohawk descent, convinced him that his hunting activities were harmful to the environment. He then set about spreading his new ecological convictions and became an early conservationist with Dominion Parks Branch (now Parks Canada). The author of *Tales of an Empty Cabin* (1936) wrote various successful novels that delighted the young Riopelle. In 1936, the artist attended a talk given by Grey Owl. In 1938, Archibald "Grey Owl" Belaney passed away in Beaver Lodge, Saskatchewan, now a popular tourist destination. In this large painting executed in Paris, we can make out the famous fur trapper's cabin by the lake from the profusion of coloured strokes rendering the Canadian forest. This Englishman who had usurped an Indigenous identity, this fur trapper who had taken up the cause of environmental protection, had all the elements needed to capture Riopelle's interest.
– FMG and AR

110
Jean Paul Riopelle
*L'étang – Hommage
à Grey Owl*
1970
Oil on canvas

110

RIOPELLE AND

KRISTA
ULUJUK ZAWADSKI

INUIT

STRING GAMES

String games, or *ajaraaq* in Inuktitut, have always been a part of my life. From my earliest memories in Igluligaarjuk (Chesterfield Inlet) on the western shores of Hudson Bay, I can vividly recall the laughter and jovial times we spent playing *ajaraaq* at home, at school and while camping at our cabin on the land. String figures are designs created with a piece of string tied into a loop, such as the commonly known cat's cradle. String games make use of string figures to play or tell stories. One such example of a string game among Inuit is to see who can create figures the fastest. During the Fifth Thule Expedition in the early 1920s, anthropologist Knud Rasmussen collected this story from the Natsilik Inuit:[1]

Tuutannguarjuk is the spirit of the string figures. It has its name after a certain string figure that is called by the very name of tuutannguarjuk. It is a dangerous spirit that sometimes attacks women, and may even carry away those who become too eager to play with string figures. There was once a child who at night, instead of sleeping, lay awake and made string figures on the platform. While the child lay there tuutannguarjuk came in and started to make string figures too, using his own intestine as string. When he was in the middle of one of the figures he said suddenly: "Let us see which of us can make tuutannguarjuit quickest." The people of the house were asleep, that is why tuutannguarjuk was so bold. He was finished first, and was just going to spring at the child when one of the sleeping men awoke suddenly and sat up. At the same moment tuutannguarjuk jumped to his feet and fled out through the passage, and the man's light sleep thus saved the child from being carried away.[2]

The string game played by the young Inuk in the story is an example of a type played by Inuit. There are many other games. String games are played near the end of the National Film Board of Canada production *Tuktu and the Clever Hands*.[3] The joy expressed by Inuit in the film is reminiscent of my own experience with string games. The string figures we learned and taught each other as children, accompanied sometimes with traditional stories or recollections of past *ajaraaq* played, were often complex and included many steps that today, as an adult, I find difficult to remember. However, the fond memories of the games themselves remain, which motivates me to continue this tradition with my children as they grow up. This is common with other Inuit as well.

In 2013, I had the privilege to attend Michael Arvaarluk Kusugak's storytelling at the Museum of Anthropology, University of British Columbia (112). Arvaarluk shared stories from his childhood and brought them to life with fluid motions of his hands and the piece of string he brought with him. He captured the audience with a figure of a caribou walking, as well as talking about the importance of *qulliit* (seal oil lamps) among Inuit while creating a figure of one with the string. The movement he brought to the string to tell the Inuit stories was captivating and a testament to the nature of string games for Inuit, who believe *ajaraaq* are important in building personal relationships as well as passing on oral histories and traditions.[4] Furthermore, *ajaraaq* are "like picture shows and also developed important skills. As the person demonstrated the game, you had to guess what it would become. The games build memory, observation and creativity skills."[5]

Arctic string figures have been documented by anthropologists for over a century. Anthropologist Franz Boas conducted ethnographic fieldwork in Baffin Island's Cumberland Sound in 1888. In his ethnography *The Central Eskimo*, he wrote, "The women are particularly fond of making figures out of a loop, a game similar to our cat's cradle. They are, however, much more clever than we are in handling the thong and have a great variety of forms."[6] Later anthropologist Diamond Jenness collected over two hundred string figures and accompanying stories or songs for study, and analyzed the distribution of string figures across the Arctic. He noted there were often rules for playing *ajaraaq*, including not being able to create string figures at certain times of the year: "From Kotzebue Sound, in Alaska, to Kent Peninsula, at the eastern end of Coronation Gulf, there was a taboo against playing the game except in the winter, when the sun no longer rose above the horizon."[7] It was believed that the sun might get tangled in the string figures and be prevented from rising back up to the sky. Although taboos or rules for *ajaraaq* were not the same for each group of Inuit across the Arctic, similar beliefs were documented in other areas of the Canadian Arctic. Anthropologist Knud Rasmussen documented one such rule among the Iglulingmiut (Inuit from Iglulik): "Boys who have not yet caught bearded seal or walrus must not play cat's cradle (string figures). If they do, then they are liable to get their fingers entangled in the harpoon lines and be dragged out into the sea."[8]

Jean Paul Riopelle took up his string game theme in 1969, first introducing the use of knots and strings in the execution of *La Joute* (100, 101), which depicted a fictional team of players of the game *jeu de drapeau* (capture the flag).[9] Riopelle was inspired by Guy Mary-Rousselière's book *Les jeux de ficelle des Arviligjuarmiut* (113), as pointed out by Riopelle's friend the artist Roseline Granet: "He loved working on the *Jeux de ficelles*. I remember very clearly: he had taken a book on string games to the studio he'd rented in Meudon. He steeped himself in the subject, and for the first time he began using acrylic. Then, as always when he began to paint, he was totally happy. The

1. The *Natsilingmiut*, or Natsilik Inuit, live in the Central Arctic, on the Arctic Coast, north of Hudson Bay. Their traditional lands are on the Boothia, Adelaide and Simpson Peninsulas and King William Island. They have been featured in the film series *Netsilik Eskimo Series*, National Film Board of Canada, 1967, producer-director Quentin Brown. See Knud Rasmussen, *The Netsilik Eskimos: Social Life and Spiritual Culture*, vol. 8, no. 1–2 (Copenhagen: Gyldendalske Boghandel, 1931).

2. Knud Rasmussen, *Intellectual Culture of the Iglulik Eskimos*, vol. 7, no. 1 (Copenhagen: Gyldendalske Boghandel, 1929), p. 248.

3. *Tuktu and the Clever Hands*, National Film Board of Canada, 1968, director Laurence Hyde, 14 min 8 s.

4. Inuit Heritage Trust, *Inuit Contact and Colonization*, 2008, http://www.inuitcontact.ca (accessed December 5, 2018).

5. Ibid.

6. Franz Boas, Sixth Annual Report of the Bureau of Ethnology: *The Central Eskimo* (Washington, DC: Smithsonian Institution, 1888), pp. 569–570.

7. Diamond Jenness, *Report of the Canadian Arctic Expedition, 1913–18*, vol. 13, *Eskimo Folk-lore. Part B, Eskimo String Figures Southern Party, 1913–16* (Ottawa: F. A. Acland, Printers to the King's Most Excellent Majesty, 1924), p. 181.

8. Rasmussen, *Intellectual Culture of the Iglulik Eskimos*, p. 177.

9. See Yseult Riopelle and Gilles Daigneault, *Riopelle. Mémoires d'ateliers* (Montreal: Catalogue raisonné de Jean Paul Riopelle, 2010).

111
Jean Paul Riopelle
Avatac (quadriptych)
1971
Acrylic on lithographs
mounted on canvas

111

111 | "I do not remember ever learning to make the *avataq*, a float to keep harpooned seals, whales and walruses from sinking. One day, I will ask an elder to teach it to me."
– Michael Arvaarluk Kusugak

The series *Jeux de ficelles*, executed in Paris, was inspired by the book *Les jeux de ficelle des Arviligjuarmiut* (1969) written by the Canadian anthropologist Guy Mary-Rousselière. Some works from the series faithfully reproduce forms shown in the book, while others are looser improvisations. *Avatac*, in acrylic over a lithograph, depicts patterns inspired by *ajaraaq*, the string games documented by Mary-Rousselière. As the title reveals, the central motif is an *avataq*, which as the Avataq Cultural Institute tells us is a traditional hunting float made of one complete sealskin. It is flanked by the figures of a polar bear, lynx and walrus, represented with greater freedom than is seen in traditional Inuit *ajaraaq*. – AR

112

112 | String games are played around the world, and we, Inuit, have spent many evenings playing with string. Some of these figures are very simple, others much more elaborate. I once spent a very enjoyable afternoon sitting on the floor in my hotel room in Yellowknife, Northwest Territories, trading string figures with Abe Okpik, who was, once upon a time, commissioned to introduce us, Inuit, to surnames. That is a story for another day. But one of our great pastimes was trading string figures, like trading cards; you show me one and I will trade you another. Abe grew up in the eastern Arctic, away from the coast. I showed him a whale I learned many years ago. The whale is beached. It transforms into a seagull that eats its *maktaaq* (skin). The seagull, in turn, transforms into a polar bear that eats its meat. Finally, it transforms into an Arctic fox that nibbles and cleans its bones and then walks away. Abe told me he has noticed that coastal people learn figures of sea animals and inland people learn figures of land animals. – MAK

112
Film still with Michael Arvaarluk Kusugak from *Storytelling Night* (2008)

The storyteller and children's book author Arvaarluk (Michael Kusugak) grew up in Repulse Bay, Nunavut. He incorporates the string games he learned in his community into the stories he tells, as shown here at the 2008 edition of the Alianait Arts Festival in Iqaluit, Nunavut.

113
Cover of Guy Mary-Rousselière, *Les jeux de ficelle des Arviligjuarmiut* (1969)

For his *Jeux de ficelles* series (1971–72), Riopelle was greatly influenced by the anthropologist Guy Mary-Rousselière's book *Les jeux de ficelle des Arviligjuarmiut*. Published in 1969 as a bulletin issued by the National Museums of Canada, the document describes and examines 112 string figures made by Netsilik Inuit in Pelly Bay. Riopelle used it as a starting point for a series of acrylics on paper.

114
Poster for the exhibition *Riopelle: ficelles et autres jeux* presented by the Canadian Cultural Centre and the Musée d'art moderne de la Ville de Paris, 1972

10. Granet cited in Michel Waldberg, ed., *Riopelle vu par...* (Paris: Centre culturel canadien, 2004).

11. Guy Mary-Rousselière, *Les jeux de ficelle des Arviligjuarmiut*, Bulletin 233 (Ottawa: National Museums of Canada, 1969), pp. 99–100.

12. Bernard Lamarche, *Riopelle. Impressions sans fin* (Quebec City: Musée national des beaux-arts du Québec, 2005).

13. Riopelle's interest in knots and strings was also fostered by his love of sailing. His personal library included Clifford W. Ashley's *The Ashley Book of Knots: Every Practical Knot—What It Looks Like, Who Uses It, Where It Comes From, and How to Tie It* (New York: Bantam Doubleday Dell, 1944.).

14. Guy Robert, *Riopelle, chasseur d'images* (Montreal: Éditions France-Amérique, 1981), p. 135.

15. Simon Blais. *Riopelle, tigre de papier : œuvres sur papier 1953-1989* (Laval: Les 400 coups, 1997).

16. Simon Blais, *Jean Paul Riopelle : pastel* (Montreal: Éditions Simon Blais, 2004), p. 120.

17. Robert Enright, "The Inside Animal: Jean Paul Riopelle's Eccentric Bestiary," in *Riopelle : Les migrations du bestiaire : Une rétrospective*, exh. cat., ed. Yseult Riopelle (Montreal: Kétoupa Édition, 2014), p. 30.

18. Marie Routledge and Ingo Hessel, "Contemporary Inuit Sculpture: An Approach to the Medium, the Artists, and Their Work," in *In the Shadow of the Sun: Perspectives on Contemporary Native Art*, exh. cat., ed. The Canadian Museum of Civilization (Ottawa: University of Ottawa Press, 1993).

19. Heather Igloliorte, "Arctic Culture/Global Indigeneity" in *Negotiations in a Vacant Lot: Studying the Visual in Canada*, eds. Lynda Jessup, Erin Morton and Kristy Robertson (Montreal: McGill-Queen's University Press, 2014), p. 159.

20. Robert, *Riopelle, chasseur d'images*.

string theme was related to the *Fountain*, which I think came just after."[10] Riopelle's paintings in this series are more abstract than the figures drawn in *Les jeux de ficelle des Arviligjuarmiut*, but one painting can be most certainly correlated to a string figure in Mary-Rousselière's book: the artist's *L'esprit de la ficelle* (121) closely resembles the publication's illustration of the Tuutannguarjuk string figure.[11]

The series can be interpreted to represent two distinct categories: the string figure as a central motif, and the string figure as a point of departure for improvisation. Riopelle's *Jeux de ficelles* series, composed of almost one hundred acrylics on paper and heightened lithographs, was first exhibited in 1972 at the Canadian Cultural Centre and the Musée d'art moderne in Paris (114). His use of acrylics and reworked lithographs in this series depicts string figures as malleable forms of expression, evoking thoughts of fluidity and communication. It is evident, as the art historian Bernard Lamarche has pointed out, that this series enabled "Riopelle to explore new levels of expression through the medium of drawing,"[12] acrylic painting, as well as the medium of knots and string.[13] Through the use of visual motifs inspired by the string games, the painting from this period in Riopelle's career was a turn from his previous work with oil paints to acrylic.[14] It is here that acrylic is used regularly for the first time by Riopelle,[15] for depicting "the famous string games of the Inuit with a certain austerity, as if he were tired of sculpting his luxuriant oil paintings,"[16] as the gallerist Simon Blais has stated. Furthermore, it is here that Riopelle had included written titles on the front of the paintings—the only time he presented a series in this way—perhaps as a way to communicate the meaning of the string figures for a non-Inuit audience. The art critic Robert Enright describes this particular series as "among his most important works on paper."[17]

The paintings Riopelle created in the *Jeux de ficelles* series allowed him to explore modernist "primitivism," as an aesthetic ideal, more deeply in his work, which lines up well with the history of Inuit art itself. The writers Marie Routledge and Ingo Hessel highlight the role of Inuit art in the creation of a Canadian nationalistic image.[18] Through the use of Inuit art, the broader Canadian public was able to promote a national image by building on the theme of Canada as a place of northern peoples. Furthermore, the art historian Heather Igloliorte points out that Inuit art, particularly carvings, has had appeal to the broader Canadian public from the 1940s onward, as "primitive art has begun to be closely associated with modernism and modern art of the European avant-garde."[19] Riopelle would have been no stranger to these Canadian underpinnings of nationalistic image-building through Inuit and their art, and was clearly influenced by Inuit art and culture in his work.

Riopelle was influenced by Inuit art, as demonstrated in his *Hiboux* (103-109) and *Jeux de ficelles* series (1969–1972) (111, 119, 121, 122, 125), as well as his *Rois de Thulé* series (1973) (72-77, 126, 135, 137, 138), after his first trip to Nunavik in 1972, and his *Icebergs* series (1977) (178-181, 185), after his trip to Nunavut (Pangnirtung, Baffin Island) in 1969, 1971 and 1977. The titles of some of the works speak to important aspects of Inuit life: *Au bout de la ligne du harpon* (1972) and *Avatac* (1971) (111) reference the hunting practices of Inuit. As a known outdoorsman who liked to spend time with nature, this was possibly where Riopelle felt most connected to Inuit. Although, as Guy Robert writes, "the figures drawn by Riopelle go far beyond the repertoire of [Inuit] string games, he simplifies the complex counter-curves of orthodox Ayarak [sic] or creates new ones, as the mood takes him."[20] This is reminiscent of the *ajaraaq* I played as a young girl in Nunavut; you learn how to create the string figures, as well as the stories that go with them, and along the way you may also create your own string figures to share with your peers.

Ajaraaq is an important aspect of Inuit culture, as well as an important aspect of Inuit social life and the socialization of children. Inuit art depicting *ajaraaq* often show an Inuk with string in hand (115-117), whereas Riopelle's depiction of string figures excludes the performative aspect through omission of a human figure. Although his art departs from Inuit art in this sense, he nevertheless attempts to include people through titles, such as *Serge et Gauguin jouant à la ficelle* (1971) (122). The importance of *ajaraaq* is exemplified by the aforementioned Arvaarluk's storytelling, when he cites his grandmother and her role in his life as a major influence in his appreciation of stories and storytelling. Riopelle's *Jeux de ficelles* series is a catalyst to do what *ajaraaq* does for Inuit, allowing for the discussion of stories and evoking in people a sense of nostalgia that might inspire them to partake in joyful practices.

113   114

115

116

115
Luke Akuptangoak
Hands with String Game
(Beluga Whale)
1978
Stone, sinew

116
Noah Arpatuq Echalook
*Woman Playing a String
Game*
1987
Dark green stone, ivory, hide

117
Noah Arpatuq Echalook
The String Game
1986
Soapstone, sinew

117

118

118 | "I only draw what I think, but sometimes I think the pencil has a brain too," declared the artist Pudlo Pudlat in 1978, setting the tone for a unique body of work. In his desire to establish a link between his cultural tradition—its shamanic past—and the modernity he gladly absorbed, the artist revealed with acuity and poetry the meeting of two worlds. The airplane, which enables this meeting, was of particular interest to Pudlat. – JDR

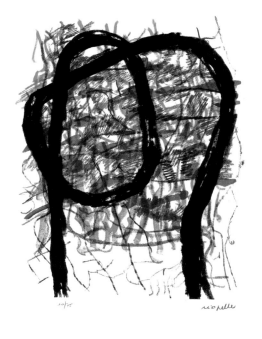

119a

b

118
Pudlo Pudlat
Untitled No. 13
1976
Watercolour and coloured
pencil on paper

119
Jean Paul Riopelle
Plates from the album
Parler de corde
a. Pl. 3, *L'Indien*
b. Pl. 4, *Avion à flotteurs*
c. Pl. 8, *Le call*
d. Pl. 9, *Original*
1972
Lithographs, 10/75

Riopelle said: "You want to
hunt a moose? You have
to be a moose. That's not
for everyone. I've drawn
all that. The print is called
*Champlain Hunting the
Moose* [*Le call*]. There are
also [string figures]. Very
important for the Indians
and Inuit."

c

d

120
Jean Paul Riopelle
Avion à flotteurs
1971
Acrylic on the lithograph
(*Suite Radisson*)
mounted on canvas

121
Jean Paul Riopelle
L'esprit de la ficelle
(triptych)
1971
Acrylic on lithograph
mounted on canvas

121

121 | What Riopelle and Mary-Rousselière call "The Spirit of the String," I have only heard of as *ajaraaq*, a generic term for string figures. I have never heard of it referred to as a spirit, but Europeans have always been enamoured of spirits. It is one of the easiest of the string figures to learn, so it was one of the first ones we were taught. In the National Film Board of Canada's Netsilik film, *At the Winter Sea Ice Camp: Part 2* (1967), Itimangnaq calls this figure Tuutannguarjuk, which I presume to mean a pair of labrets or chin ornaments. He recounts a story of a young person who stayed awake late at night, playing with string, when Tuutannguarjuk challenged him to see who could complete the Tuutannguarjuk figure first; he was playing with his intestines. If he won the game, he would carry the young person away. An adult awoke just before they began to play, and Tuutannguarjuk rushed out of the entranceway, carrying his intestines. After learning this figure, we progressed to other, more elaborate ones. When we learned a new figure, we were told to rub it on our foreheads, so we would not forget it. It does not work, of course, since I have forgotten many of the figures I learned. – MAK

123

122
Jean Paul Riopelle
*Serge et Gauguin
jouant à la ficelle*
(triptych)
1971
Acrylic on lithographs
mounted on paper

123
Jean Paul Riopelle
Ménage à trois-Pistol
(triptych)
1972
Acrylic on lithographs
mounted on canvas

124
Jean Paul Riopelle
Paysage
1971
Acrylic on lithograph
mounted on canvas

125
Jean Paul Riopelle
Tyuk (triptych)
1971
Acrylic on lithographs
mounted on canvas

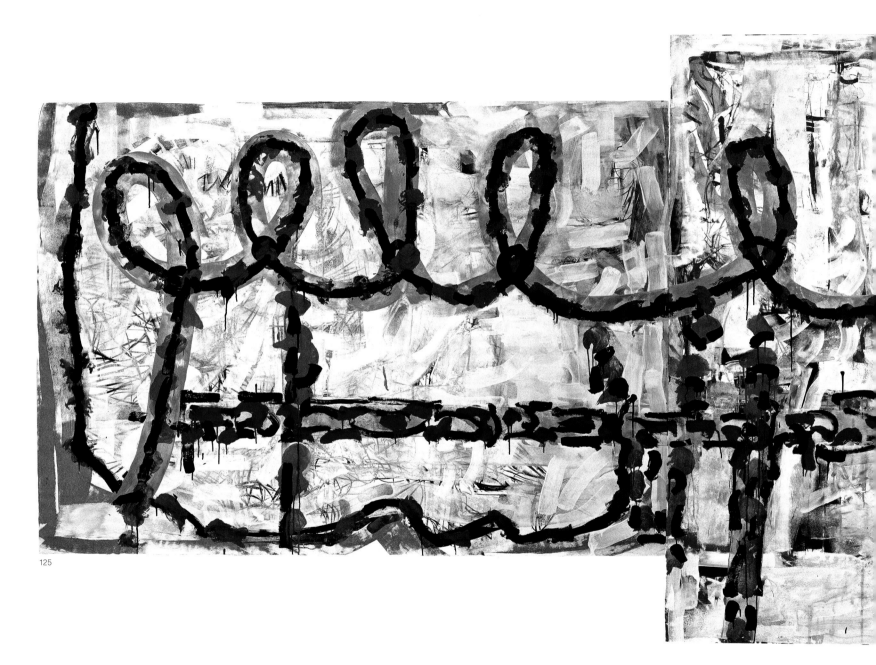

125

RIOPELLE AND THE REPRESE OF THE

MARI KLEIST

THE OF THE

NTATION
OTHER:

KINGS
ARCTIC

Like Inuit art practices, Western art depicting Inuit and their culture cannot easily or fairly be generalized, as Inuit are diverse and inhabit a geographically vast area. When Western artists depict Inuit, they often produce a stereotypic narrative, in many cases from a bygone era, which may be interpreted as a way of "othering." Inuit culture and art has for centuries been a source of interest for Westerners, as it represents for them a culture that is "exotic" and thus has the appeal of the Other, that which is different from their own image of Western culture. This ontology typically produces a fixed image of the Other and becomes problematic, as representations of Inuit and their culture tend to become stereotypically reproduced with a touch of ethnocentrism. Overall, ways of understanding and interpreting art, including Indigenous art, have commonly been based on historical Western perceptions of the role of art[1] and what it should be.

Yet in these representations of Inuit and their culture there is also no doubt an individual experience or story from the point of view of the artist, an individual and personal sensation and experience that fuels the artist's imagination and prompts him or her to create the artwork and share it with a broader audience. Riopelle's *Rois de Thulé* series from 1973 (**72-77, 126, 135, 137, 138**) is obviously a product of this type of representation, in his case stoked by his fascination with a people who mastered life in the North, in my hypothesis not only Inuit, but also Dorset people.

ROIS DE THULÉ: RIOPELLE AND THE NORTHERN GAZE

The title of Riopelle's *Rois de Thulé* series of works has been interpreted by art historians to have an association with the artist's admiration for Jean Malaurie's 1955 book *Les derniers rois de Thulé* (*The Last Kings of Thule*) (**41**), which he had read. However, the question remains whether Riopelle's facial imagery is meant to represent the particular group of Inuit of the Thule region in Greenland—the Inughuit of Avanersuaq, which were represented in Malaurie's book—because any diversity of Inuit or Arctic peoples is lacking in Riopelle's representations. Moreover, no formal similarities can be found between the book's illustrations and Riopelle's drawings.

The title *Rois de Thulé* is very ambiguous: who, in fact, do the faces illustrated represent? Is it the Inuit of the Thule region, as Malaurie's title implies? Is it another Inuit group?[2] Or is it the people of the Far North in general, as in the concept of *Ultima Thule*, which refers to the northlands beyond the known lands, as defined by writers of antiquity, such as Pytheas of Massalia? All these questions perhaps imply that Riopelle's series combined a variety of references that informed his northern imaginary. However, none of these hypotheses points to any direct formal inspiration for the series.

Riopelle's *Rois de Thulé* images have been interpreted to be highly reminiscent of Henri Matisse's illustrations for Georges Duthuit's *Une fête en Cimmérie* (**40**).[3] Although the former's choice of subject may be inspired by the latter's Inuit portraits, I see a clear difference between their works. Riopelle's drawings do not directly strike me as similar to the Inuit face depictions by Matisse in his Inuit portraits (**127**). Not surprisingly, Matisse's likenesses mimic "emotive" faces, because they reproduce the Inuit faces represented in photographs illustrating Knud Rasmussen's publication *Across Arctic America: Narrative of the Fifth Thule Expedition* (1927) (**128-130**) and Gontran de Poncins' publication *Kablouna* (1941). In contrast, Riopelle's series presents synthesized, outlined faces and complex, elaborated and more abstracted forms in coloured compositions (**135-138**) that differ from Matisse's Inuit portraits, which are, most of the time, isolated figures drawn in black on a white background. Yet again it seems to be an indirect inspiration that fueled Riopelle's interest in the subject more than an artistic and formal influence.

FROM THE KINGS OF THULE TO THE KINGS OF DORSET

As an Arctic archeologist from Greenland specialized in the Dorset culture, I instantly recognized particular aspects of the work of the Dorset people in the facial representations found in Riopelle's *Rois de Thulé* series. At first glance, I immediately envisioned the accumulation of linear facial engravings made by the Dorset people in Qajartalik (**132**), in the Kangiqsujuaq area in Nunavik,[4] as well as the known pre-Dorset and Dorset maskettes (miniaturized carved masks) and multiple face carvings on caribou antler (**131**) or walrus ivory pieces.

The unique petroglyph site with engraved facial images on soapstone (steatite) outcrops in Qajartalik was first reported by the anthropologist Bernard Saladin d'Anglure in the early 1960s,[5] although Inuit living in the area had for decades known of the exceptional depictions near the soapstone quarry.[6] Petroglyphs are extremely rare in the eastern Arctic,[7] and the only known examples of rock art are documented in three sites;[8] they are all made by the Dorset people, who inhabited eastern Canada and Greenland for more than two thousand years prior to the migration of early Inuit (also known as Thule people, who are the direct ancestors of the contemporary Inuit with no immediate ancestry to the Dorset).

1. See Alfred Gell, *Art and Agency: An Anthropological Theory* (Oxford: Clarendon Press, 1998), and Ingo Hessel, *Inuit Art: An Introduction* (London: British Museum Press, 1998).

2. See Robert McGhee, *Ancient People of the Arctic* (Vancouver: UBC Press, published in association with the Canadian Museum of Civilization, 1996).

3. See Hélène de Billy, *Riopelle* (Montreal: Art Global, 1996).

4. See Daniel Arsenault, "The Aesthetic Power of Ancient Dorset Images at Qajartalik, A Unique Petroglyph Site in the Canadian Arctic," in *Boletín del Museo Chileno de Arte Precolombino* (Santiago de Chile), vol. 18, no. 2 (2013); Mari Hardenberg, *Trends and Ontology of Artistic Practices of the Dorset Culture 800 B.C.–1300 A.D* (København: Københavns Universitet, Det Humanistiske Fakultet, 2013); McGhee, *Ancient People of the Arctic*; P. S. Taçon, "Stylistic Relationship between the Wakeham Bay Petroglyphs of the Canadian Arctic and Dorset Portable Art," in *Rock Art Studies: The Post-Stylistic Era, or Where Do We Go from Here?, Papers Presented in Symposium A of the 2nd AURA Congress, Cairns, 1992*, eds. Michel Lorblanchet and Paul G. Bahn (Oxford: Oxbow Books, 1993).

5. Bernard Saladin d'Anglure, "Découverte de pétroglyphes à Qajartalik sur l'île de Qikertaaluk," *North/Nord*, vol. 9, no. 6 (1962).

6. See Daniel Arsenault, Louis Gagnon, Daniel Gendron and Claude Pinard, "Kiinatuqarvik: A Multidisciplinary Archaeological Project on Dorset Petroglyphs and Human Occupation in the Kangirsujuaq Area," in *Contributions to the Study of the Dorset Palaeo-Eskimos*, ed. Patricia D. Sutherland (Gatineau: Museum of Civilization, 2005).

7. See Taçon, "Stylistic Relationship . . . ."

8. The Qajartalik site is much larger and richer in the number of visual representations than Nuvukulluk and Upirnivik, two other petroglyph sites located in the same marine area, south of Kangiqsujuaq, Nunavik.

126
Jean Paul Riopelle
Rois de Thulé
1973
Mixed media on paper

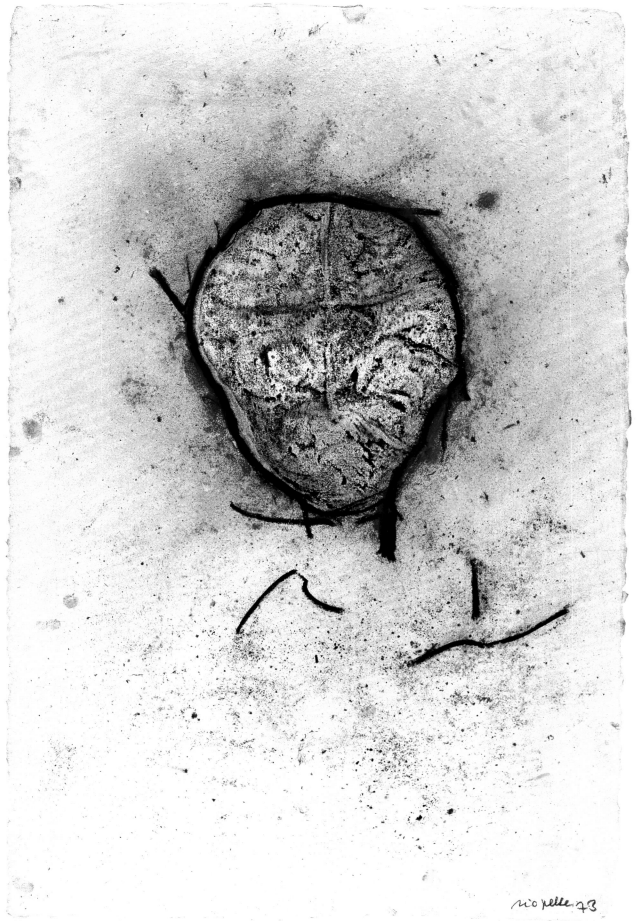

127a

b

c

d

127
Henri Matisse
Pls. 2, 16, 18, 20, 1, 3,
9, 11 of the series
of original lithograph
illustrations (31 in
total) in Georges
Duthuit, *Une fête en
Cimmérie* (1963)
1948–49

e

f

g

h

139

I believe that in his representation of the North, Riopelle chose to portray faces greatly inspired by the Dorset rock engravings that were initially brought to public attention on a few occasions in the 1960s and 1970s. Riopelle was possibly a reader of *The Beaver: A Magazine of the North*,[9] and because a couple of articles about the Dorset petroglyph sites were published in this widely distributed magazine, it could be cautiously hypothesized that Riopelle might have read these articles and been inspired by the visual images illustrating them. These unique examples of prehistoric rock art—a regional heritage from the deep past—could have fascinated Riopelle and inspired him to portray these in his artwork. Furthermore, in Paris in 1972, Riopelle visited the exhibition presented by the Canadian Eskimo Arts Council at the Grand Palais, *Sculpture of the Inuit: Masterworks of the Canadian Arctic* (**42**),[10] which included Dorset facial carvings. He would also have seen many of these pieces in the 1971–72 "Eskimo World" issue of *Canadian Art* (**133**), which he had in his possession.

Dorset people were skilled carvers with a unique carving tradition that distinctively depicted and symbolized the human figure in a manner typically without direct parallels in other circumpolar native cultures.[11] The facial engravings carved as petroglyphs or on antler and ivory are commonly deemed unlike any Inuit carvings,[12] because early Inuit did not commonly elaborate facial features (including eyes, nose and mouth) or expressions (such as mood) like the Dorset people did, and rarely elaborated arms and feet in their miniature carvings when depicting the human form in sculpture. For the Dorset people, it was important to render these inherent features and expressions in their carvings.

In Riopelle's *Rois de Thulé*, we see the same facial imprint represented in by far the majority of the series, as he favoured the same wooden log (**19, 20**) as a matrix in the production of the series. However, in examining the works, I notice that Riopelle used the same imprint in different ways and with slightly different features, but the face is nonetheless frequently circled by a recurrent and large oval outline. In some works of the series, more abstracted form has been applied (**136**).

Two particular works in the series seem to me especially similar in composition to the actual petroglyph in the soapstone quarry at Qajartalik that bears a series of different engraved human faces in frontal view (**132**). These two particular drawings by Riopelle exhibit parallelism to this petroglyph, and may point to one of his unknown inspirational sources: the Dorset petroglyphs. In Riopelle's images, the faces are positioned side by side, upside down in relation to the other faces, just like in the Dorset petroglyphs and the Dorset face clusters found on sections of caribou antler and walrus ivory.

By using wood to define his motifs, Riopelle combines materials that have hints of organic character in his facial representations. For example, the colours of the natural surroundings of the petroglyph site seem partly represented in Riopelle's work with the use of black charcoal and colourful pastel in green, blue, yellow and orange/red (**126**). The choice of colours and grainy textured surfaces appear to represent the rock outcrops, Arctic lichens, landscape, sky and sea.

Riopelle had travelled up North, visiting Pangnirtung in Baffin Island, Nunavut, in 1969 and again in 1971, both times with Theo Waddington, who was then a gallery owner promoting Inuit art in Montreal and Toronto. A few years later, in 1972, the artist once again visited the North, this time staying in the Southern Hudson Bay and James Bay regions in northern Quebec. Having travelled up North on various occasions, Riopelle became familiar with the landscape and environment of Nunavik and Nunavut, which likely inspired his artwork.

That being said, we can ask if it is Dorset people, and not the Inuit, whom Riopelle is representing, or perhaps simply both interchangeably? In my opinion, it is instead the Dorset petroglyphs that are his primary source of inspiration. Due to the striking resemblance between Riopelle's facial representations and the Dorset engravings in Qajartalik, I see the artwork of the *Rois de Thulé* series as being by a Euro-Canadian artist who was inspired by petroglyphs.

Artists have the freedom to express their own perceptions of what they see and/or what they want to convey through their artwork. They have a freedom of expression, and with that they also have a responsibility with regards to what they express and make public. This is even more pronounced if what they portray or convey involves other peoples and cultures. Here, sensitivity is a virtue.

9. Communicated by Huguette Vachon. See Fred Bruemmer, "The Petroglyphs of Hudson Strait," *The Beaver*, vol. 304, no. 1 (1973); George Swinton, "Prehistoric Dorset Art: The Magico-religious Basis," *The Beaver*, vol. 298 (Autumn 1967); and William E. Taylor, Jr., "Prehistoric Dorset Art: The Silent Echoes of Culture," *The Beaver*, vol. 298 (Autumn 1967).

10. See Guy Robert, *Riopelle, chasseur d'images* (Montreal: France-Amérique, 1981).

11. See Mari Kleist, "Anthropomorphic Images of the Late Dorset Culture," in *North Atlantic Archaeology Journal*, vol. 5 (2018).

12. See Taçon, "Stylistic Relationship . . . ."

128   129   130

128
"Qingaruvdliaq, the woman who knew all the men's songs and prompted them when they forgot the words"
Ill. in Knud Rasmussen, *Across Arctic America: Narrative of the Fifth Thule Expedition* (1927)

129
"Native from Pelly Bay"
Ill. in Knud Rasmussen, *Across Arctic America: Narrative of the Fifth Thule Expedition* (1927)

130
"Tatilgaq, who described the Native Methods of Hunting"
Ill. in Knud Rasmussen, *Across Arctic America: Narrative of the Fifth Thule Expedition,* (1927)

131
Dorset
Antler with carved faces
N.d.
Caribou antler

132
Petroglyphs at Qajartalik, Nunavik
2004

"The Qajartalik petroglyphs are unique manifestations of Dorset era artistic expression. Qajartalik appears to be the only place where Dorset era peoples transposed onto soapstone, and on an enormous scale, the distinctive figures usually found on much smaller artifacts made of bone, ivory or horn. In the early 1960s, Bernard Saladin d'Anglure documented 95 carvings at Qajartalik . . . During his later expeditions (from 1996 to 1998) with Avataq [Cultural Institute], we were able to identify an additional 70 petroglyphs, bringing the site's total to 165. Some of Qajartalik's petroglyphs are only visible in adequate light, and while most of them portray anthropomorphic features, they are not overt representations of human figures." (Avataq Cultural Institute)

131

132

THE ESKIMO WORLD

ᐃ ᓄ ᐃᑦ ᓴ ᓇ ᐅᒐᖅ

artscanada

December 1971/January 1972

Special Issue Price $3.00

133

133 | Riopelle had a copy of this 1971–72 issue of *artscanada* devoted to Inuit art. On the cover is a mask from Cape Dorset, Nunavut, found in 1970 by anthropologist Guy Mary-Rousselière, who told the ethnomusicologist Jean-Jacques Nattiez, when they were both in Mittimatalik (Pond Inlet), Nunavut, in the 1970s, that the mask "had inspired a work by Riopelle." He was probably referring to the *Rois de Thulé* series, in which the predominant motif is a face or a mask. Dorset art, which predates the Inuit culture, may have been one of the northern inspirations for this series, whose sources lend themselves to various interpretations. – AR

133
Cover of "The Eskimo World" issue of *artscanada* (1971–72)

134
Mattiusi Iyaituk
A Young Hunter's First Catch (I)
1979
Soapstone, caribou antler, walrus ivory

134

135
Jean Paul Riopelle
Untitled
From the series
Rois de Thulé
1973
Acrylic and
gouache on paper

136
Jean Paul Riopelle
Untitled
1973
Gouache on paper

136

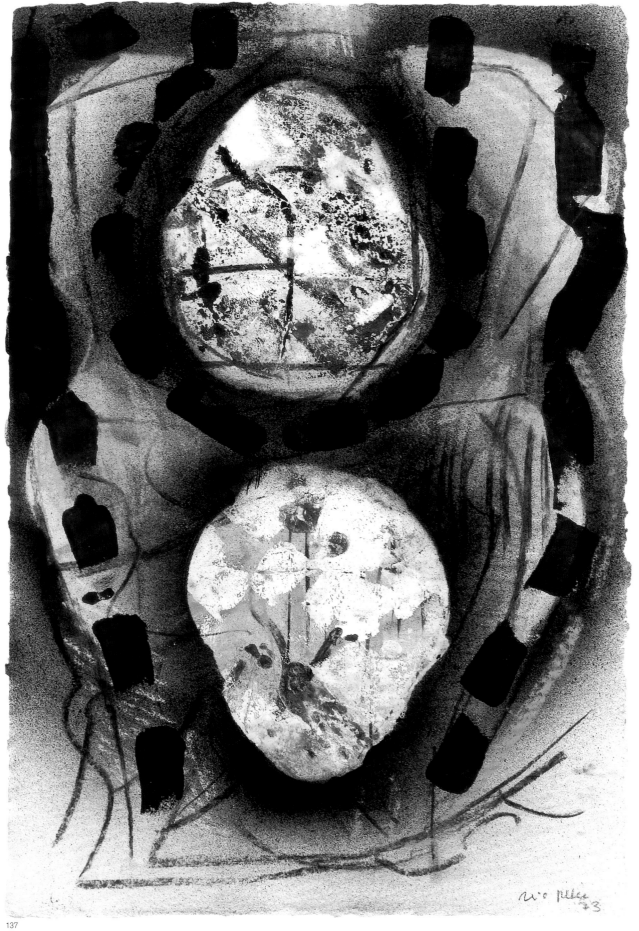

137
Jean Paul Riopelle
Les rois de Thulé
1973
Mixed media on paper

138
Jean Paul Riopelle
Les rois de Thulé
1973
Mixed media on paper

séquelle 73

139a

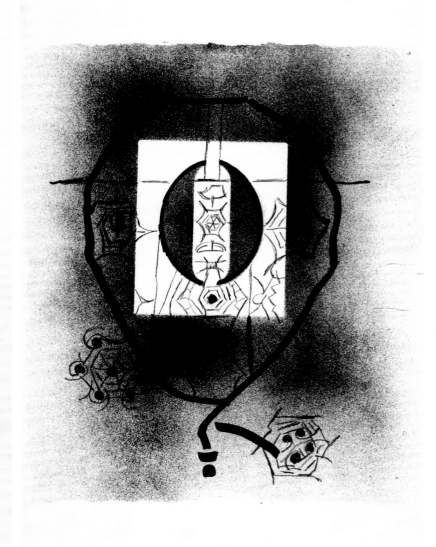

b

139
Jean Paul Riopelle
Pls. *L, O, P, W-X*
From the series of illuminated
letters *L'alphabet de Thulé*
About 1979
Lithographs

About 1979, Riopelle returned
to the subject of Thule, which
he had explored earlier, in
twenty-five lithographs (trial
proofs). In addition to the
letters of the alphabet (with "Q"
missing), he revived the shape
of the Inuit face or mask from
the *Rois de Thulé* series (1973).
The abundance of snowflakes
adds to the northern theme.

A contract unearthed by Yseult
Riopelle reveals that the writer
and art critic Michel Waldberg
was to write a poetic work
composed of texts on each letter
of the alphabet. The publication
accompanied by lithograph
prints (99 sheets and 26 artist
proofs), never came to be.

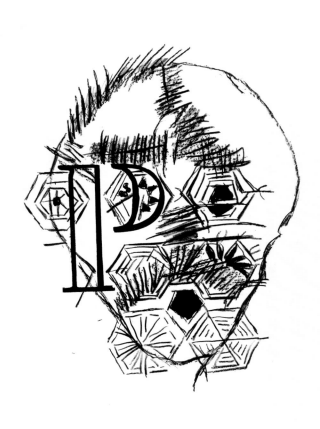

c

i

d

RIOPELLE MEMORY PLACES:

LAND OF

AND THE OF

ANDRÉANNE ROY

A VOYAGE TO THE TITLES

The 1970s undoubtedly represent Jean Paul Riopelle's great Canadian decade.[1] Although he had returned periodically to his homeland since settling in France in 1947, it was during these years that he began re-engaging with the Canadian territory, in both his life and his work. Spurred by his passion for hunting and fishing, he travelled widely in northern Quebec over the course of the decade, with forays into Nunavik and Nunavut. Despite his claim that he did not believe in "taking root, but in uprooting"[2] he established home bases in Estérel, in the Laurentians, and at Île-aux-Oies, in Chaudière-Appalaches. His empirical experience of the Canadian territory had a powerful influence on his work. As we shall see, the titles he gave his abstract paintings often resulted in them being read as landscapes. Some would call these abstract landscapes. Riopelle preferred the term "mental landscape"[3] to describe the works in which nature seems to have been reshaped in a comprehensive vision that fused his personal experience and his imagining of the land.

Scholars have devoted considerable study to Riopelle's relation to mimesis[4] and the naturalist character of his work. In pursuing this reflection, I intend to recast the question by exploring his landscape titles and their relationship to compositions that are the result not of the imitation of nature but of its evocation. I shall attempt to identify the impact of these titles on the works' reception and to show how they have often served as a basis for interpretation. Although the explanatory potential of an analysis of the titles is limited when it comes to Riopelle's abstract compositions —whose subject is essentially painting itself—the examination of a small corpus can shed significant light on the artist's geographic imaginary when this group of works is juxtaposed with his biographical path, for this path contributed towards the singularity of his oeuvre.

This essay focuses on the works produced in 1973 and the many references to northern territories they embody, which often evoke particular places—occasionally undefined or even imaginary places—and the natural phenomena encountered there. The year 1973, which saw the execution of the *Rois de Thulé* series (**72–77, 126, 135, 137, 138**), is decisively northern, and allusions to landscape are omnipresent.

RIOPELLE'S TITLING

"Any meaning they [titles] possess is connotative rather than denotive."[5]

The titles of Jean Paul Riopelle's painted production as a whole are astonishingly varied. If we discount the many works labelled *Untitled* and the references to nature, the notion of territory—whether North American or European— plays a predominant role. Although a good proportion of the titles were inspired by the artist's travels (Austria, Spain, Holland, etc.) and places in France (especially in the Île-de-France and Midi regions), the catalogue also includes frequent references to Canada, concentrated for the most part in the 1970s.

Jean Paul Riopelle titled his paintings after they were completed, often interpreting the results of his work made without any preconceived ideas yet fuelled by his visual experience. In these cases, the title reflects what he saw in the image when he considered it with a hermeneutic eye. Other titles seem rather to refer to external references to the work, frequently biographical events that resonated in his pictorial world. In this category are titles that evoke his travels, his interests[6] and what he was reading at the time.[7] If, as Riopelle suggested, he "travelled to find titles for the paintings [he] had already made,"[8] it seems that his wanderings possessed a heuristic dimension that led not only to the invention of titles but also to the creation of abstract works whose interpretation is crystallized by their titles. The artist aimed to communicate to the spectator "what was going on when [a] particular canvas was taking shape." He added: "Even if you select a title that doesn't suit the picture perfectly, at least it leaves a trace, it's like a marker for your memory."[9]

Gérard Genette maintained that the titles of works fulfil three distinct functions: identification, indication of the subject, and temptation of the public.[10] The first function, identification, concerns the practical need to distinguish one work from another. Ernst Gombrich showed how the widespread use of titles that began during the Renaissance was the result of the development of the art market and the increased mobility of images it gave rise to.[11] It was no doubt for this utilitarian reason that Riopelle often gave titles to his works as they were leaving his studio, at the behest of his gallerists. The question of the authorial figure arises here, for we know that the artist regularly appealed to his entourage for assistance in finding titles, holding what he called "title sessions" at which friends and family were encouraged to free-associate in front of the works. Did the artist actually have little interest in the titling process, as the frequent recurrence throughout the oeuvre of *Untitled* would seem to suggest? When asked if the titles of his paintings were important to him, he nevertheless responded: "If you don't provide one, you lose trace of the painting, in part at any rate."[12]

Is this trace related to the second of the functions identified by Genette—communication of the work's subject? This is where things get complicated: the precise nature of the link between Riopelle's titles and his works, the semiotic relation between text and image, poses a number of problems, for he was an artist who practised abstraction without entirely eschewing reality. It appears that in many of his title choices, the painter was relaying the "trace" of a visual memory, a fleeting impression. But if this is the case, did the recollection arise at the time the work was being created, and thereby serve as its inspiration, or a posteriori, when the time came to choose a title? It is a difficult question, and the answer—which likely varies from one work to another[13]—is privy to Riopelle alone. Some of the titles possess an ambiguity of meaning, moreover, that turns them into traps. The artist would probably have concurred with Umberto Eco's claim that "a title must

1. It could be argued that both the 1980s, during which Riopelle's production was shaped by his visits to Île-aux-Oies, and the 1990s, which he spent entirely in this country, were also "Canadian decades," although associated more specifically with Quebec. My assertion is based on the fact that the titles of the works from the 1970s constitute the most wide-ranging inventory of Canadian places, from the Maritimes to the Prairies and including the Far North.

2. Laurent Lamy, "Un peintre québécois connu dans le monde entier : Riopelle," *Forces*, no. 28 (July 1974), p. 40.

3. "Landscapes, if you must, but mental landscapes!" See Guy Robert, *Riopelle, chasseur d'images* (Montreal: Éditions France-Amérique, 1981), p. 181.

4. See the essay herein by François-Marc Gagnon.

5. Harry Bellet, "The Chasse-galerie," in *Jean-Paul Riopelle*, exh. cat. (Montreal: The Montreal Museum of Fine Arts, 1991), p. 34.

6. It is worth noting that many titles from the 1970s refer to the Indigenous world, particularly Indigenous toponymy. See the essay herein by Serge Bouchard.

7. As witness the *Rois de Thulé* and *Hiboux* series, as well as several later works (see Stacy A. Ernst and Ruth B. Phillips' discussion on the *Lied à Émile Nelligan* album and the silverpoint drawings from 1979 in their essay herein).

8. "Travelling is a bit like dreaming. I wonder if one doesn't make the paintings before having travelled. Maybe I travelled to find titles for the paintings I had already made. Otherwise, I'd have had to drag them out of friends." Jean Paul Riopelle, quoted in *Jean-Paul Riopelle. Peinture, 1946–1977*, exh. cat., ed. Pierre Schneider (Paris: Musée national d'art moderne, Centre Georges-Pompidou; Quebec City: Musée du Québec; Montreal: Musée d'art contemporain, 1981), p. 88. This translation taken from *Jean-Paul Riopelle*, 1991, p. 196.

9. Gilbert Érouart, *Entretiens avec Jean-Paul Riopelle, suivis de Fernand Seguin rencontre Jean-Paul Riopelle* Montreal: Éditions Liber, 1993, p. 70. Published in English as *Riopelle in Conversation* (Concord, Ont.: House of Anansi Press, 1995); this excerpt, p. 48.

10. Gérard Genette, *Seuils* (Paris: Éditions du Seuil, 1987), pp. 59–106.

11. Ernst Gombrich, "Image and Word in Twentieth-century Art," *Word & Image*, no. 3, vol. 1, (July–September 1985), pp. 213–241.

12. Érouart, *Entretiens avec Jean-Paul Riopelle*, p. 70; English version, p. 48 (trans. modified).

13. "My paintings are the results, the repercussions of my relations with reality, with nature, with what I see, with life; they reflect what I perceived or felt, and also what was happening within me at the time I was painting them, which may no longer have had anything to do with my starting point, with this travel memory or that idea of colour that suddenly arose as I was having a drink with friends.—It depends, it depends on so many things." Jean Paul Riopelle quoted in Robert, *Riopelle, chasseur d'images*, p. 272.

140
Jean Paul Riopelle
Fonte
1973
Oil on canvas

muddle . . . ideas, not regiment them."[14] Although Riopelle sometimes used polysemic effects and puns, he was nonetheless conscious of the risk that they be misunderstood: "The artist's compulsion to give everything a name can end up being misleading. And neither memory nor history may ever set things straight. . . . So the choice of a painting's title is important . . . but also very delicate, extremely dangerous!"[15]

And it is so because this communicative act, whose meaning derives from its context, is an integral part of the spectator's experience. Regardless of an artist's intention and the role he or she wishes to ascribe to titles, they have an impact on the reception of works that cannot be ignored: "A title determines . . . the interpretative movement as margins border a text,"[16] asserts Bernard Bosredon. A number of authors[17] have demonstrated that titles of works operate like guides to interpretation that launch the active spectator on a quest for meaning. Moreover, titles are in fact performative utterances whose message modifies the spectator's state of mind, partially conditioning their reading of the work by means of the information conveyed. In light of this, I believe it is worth examining the part played by the titles in the reception of a group of works by Riopelle from 1973 under the genre of landscape.

A PICTORIAL JOURNEY INTO BOREAL TERRITORY

"I don't know if I precede the landscape I'm painting, or if the landscape precedes me."[18]

From the late 1960s on, Riopelle began returning to Quebec more frequently to go hunting and fishing with his friend Champlain Charest. Exploration of the land was central to their expeditions, and it is significant that the first painting by the artist that Charest acquired, whose official title is *Cape tournante* (143), Riopelle called "The Map of Canada." In this case, the artist was switching from a referent external to the work (Cap Tourmente, one of his hunting destinations) to an internal one—the formal similarity he had observed between the painting and the map of Canada's territory. As he pointed out, "it even shows Hudson Bay."[19] The title of the second work Charest acquired, *Sainte Marguerite* (145) is equally interesting, for although it was later sometimes taken as an allusion to the village of Sainte-Marguerite near Estérel, where in 1974 Riopelle would establish his Canadian studio, it actually referred to the island of Sainte-Marguerite, off the south coast of France. The

painting could be interpreted either as representing the shape of the island or as an aerial view of its fortress—visual associations of the kind prompted by the appearance during the 1960s of more circumscribed, solid forms that lend themselves to comparison with elements of reality.

In 1972, Riopelle and Charest flew out from Abitibi to the east coast of James Bay, where it connects to Hudson Bay, to go goose hunting. A year later, a number of titles evoke places they visited. With *Sucker hole à Matagami* (144), Riopelle's title is richly narrative. A "sucker hole" is a meteorological phenomenon that makes flying risky, but it is not clear if in executing the work the artist was recalling an event that actually took place, or whether the title was suggested by the formal characteristics of the image. Certainly, the bipartite composition showing two masses emerging from a dark ground could suggest the sudden change of light and visibility that characterizes this trick of the weather. Another painting speaks to the importance of flying in the artist's life: *Capitaine Tempête* pays tribute to Claude Genet,[20] the pilot who accompanied Riopelle and Charest on major expeditions. In this case, the referent is more obviously external to the work and related to the fabric of the artist's life.

It is interesting to consider the impact of the artist's flights over Quebec's territory. Did the aerial views of vast stretches of land they offered result in the production of works representing a topographical vision of the country? Several of the paintings from 1973 seem to suggest this. The broad black lines of *Au-delà du 52ᵉ* (149) could be interpreted as roads seen from the air. On the other hand, they may arise from a spontaneous artistic gesture identified after the fact as a "5," which in turn triggered the reference to the 52nd parallel.[21] Similarly, the broad white bands of *De la grande baleine* (152) might embody the memory of having flown over the Great Whale River and its tributaries. But the designation is ambiguous, for *baleine* is the French word for "whale," and in 1973 Riopelle also assigned titles that include the names of other animals, such as *Du caribou* and *Du grand cormoran* (great cormoran). So is the reference territorial or faunal? Riopelle alone knows, and it would hardly matter were it not for the fact that the title partially conditions the spectator's analysis. It seems possible that *Fort George* (150), though it dates from 1975, was also inspired by the visual impression left by a flight over Chisasibi (a Cree village, formerly known as Fort George, located at the mouth of the La Grande River) made during the same expedition of 1972. "I see everything I create as part of what I see, what I have seen in the past, yesterday or years ago,"[22] said the artist. It is worth noting, too, his passion—attested by his daughter Yseult—for studying maps, both terrestrial and marine.

14. Umberto Eco, "Postscript," in *The Name of the Rose* (Boston; New York: Houghton Mifflin Harcourt, 2014), p. 543.

15. Érouart, *Entretiens avec Jean-Paul Riopelle*, pp. 70–72; English version, pp. 48–49.

16. Bernard Bosredon, *Les titres des tableaux: une pragmatique de l'identification* (Paris: Presses universitaires de France, 1997), p. 46.

17. Notably John Fisher, Jerrold Levinson, Margery B. Franklin, Robert C. Becken and Charlotte L. Doyle, Stephen Bann, Ernst Gombrich and Bernard Bosredon.

18. Lamy, "Un peintre québécois connu dans le monde entier: Riopelle," p. 44.

19. Hélène de Billy, *Riopelle* (Montreal: Art Global, 1996), p. 203.

20. Thanks to Champlain Charest for having shared his reminiscences with me over the course of several conversations.

21. According to the geographer Louis-Edmond Hamelin, who coined the term "nordicity" in the 1960s, the "Middle North" starts between the 48th and 52nd parallels. "Quebec's north begins at the 50th degree of latitude; it stretches from Sept-Îles, in the east, to Lac Matagami, in the west, which in my vocabulary I call the Middle North." See Daniel Chartier and Jean Désy, *La nordicité du Québec, entretiens avec Louis-Edmond Hamelin* (Quebec City: Presses de l'Université du Québec, 2014), p. 40.

22. Helen Duffy, "Jean-Paul Riopelle," in *The Laurentians: Painters in a Landscape*, exh. cat., ed. Mela Constantinidi (Toronto: Art Gallery of Ontario, 1977), p. 64.

141

142

141
Riopelle
Ill. in the exhibition catalogue *Jean-Paul Riopelle, Jean-Julien Bourgault* (1991)

142
Riopelle
Ill. in the exhibition catalogue *Riopelle: œuvres vives* (1993)

143
Jean Paul Riopelle
Cape tournante
About 1967
Oil on canvas

143

144

23. Guy Robert, *Riopelle ou la poétique du geste* (Montreal: Éditions de l'Homme, 1970), p. 71.

24. Paul Auster, "Introduction," in *Jean-Paul Riopelle: Paintings from 1974, Pastels from 1975*, exh. cat. (New York: Pierre Matisse Gallery, 1975).

25. It was during this same year, 1973, that Riopelle executed some seventy works on paper on the theme of the Kings of Thule. For more on this series see the essays by Florence Duchemin-Pelletier and Mari Kleist in this catalogue.

26. Jean-Marc Poinsot, *Quand l'œuvre a lieu: l'art exposé et ses récits autorisés* (Geneva: Musée d'art moderne et contemporain; Villeurbanne: Institut d'art contemporain, 1999), p. 247.

27. "The process of making the artist into a hero after the fact is constitutive of biographical reconstruction, which invents nothing but emphasizes, highlights, erases, and touches up." See Nathalie Heinich, *La gloire de Van Gogh: essai d'anthropologie de l'admiration* (Paris: Les Éditions de Minuit, 1991), p. 113. Published in English as *The Glory of Van Gogh: An Anthropology of Admiration* (Princeton, New Jersey: Princeton University Press, 1996); this excerpt pp. 72-73.

Other paintings make reference to particular places, such as *Baie James* (147) and *Il a neigé sur Opinaca* (146). The artist provides no details that allow us to identify the location. On the contrary: "He retains, of the sources and resources offered by closely observed nature, only the schemas of visual, pictorial elements, which enable him to structure his emotions and present us with renderings, dynamic renderings stripped of their anecdotal and touristic references."[23] In these cases, it is the chromatic range that has the potential to evoke memories of the places in question. *Baie James* possibly conjures the fall colours, lakes and rivers of an area Riopelle visited: dominated by tones of red, orange and blue, it is an all-over composition in which land and water seem to merge. With its chilly palette, the more narratively titled *Il a neigé sur Opinaca* appears to summon the climate of the named region (the Opinaca is a river that flows into James Bay). "The almost limitless energy we find in his canvases does not speak of an abstract program to become one-with-nature, but of a tangible need to be present, to be here, to see the thing that is,"[24] wrote Paul Auster in his introduction to the catalogue of Riopelle's 1975 exhibition at the Pierre Matisse gallery in New York. Never, though, should we forget the appreciable part played by reverie and imagination in the artist's formal approach.

It is not clear why Riopelle titled two of his 1973 works *Coral Harbour*, which is the name of an Inuit village also known as Salliq (or Salliit) located on Southampton Island in Nunavut, north of Hudson Bay. According to his travel companions, Riopelle never went there. Did the artist dream of this region? Did his fascination for the North transcend what he was able to learn through concrete experience? More importantly, did he need to visit a place in order to develop a "mental landscape" of it that could become the source of an abstract image? By the same token, does the title *Iceland* (151) refer to the country of Iceland, in which he never set foot, or was it some generic, undefined "land of ice" he wished to evoke? With its central mass surrounded by white, perhaps the painting alludes to Iceland as one of the possible sites of the mythical island of Thule described by Pytheas.[25]

Other works from 1973 may evoke the 1972 trip without making reference to specific places. The triptych titled *D'un long voyage* (148) is undoubtedly one of the masterworks of 1973. For those eager to identify representational elements in Riopelle's abstract oeuvre, the two side panels, made using the decalcomania technique, appear to portray the horizon line characteristic of traditional landscapes, and the central section seems more like an aerial view. We might be tempted to identify the shorelines of James Bay and Hudson Bay—because Riopelle's abstractions readily lend themselves to analogical interpretations—but is this what the artist intended?

Over the course of 1973, Riopelle constructed a coherent ensemble of references to northern territories and nordicity. The titles from that year actually represent a kind of personal "lexicon of the North" made up of a comprehensive northern vocabulary of which *De la toundra, Fonte des neiges, Fonte* (140), *Première neige, Chemin d'hiver, Snow Print* and *Du soleil et du gel* offer just a few examples. These titles conjure the poetry of the North, rather than particular places. I would suggest, in fact, that they have their source more in the recollection of vague impressions than in precise memories that the artist wished to capture on canvas. Although these titles were not aimed at unveiling the concrete subjects of abstract images, it seems that Riopelle used them to create an atmosphere, a sense of nature and of landscape. These elements are reconfigured, synthesized or fragmented through the prism of his unique view of the environment. Since the principal "subject" of his works is undoubtedly painting itself, Riopelle does not show us nature transparently, but rather by emphasizing the opacity of this form of expression.

An examination of Riopelle's titles from 1973 exposes their semantic relationship to the works they identify and the connection of those works to the landscape genre. To extrapolate on the ideas of Jean-Marc Poinsot, if we recognize the title as a paratext offering a description of the work's "content," whether figurative or abstract, the title can be seen as the artist's first "authorized narrative," his most reduced formulation of "the terms of the iconographical contract."[26] Furthermore, both the classification of the works as landscapes supported by titles that evoke "what was going on when a particular canvas was taking shape" and the links between these titles and the events of the artist's life represent elements of individuation that play a role in the elaboration and preservation of Jean Paul Riopelle's artistic persona. Many critics and commentators have discussed these elements, thereby contributing to the creation of the artist's "legend"[27] —his image as an explorer of the vast expanses of Canada.

This abstract corpus, whose landscape titles appear to be linked to referents both internal and external to the work, clearly illustrates how titles act as linguistic complements that are an integral part of the spectator's aesthetic experience. It also reveals how titles, through their expressive properties, help shape the interpretative movement by triggering a dialogue between themselves, the work and the spectator. The spectator's reception is a product of their relationship with their own imagination. Riopelle deconstructs the traditional perception of landscape, thereby thwarting our cultural habits, and it is perhaps in the gap between the horizon of expectation created by his landscape titles and his images devoid of either vanishing point or perspective that some aspect of our aesthetic experience plays out.

144
Jean Paul Riopelle
Sucker hole à Matagami
1973
Oil on canvas

145

146

150

151

149
Jean Paul Riopelle
Au-delà du 52ᵉ
1973
Oil on canvas

150
Jean Paul Riopelle
Fort George
1975
Oil on canvas

151
Jean Paul Riopelle
Iceland
1973
Oil on canvas

152
Jean Paul Riopelle
De la grande baleine
(triptych)
1973
Oil on canvas

RIOPELLE INDIGENO PLACE

SERGE BOUCHARD

THE CALL OF

AND
US
NAMES:

THE LAND

Because of the titles Jean Paul Riopelle gave to many of his works, some people have thought he was very much taken with the worlds of Indigenous peoples. In the eyes of the French intelligentsia of the 1950s, the young artist had the stamp of a legend: his flamboyant style, free spirit and exceptional raw strength (which was later compared to that of the "majestic moose, quiet and still, but quick to charge")[1] made him seem the epitome of a Canadian from the great outdoors, naturally attuned to Indigenous peoples. Later on, his repeated visits to the Arctic and Subarctic gave rise to the belief that he knew a great deal about First Nations peoples and had experienced their realities. But Riopelle was above all a fisherman and a hunter, of game as much as of images.[2] His trips to the North do not appear to have been prompted by a serious curiosity about Indigenous peoples.

Riopelle's immersion in untamed nature was in fact driven by his love of hunting and fishing. He lived this great love most intensely in the 1970s, when he came back to Quebec frequently and could count on his friend Champlain Charest, a pilot and owner of a seaplane.[3] At the time, a seaplane was a rare luxury for diehard hunters, a precious toy. A floatplane made everything accessible. Every lake and river, every remote corner in the wilds of Quebec offered up its secrets and bountiful game.

Riopelle was already more than an exotic Canadian in Paris in the early 1950s. He came across as a *coureur de bois*, which he did not mind. But at that stage in his life, had he travelled up and down the vastness of his country's wilderness, encountered the people who had lived there since time immemorial and become familiar with their history and culture? More importantly, had he earned the nickname "superior trapper" given to him by André Breton?[4] In truth, Riopelle was, like the majority of French Canadians, almost entirely oblivious of the peoples and realities of Quebec's northern regions.

Nevertheless, the artist appears to have had a certain attachment to Indigenous place names since his youth, an indication of interests rarely evidenced at the time. From 1945 to 1985, Riopelle gave some of his paintings titles that show his curiosity and respect. *Ontario* (1945 and 1947–48), *Hochelaga* (1947; Iroquois for "beaver path" or "big rapids")(**3**),

Mitchikanabikong (1975; Algonquin for "stone barrier") (**160**), *Kakwa* (1974; Cree for "porcupine") and *Mascouche* (1975; Cree for "little bear") (**159**) are from a long list of titles featuring Indigenous terms that the average Canadian had never wondered about. "Ontario" is an Iroquoian word, probably Huron-Wendat, perhaps also Iroquois. Its meaning relates to the beauty of that Great Lake, which does indeed boast gleaming water. Moreover, the great historical figure Handsome Lake was a prophet and reformer among the Iroquois people to the south of Lake Ontario. These are things that Riopelle played with. Starting with place names, animal terminology or sometimes even the "Indian" logic that named places after natural features, he came up with titles like *Point de rencontre – Quintette* (1963) (**11**), *Au pays du carcajou* (1976) and *Où un ours est chassé* (1985–89), that opened doors through which the viewer could enter these unknown worlds. By idealizing such words and expressions, the artist touches on the wealth and magnitude of lost languages, the sounds of history.

Quebec's North was gradually discovered during the Quiet Revolution. René Lévesque, then the Liberal Minister of Natural Resources, went on a long trip to James Bay, Hudson Bay and Ungava Bay in the early 1960s; he returned to Quebec City furious. Essentially, he told reporters that these regions had been sorely neglected and that it was high time to attend to them. Before 1970, only a handful of scientists and eccentrics had dared venture to the North to penetrate the veil of collective ignorance. Jacques Rousseau, a colleague of Frère Marie-Victorin, had inventoried the flora of the boreal zone as far as the tundra and, in the 1950s, had written many articles on Cree culture for the readers of *La Patrie*. The forest engineer Paul Provencher had captured the Inuit culture of the north coast and Labrador in a wonderfully rich collection of photographs. But little attention was paid to the work of these eccentrics.

The North was late in entering Quebec's collective imagination. The watershed moment came when the James Bay hydroelectric project was announced in 1970. Quebecers then learned about the Cree through their land claims and the court battles they initiated to assert their ancestral rights over the James Bay territory. Quebecers also discovered the boreal forest, the North's vastness, extending towards the taiga and the Inuit tundra. The province's Indigenous peoples henceforth factored into the political agenda of the government. Journalists had to become familiar with new material, learning the names of First Nations and place names like Caniapiscau, Némiskau, Chibougamau, Matagami, Mistissini and Kegaska. Riopelle came back to Quebec in this climate of change accelerated by agreements with the Cree and Inuit and by the opening of the North to hunters and fishermen hungry for unspoiled lands. He does not appear to have taken much interest in the contemporary work of Quebec anthropologists, including the major studies of Rémi Savard, in particular, and Madeleine Lefebvre. As far as we know, Riopelle's library contained publications on Inuit and Northwest Coast art, but apparently no serious ethnographic

1. Raymond Bernatchez, "La vie, la mort, rien d'autre," *La Presse* (Montreal), March 14, 2002. Quoted in Francine Couture, "La mise en légende de Riopelle ou l'héroïsation d'un artiste moderne," *Revue canadienne d'esthétique / Canadian Aesthetics Journal*, vol. 7 (Fall 2002). https://www.uqtr.ca/AE/Vol_7/libres/couture.html#_ftn14 (accessed April 28, 2020).

2. See Guy Robert, *Riopelle, chasseur d'images* (Montreal: Éditions France-Amérique, 1981). In the mid-1980s, the artist stopped killing animals but continued to go hunting.

3. Riopelle also went hunting and fishing in France, around Vétheuil, Ile-de-France, in Champagne and around the Baie de Somme, Picardie. He mostly went boar hunting with the painter Paul Rebeyrolle.

4. Elisa Breton, André Breton and Benjamin Péret, "Aparté," in *Riopelle à La Dragonne*, exh. cat. (Paris: Galerie Nina Dausset, 1949), [n.p.].

153

154

153
Riopelle standing in front of *Micmac* (1975) About 1976

154
Unidentified person, Riopelle, Kenny Brien (guide) and Louis Gosselin at the camp of Vieux poste du lac Mistassini, north of Chibougamau About 1975–76

In the mid-1970s, Riopelle went twice to the Vieux poste du lac Mistassini, a fishing camp employing Cree guides.

155
Jean Paul Riopelle
Micmac (diptych)
1975
Oil on canvas

155

156

156 | In the mid-1970s, at a time when Riopelle travelled around Quebec hunting and fishing, he seems to have developed a new sensitivity to Indigenous peoples. This led him to borrow the names of their lands and Nations from their languages when giving titles to his works. However, in the case of *Tête de boule 1, 2, 3* (meaning ball-head or round-head), the artist chose a name formerly used by the French colonists to refer to the Atikamekw but now considered pejorative. This work in the form of a triptych, in which the medallion shapes may call to mind heads, could indicate that the title refers to the three Atikamekw bands (Wemotaci, Manawan and Opitciwan). This painting may be contemporaneous with Riopelle's acquisition of a hunting canoe made by the noted Atikamekw bark canoe maker César Newashish. – AR

156
Jean Paul Riopelle
Tête de boule 1, 2, 3
(triptych)
1974
Oil on canvas

157
Jean Paul Riopelle
Muscowequan
1976
Oil on canvas

study on Canada's eastern First Nations. Nevertheless, Riopelle exemplified the newfound interest in Indigenous cultures and their place names, giving his works titles like *Mistassini* (1975), *Kegaska* (1974) and *Matosipi* (1975), among many others. Some titles relate directly to areas where he had travelled, particularly after his big trip in 1972 to Matagami (*Sucker hole à Matagami*, 1973) (**144**), James Bay (*Baie James*, 1973, **147**; *Il a neigé sur Opinaca*, 1973, **146**) and all the way to southeastern Hudson Bay (*De la grande baleine*, 1973) (**152**). These territorial references went beyond the borders of Quebec and the places Riopelle had been to, extending into the Maritimes (*Kouchibouguac*, 1974), Ontario (*Mattawa*, 1976; *Mitchiging*, 1976) and the Prairies (*Muscowequan*, 1976) (**157**), *Kee-See-Kons* (1974). He also used the names of First Nations in the titles of his works (*Saulteaux*, 1974; *Micmac*, 1975 (**155**); *Iroquois silencieux*, 1977). Titles for a series of works on paper from 1974, all beginning with the letter "K," and a series of oils on canvas from 1975 and 1976 beginning with the letter "M," are taken from Indigenous sources. Could the artist, who would give titles to works after their completion, have used an Indigenous dictionary?

Back at home and having the means to engage in the activities he loved, Riopelle had the North as his playground. A seaplane at his disposal, he went fishing for Arctic char in the tundra's most tranquil lakes. He went hunting for caribou in the taiga, all the moose he wanted in the boreal forest and geese on Hudson Bay. Sources of inspiration for his art were abundant: he saw the North from the sky, appreciated the light, had the feeling of diving into nature, became himself a moose, talked to the animals—smelled them, pressed against them—communed with wolves and embodied an owl's spirit. His flights over land he did not walk through were points of light in the sky, the reflections of a reclusive moon, the aerial spirit of all the animals he had killed, all the fish he had caught, the lake waters that bore his canoe, the Arctic air, the Subarctic quiet. All this fuelled his work, all this obsessed and pursued him. This is what led sociologist of Huron-Wendat art Guy Sioui Durand to say that Riopelle thought like an Indigenous hunter.

To be sure, Riopelle immersed himself in nature, but he did not immerse himself deeply in the nature of Indigenous peoples. There is no evidence that would lead one to even imagine him experiencing immersion in any Indigenous community. It appears that culture and politics were not his favourite subjects. In the manner of well-to-do outdoorsmen who rely on the services of outfitters (whom the Indigenous derisively call "those gentlemen") he did in fact spend time with Cree guides, namely at Lake Mistassini (**154**), Inuit guides in Pangnirtung and perhaps Innu guides. And as a hunter who developed an interest in canoes, he did make his way to Manawan, on Lake Kempt, to meet the famous artisan César Newashish, who built traditional bark canoes and whose craft had been brought to light by documentary maker Bernard Gosselin for the National Film Board. But meeting Newashish and receiving a custom-decorated canoe from him does not make Riopelle an expert on the history and culture of the Atikamekw, a nation he referred to by the outdated derogatory name "Têtes-de-Boule" (**156**). Nowhere do we see him take an interest in the dramatic sedentarization of Canada's First Nations. His interest lay elsewhere, in the realm of the imagination and not politics.

One does not have to be Indigenous to tap into one's animal spirit. Riopelle was a woodsman; he knew an animal's shape and movement, the aura that emanates from it and the shadow that envelops it. He ultimately became that "peerless trapper," André Breton's Wild Man, he who, from his home in the Laurentians, would soar, take off from the surface of Lake Masson and fly over a spruce-covered continent, as in tales about the Chasse-Galerie; a legend, himself soul-searching.

157 | In the 1970s, Riopelle made many paintings with titles relating to Canadian territory as well as to First Nations and Indigenous cultures in the boreal zone. The titles refer not only to communities living in the areas he had visited, but also to others he could only discover through literary sources, for example *Muscowequan*. In 1975 and 1976, Riopelle probably named a large number of works after Indigenous words beginning with the letter "M," which makes one think he took them from an Indigenous dictionary. *Muscowequan*, painted in Estérel, refers to the Saulteaux (Anishinaabe) First Nation, whose territory lies 140 km northeast of Regina, Saskatchewan. – **AR**

158

158
Jean Paul Riopelle
Lac du Nord-Est
1975
Oil on canvas

159
Jean Paul Riopelle
Mascouche
1975
Oil on canvas

160
Jean Paul Riopelle
Mitchikanabikong
(triptych)
1975
Oil on canvas

159

ICEBERGS:

"AMONG WORLD'S

SCU

RIOPELLE THE MOST BEAUTIFUL LPTURES"

FRANÇOIS-MARC GAGNON
AND ANDRÉANNE ROY

François-Marc Gagnon's original
essay has been completed by Andréanne Roy.

The *Icebergs* series constitutes the furthest point Jean Paul Riopelle ever took nordicity. Far from being an abstract concept, the North was for the artist an expanse of Quebec and Canada's territory that could be visited and, beyond being seen, be grasped through all the senses by way of immersion.

Riopelle travelled to the Far North several times. He first went to Pangnirtung (Baffin Island, Nunavut) in 1969, then again in 1971, both times with the gallery owner Theo Waddington, who sought to acquire Inuit sculptures, and his friend Dr. Champlain Charest. The artist returned with the latter to the coastal areas of James Bay and Hudson Bay in 1972 and to George River, which flows north to Ungava Bay, about 1975–76. In Pangnirtung in July 1977, the two men met up with Claude Duthuit, whose father, Georges, was one of Riopelle's greatest advocates in Paris. Claude immortalized Riopelle in a photo showing him emerging from an "ice whale" (**161**). Their expeditions to Baffin Island were to fish char and hunt caribou: twenty years later, Champlain Charest still remembered the friendship that grew up between them and their Inuit guide Jaco Kunilusie despite the language barrier.[1]

A set of picture postcards sent to Joan Mitchell (**164-168**) indicate just how clear Riopelle's ideas on nordicity were in his mind. His comments regarding the cards' illustrations point to his fascination with the area and its landscapes ("Fishing and hunting among the world's most beautiful sculptures") (**164**), as well as his interest in Inuit culture ("To be toasty warm, a seal or walrus coat") (**165**). As Riopelle explained, such first-hand knowledge of the area had an effect on the *Icebergs* series:

Obviously, if I'd gone to the Mediterranean I'd never have come back with paintings like those, but in the Arctic nothing is clear-cut. All is not black and white. The sky, though, seems black, really black. If I painted a sky that way, no one would believe me. And on the ground, there's not even white snow. There's ice that is grey, transparent.

The icebergs are fantastic to see, they're like white mushrooms that melt, alter, shift until they find a new equilibrium. If they weren't perfectly balanced, they wouldn't stay put. That's sculpture! But the most extraordinary thing is to hear them. They make an incredible noise as they turn, like an explosion.[2]

Icebergs became Riopelle's favourite subject in 1977. The inspiration he drew from his experience with nature in the North took form in compositions that reveal a complex relationship with mimesis. The series of some thirty works was in fact painted in Estérel, in the Laurentians of Quebec, and in Saint-Cyr-en-Arthies, Île-de-France.

MIMESIS

Involved verbal descriptions of Riopelle's paintings often prove to be inadequate: his pictures are elusive at every turn and defy being pigeonholed. Giving precedence to colour, Riopelle dissociated his painting from discourse. His art seems to embody an aphorism of the poet Simonides of Ceos (556–467 BCE), as handed down by Plutarch: "Painting is silent poetry, poetry is eloquent painting."[3]

Although there are many *Untitleds*, *Compositions* and *Paintings* in Riopelle's oeuvre, some of the works in the *Icebergs* series have literary titles that perfectly demonstrate his notion of mimesis. These more evocative names do not correspond to faithful representations of the real. A painting reduced solely to its subject loses its specificity, to edge towards "literature." Identifying himself with neither abstraction nor figuration, Riopelle described his surprising approach as follows:

My most "abstract" paintings, according to some, are for me the most figurative, in the true sense of the word. On the other hand, the geese, owls, moose . . . Those paintings into which people read meaning, are they not more abstract than the others? Abstract: "abstraction," "to abstract," "to extract from," "to derive from" . . . My approach is the exact opposite. I don't take anything from Nature, I move into Nature. . . . I depart from the real only as much as I have to: I don't put it behind me entirely, I keep my distance where reality is concerned. What distance? The right distance.[4]

A dictionary definition of the verb "abstract" reads "to move (a person or thing) away, withdraw";[5] the noun "abstraction" is defined as "the action of withdrawing or secluding."[6] As such, the animals in Riopelle's bestiary could be labelled "abstracts." They are withdrawn from nature, secluded and . . . true to life. In 1947, when Riopelle was fully committed to working in a non-figurative style, he declared, "I no longer pick up a brush until I've entirely re-immersed myself in nature and can document it."[7] Although it is difficult to determine what he means by the "right distance" from reality,

1. Interview with Champlain Charest by Hélène de Billy, 1995, Fonds Hélène de Billy, Library and Archives Canada.

2. *Jean-Paul Riopelle*, exh. cat. (Montreal: The Montreal Museum of Fine Arts, 1991), p. 198.

3. Plutarch, *Moralia*, "De gloria Atheniensium," section 3, quoted from Susan Ratcliffe, ed., *Concise Oxford Dictionary of Quotations*, 5th edition (New York; Oxford: Oxford University Press, 2006).

4. Gilbert Érouart, *Riopelle in Conversation* (Concord, Ontario: House of Anansi Press, 1995), p. 25.

5. *Oxford English Dictionary*, second edition, s. v. "abstract."

6. Ibid., s. v. "abstraction."

7. Guy Viau, "Six peintres canadiens. Reconnaissance de l'espace," *Notre temps* (Montreal), July 12, 1947, p. 5.

161
Claude Duthuit
photograph of
Riopelle in
Pangnirtung, Nunavut
July 1977

162
Claude Duthuit
photograph of
Champlain Charest
in Pangnirtung,
Nunavut
July 1977

161

162

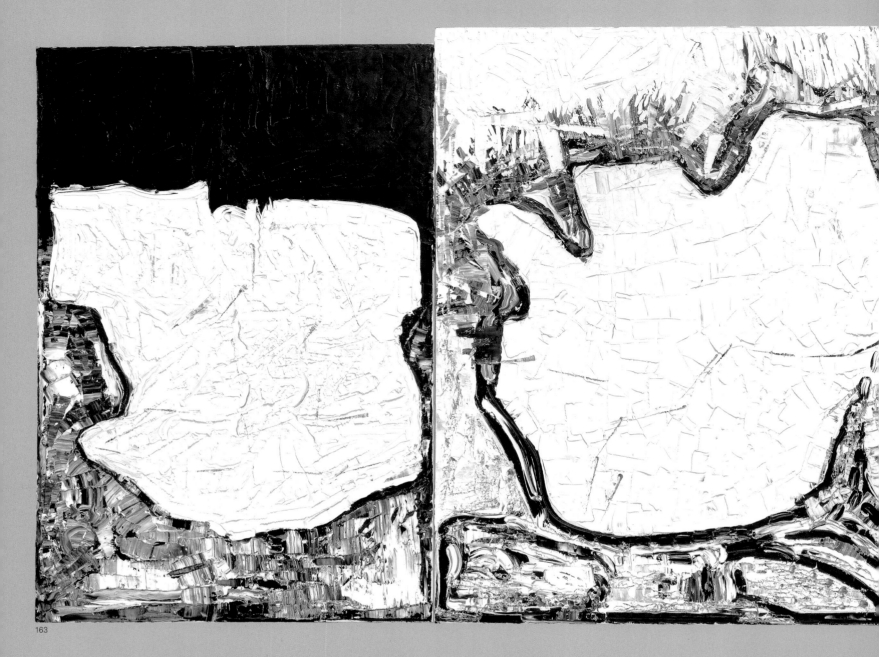

163

163 | The icebergs of Pangnirtung (Baffin Island, Nunavut),
which Riopelle visited in 1977, were the inspiration for
his depictions bursting with nuanced evocations of the
northern landscape rendered in black and white contrasts.
This first-hand experience of Canada's Far North was a
source of artistic renewal for Riopelle: adopting a greater
economy of colour conjured the land in works where
the artist played with the thin line between abstraction
and figuration. In this composition with imposing white
masses, Riopelle captures the powerful impression the
grounded icebergs and the ice floes had on him when he
was among them fishing for Arctic char. The *Icebergs*
series is the artist's last significant series in oil. – AR

163
Jean Paul Riopelle
Pangnirtung (triptych)
1977
Oil on canvas

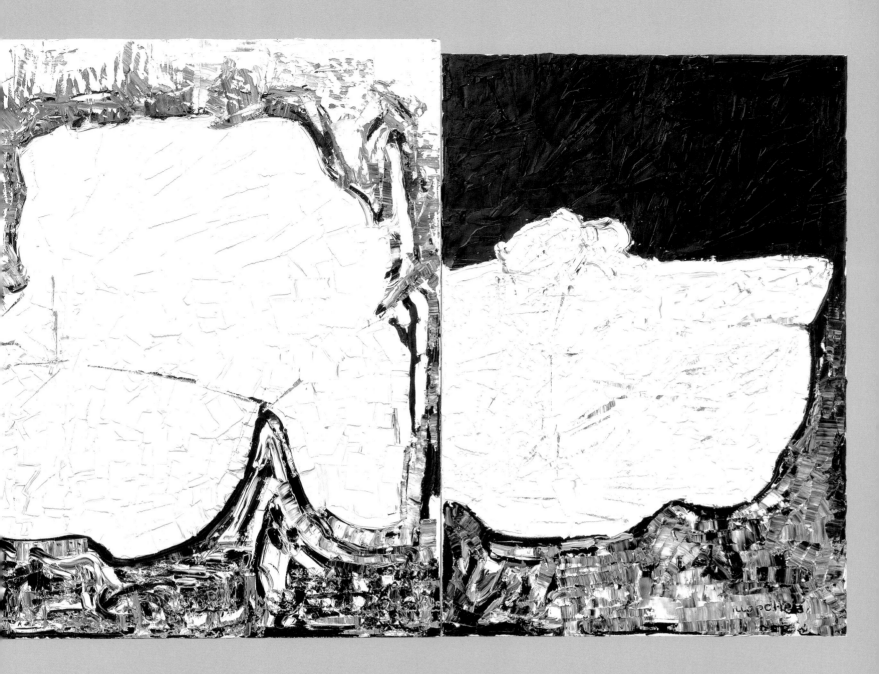

Riopelle seems to concur with Plato, who accused painters of ignoring the truth and seeking only to render an illusion of reality through resemblance. Plato's view is well known:

The art of representation, then, is a long way from reality; and apparently the reason why there is nothing it cannot reproduce is that it grasps only a small part of any object, and that only an image. Your painter, for example, will paint us a shoemaker, a carpenter, or other workman, without understanding any one of their crafts; and yet, if he were a good painter, he might deceive a child or a simple-minded person into thinking his picture was a real carpenter, if he showed it them at some distance.[8]

Following Riopelle's logic, Plato's painter would not be the "right distance" from the subject. Because "the only way to know nature is to take part in it,"[9] Riopelle's art practice comes closer to the truth than the so-called realist views devised by academic painters concerned with creating the illusion of the real.

METHEXIS

By moving "*into* Nature," Riopelle sought to dissociate mimesis from resemblance and illusion. Rather than mimesis in the usual sense, his approach had more to do with *methexis* (participation): "To reconcile with nature, you mustn't describe *it*, but instead *yourself* become natural."[10]

The aforementioned photo by Claude Duthuit suggests Riopelle's inclination towards *methexis*. The artist is shown inside the body of an "ice whale" that is sprawled on the ground. He forms part of it. He feels it through his own body. The sense of sight has little to do with this way of apprehending: "Painting testifies to what happened inside

of me in front of the real thing . . . You don't see nature. To make it felt, it's best to use its methods."[11] The viewer eagerly looking to find an exact likeness of nature will not immediately subscribe to Riopelle's participative approach, which requires that the artist keep a certain "distance where reality is concerned" and avoid academy-style copying. Yet in maintaining distance from the real, the painter does not entirely "depart from the real." It is imperative to remember one thing: Riopelle does not intend to create a realistic illusion by making a detailed depiction from a deliberately selected perspective on reality. Instead, as Guy Robert has remarked, "from the sources and resources of closely observed nature, [Riopelle] retains only the framework of visual and pictorial elements that allow him to structure his emotions and present us with versions, dynamic visions, divested of their anecdotal and touristic references."[12]

Some works in the series, including *Cap au nord* (**176**) and *Paysage d'autrefois* (**6**), nevertheless correspond to the landscape tradition. *Cap au nord*'s two-part composition depicts an iceberg and its reflection in the water. The artist applies strokes of black paint to capture the mirroring of the heavy mass off the snow and the rippling, shimmering water. The intense glare of the light is transposed here in visual elements intended to re-create the impression left on the visitor to the North, where "nothing is distinct."

In *Soleil de minuit* (**177**), the circle—a figure associated with both centrifugal and centripetal forces—relays the artist's approach, which always aims for the "right distance" from the subject, in other words, not too far, and not too close. The black-saturated circle and the contrast of white against a grey ground do not replicate the sun, but rather convey the odd impression the sun would make on a person seeing it from there. The paradox of the "midnight sun,"[13] a phenomenon peculiar to the polar regions, thus perfectly suits the artist's purpose.

Although in *Soleil de minuit* colour defines the forms, in other paintings, such as *Pangnirtung* (**163**), *Titanic I*, *Titanic II* and *Iceberg I* (**178**), the forms are separated from the background by contour lines. Thickly applied black paint demarcates masses and renders all the heaviness and monumentality of the icebergs. By transmitting their massive presence and capturing the feeling of translucency and the play of shadow and light, these works from the *Icebergs* series become even "truer" than illusionistic representations of reality.

8. Plato, *The Republic of Plato* (New York; London: Oxford University Press, 1960), p. 328.

9. Laurent Lamy, "Un peintre québécois connu dans le monde entier : Riopelle," *Forces*, no. 28 (July 1974), p. 45.

10. Pierre Schneider, *Riopelle : signes mêlés* (Paris: Maeght; Montreal: Leméac, 1972), p. 64.

11. René Viau, "Entretien avec Riopelle," in *Riopelle : laves émaillées*, by René Viau, Jean-Louis Prat and Pierre-Jean Meurisse (Toulouse: Art'poche, 1992), pp. 26 and 54.

12. Guy Robert, *Riopelle ou la poétique du geste* (Montreal: Éditions de l'Homme, 1970), p. 71.

13. The midnight sun, also known as the polar day, occurs in the summer months in the Arctic and the Antarctic circles, when the sun remains visible for several consecutive days. The opposite phenomenon is called the polar night, when the sun stays below the horizon in the winter months. The closer one is to the poles, the longer these two natural phenomena last.

164

165

166

167

168

164
"Eskimo Hunt on the Arctic"
Postcard sent by Riopelle to
Joan Mitchell in 1977 on
which he wrote: "La pêche et
la chasse au milieu des plus
belles sculptures du monde,
grande amitiée [sic], JP."
[Fishing and hunting among
the world's most beautiful
sculptures, Your dear friend, JP.]

165
"The Arctic Walrus"
Postcard sent by Riopelle to
Joan Mitchell in 1977 on which
he wrote: "Pour avoir bien
chaud, un manteau de phoque
ou de morse, grande amitiée
[sic], JPR" [To be toasty warm,
a seal or walrus coat, Your dear
friend, JPR]

166
"Crater Lake N.W.T."
Postcard sent by Riopelle to
Joan Mitchell in 1977 on
which he wrote: "Il eu neiger
[sic] et la pêche était bonne à
'Pangnirtung', Grande amitiée
[sic] JP" [It snowed and the
fishing was good at Pangnirtung,
Your dear friend, JP]

167
"The Arctic White Whale"
Postcard sent by Riopelle to
Joan Mitchell in 1977 on which
he wrote: "Tous ici pense
[sic] que tuer le bœuf pour
manger est un scandle [sic],
grande amitiée [sic] riopelle"
[Everybody here thinks it's a
scandal to eat beef, Your dear
friend riopelle]

168
"Pangnirtung Fiord"
Postcard sent by Riopelle to
Joan Mitchell in 1977 on which
he wrote: "A gauche sur la
carte vestiges d'une citée [sic],
du dernier des rois de Thulé,
grande amité [sic] JP" [On the
left of the postcard, the vestiges
of a town of the last king
of Thule, Your dear friend JP]

When colour is involved—for example the ochre and blue in *Iceberg V* (**185**)—line, although more subdued, remains present. Riopelle said of his palette, "If I dared to paint my series of icebergs in the 1970s, it's because the colour white doesn't exist in nature. If snow were really white, no painter would be able to render it. If snow were white, I wouldn't have taken the chance."[14] Over the coloured background, Riopelle superimposes a network of black lines recalling the Inuit string games that caught his attention in 1971–72. The composition emits a sense of emerging lightness.

RIOPELLE AND HARRIS, AT OPPOSITE POLES

Riopelle's approach was driven by his first-hand knowledge of the Far North—which he not only saw for himself but also "practised" by way of hunting and fishing—and it set him apart from many other abstract and figurative artists who looked to nature for inspiration. Comparing, or rather contrasting, Riopelle's *Icebergs* series with the work of Lawren Harris elucidates this point.

Like Riopelle, the Group of Seven painter had been to Canada's Arctic: he visited Baffin Island in 1930 (**169**).[15] But what distinguishes the two artists, other than their differing characteristic techniques, has to do with the historical distance separating them. In the context of an art practice engaged in associating a nascent sense of Canadian identity with the land, Harris offered up a nationalist vision that was prevalent in his time. Some fifty years later, when Riopelle was returning more regularly to Quebec and took up the *Icebergs* series, he was motivated by entirely different, essentially apolitical factors. He, who claimed to believe not in "taking root, but in uprooting,"[16] in fact managed to remain unburdened by any ideological or nationalistic affiliations. From the inspirational sources Riopelle found in Quebec and Canada's North, he produced works expressing purely visual concerns.

Clearly, the two artists approached Canada's northern landscapes very differently. Harris, deeply devoted to theosophy and transcendentalism, attributed a spiritual dimension to northern territories: "It seems that the top of the continent is a source of spiritual flow that will ever shed clarity into the growing race of America, and we Canadians being closer to this source seem destined to produce an art somewhat different from our Southern fellows—an art more spacious, of a greater quiet, perhaps of a more certain conviction of eternal values."[17]

Harris was on a spiritual quest, whereas Riopelle fostered an essentially materialist vision, staying close to the essence of tangible things and their physical manifestations. Northern nature and its representation, while a metaphysical matter for Harris, were handled entirely in terms of physicality by the creator of the *Icebergs* series, for whom nature was as much a point of departure as a destination.

Riopelle shows the North through the prism of his experience, which he transposes into paintings that primarily capture the present moment: not the moment of observing nature, but that of the work's execution, shaped by the sensations that persist in the artist's sensory memory and in his body. Although Riopelle sought the "right distance" vis-à-vis nature, his immersive experience within the landscape, combined with his internalization of it, led him to produce an art of proximity wherein lived experience reigns supreme over the reproduction of the subject.

14. Érouart, *Riopelle in Conversation*, p. 26.

15. In 1930, Lawren Harris took his only trip to the eastern Arctic on the SS *Beothic*, a Canadian government supply ship. A. Y. Jackson was also on the expedition.

16. Lamy, "Un peintre québecois . . .," p. 40.

17. Lawren Harris, "Revelation of Art in Canada," *The Canadian Theosophist*, no. 5 (July 1926), pp. 85–86.

171 | With its palette of black, grey and white, its web of rope and its owls, *Fontaine* combines motifs from the North that marked Riopelle's output in the 1970s. The coloured plaster recalls the landscapes rendered in a limited palette in the *Icebergs* series (1977) (**178-181, 185**). The ropes tie the various components of the sculpture together, recalling the motifs of the *Jeux de ficelles* series (1971–72) (**111, 119, 121, 122, 125**), which was inspired by *ajaraaq*, the string games of Inuit. And the inclusion of plaster versions of *Hibou-Roc* and *Hibou-White Stone*, which tops the sculpture, is a nod to the series *Hiboux* (1969–70) (**103-109**).

Undertaken about 1963 and finished about 1977, this evolving sculpture started out by reusing the plaster moulds that had served in making the sculptures *La Défaite* (1962–65) (**15**) and *La Victoire et le Sphinx* (1962–65). Riopelle thus salvaged and showcased an essential element in the process of lost-wax casting in bronze. Work on the piece was begun at the Meudon foundry, and the finishing touches were added at the studio in Saint-Cyr-en-Arthies. This monumental work is on public display for the first time in this exhibition. – **AR**

169

170

169
Lawren S. Harris
Icebergs, Davis Strait
1930
Oil on canvas

170
Champlain Charest
and Riopelle standing
in the centre among
fellow travellers in the
Arctic
July 1977

171
Jean Paul Riopelle
Fontaine
About 1964–77
Painted plaster
and ropes

171

172

173

174

175

177

177 | We might be tempted to view the four panels of *Soleil de minuit (Quatuor en blanc)* as quite austere, because here Riopelle renounces the use of colour. But in fact, this set of four panels, which was inspired by a journey to the Far North, is the key to the work that will follow. The midnight sun has banished the night, but without truly negating it. Here, Riopelle is experimenting with a form of presence/absence that will be extremely important to his later development. By shining remorselessly for twenty-four hours, the midnight sun creates a need for night and makes us sense its loss. This world of constant affirmation calls out for negation. It makes us realize our need for nothingness, which is just as strong a need as our need to exist. And thus one of the panels shows a black sun and another a mere corona, like a sun being eclipsed. The work calls to mind the words of Nietzsche in his famous passage on the death of God in *The Gay Science* (1882): "What were we doing when we unchained this earth from its sun? Where is it moving to now? Where are we moving to? Away from all suns? Are we not continually falling? And backwards, sidewards, forwards, in all directions? Is there still an up and a down? Aren't we straying as though through an infinite nothing? Isn't empty space breathing at us? Hasn't it got colder? Isn't night and more night coming again and again?" – FMG

177
Jean Paul Riopelle
*Soleil de minuit
(Quatuor en blanc)
(quadriptych)*
1977
Oil on canvas

178

178
Jean Paul Riopelle
Iceberg I
1977
Oil on canvas

179
Jean Paul Riopelle
Iceberg II
1977
Oil on canvas

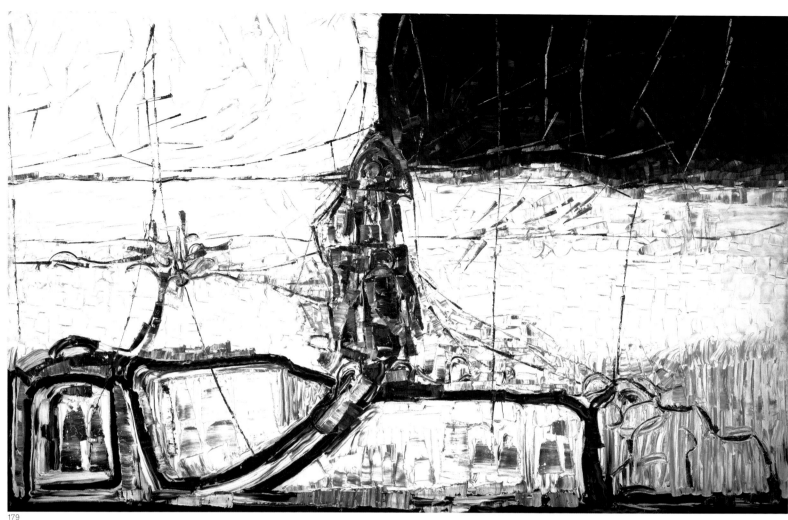

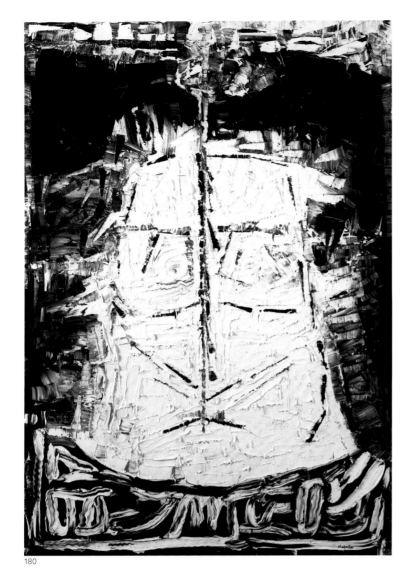

180

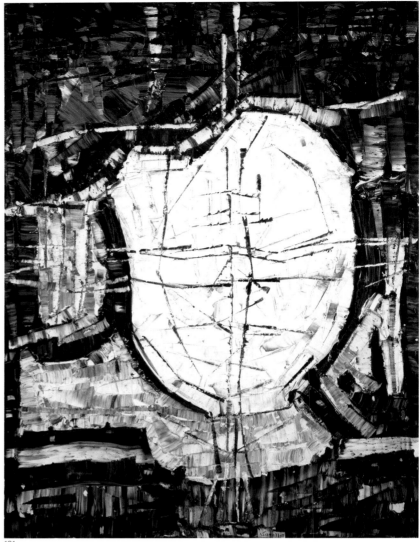

181

180
Jean Paul Riopelle
Iceberg VIII
1977
Oil on canvas

181
Jean Paul Riopelle
Iceberg XI
1977
Oil on canvas

182
Jean Paul Riopelle
Au pil de son masque
1978
Oil on canvas

182

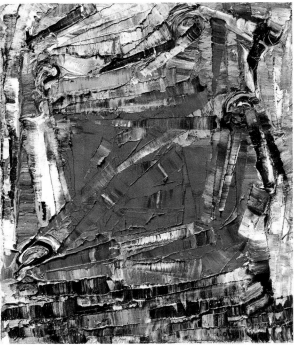

183

184

183
Jean Paul Riopelle
Rouge esquimaux
(diptych)
1977
Oil on canvas

184
Jean Paul Riopelle
Inuit
1977
Oil on canvas

185
Jean Paul Riopelle
Iceberg V
1977
Oil on canvas

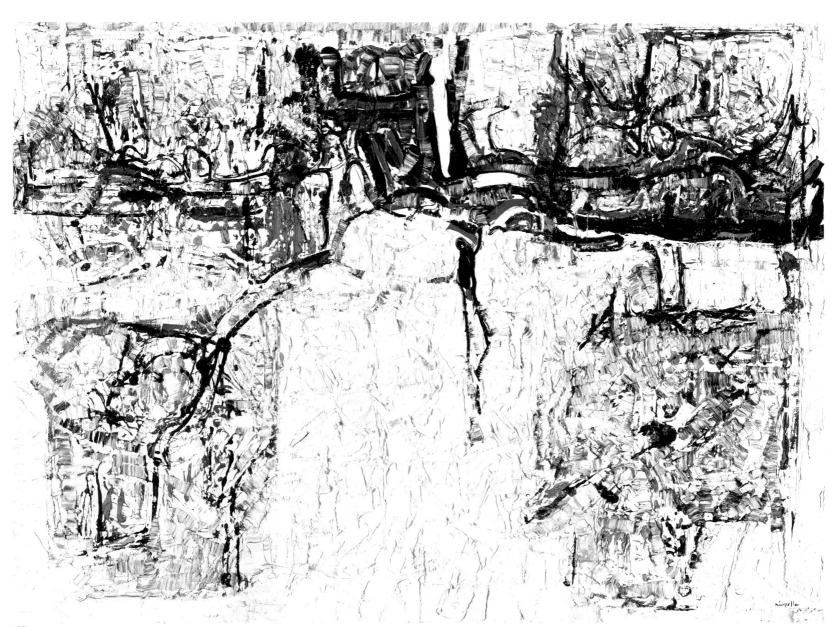

RIOPELLE AND NOR COAST

APPRO
DIALO
TRANSFO

STACEY A. ERNST
AND RUTH B. PHILLIPS

THWEST
ART:

PRIATION,
GUE,
RMATION

186 | This contemporary mask, carved by the late Beau Dick, one of the great Kwakwaka'wakw artists of our time, illustrates the artist's innovative approach to his vision of the traditional masks. His interpretation of this conventionally polychromed ghost mask presents deeply carved skeletal-like features and an innovative monochrome graphite surface. Although ghosts were believed by the Kwakwaka'wakw to live far away in their own villages, some of the departed would also return to the world of the living under certain circumstances, especially during the winter ritual events. Ghosts danced during the appearance of Winalagalis, the warrior spirit who comes from the northern underworld to preside over the winter ceremonial. The mythical being Bak'was, who was associated with the souls of those who had drowned, would also be accompanied by ghost dancers wearing this type of mask – **BHR**

186

Beau Dick
Ghost
2012
Wood, vegetable
fibre, feathers, paint

187

188

187
Georges Duthuit in front of two
masks in his collection that he
loaned to Riopelle
About 1950

188
Yseult and Sylvie Riopelle in the
apartment at 88 Rue Chardon-
Lagache, Paris XVI
(on the wall, a mask loaned by
Georges Duthuit and Riopelle's
Pleine saison [1954])
1954

In the mid-1950s, Georges
Duthuit loaned Riopelle several
works of Northwest Coast art.
This photograph of the interior
of the artist's Paris studio on Rue
Chardon-Lagache includes an
unidentified Indigenous mask
from his collection.

1. On modernist primitivism in France, see, for example, Robert Goldwater's classic study, *Primitivism in Modern Art* [1938] (Cambridge, Massachusetts: Harvard University Press, 1986); and, on post-World War II France, Daniel Sherman, *French Primitivism and the Ends of Empire*, 1945–1975 (Chicago: University of Chicago Press, 2011).

2. See Marie Mauzé, "Odes à l'art de la côte Nord-Ouest. Surréalisme et ethnographie," *Gradhiva*, no. 26 (2017); Edmund Carpenter, "Introduction," in *A Dialogue on Form and Freedom: Northwest Coast Indian Art*, exh. cat., Bill Holm and William Reid (Houston, Texas: Institute for the Arts, Rice University, 1975), pp. 9–29.

3. See Mauzé, "Odes à l'art . . ."

4. Yseult Riopelle in *Riopelle vu par...*, Michel Waldberg, ed. (Paris: Centre culturel canadien, 2004), p. 98.

5. Ibid., p. 98. We are grateful to Aaron Glass for clarifying the identities of the beings represented in this mask and for other helpful comments on this essay.

6. Yseult Riopelle located the Swinton books and photographs in Paris in June 2019; they had originally been in Riopelle's Val-d'Oise studio in France. She continues to research the relationship between the folder "Riopelle / for book / Indian Stories," now in the Kandinsky Library, Paris, but as yet uncatalogued. In consultation with Duthuit specialist Rémi Labrusse and other scholars, she has related this folder to twenty-six pages of unsigned texts datable to the period 1953–59 discovered in the Joan Mitchell Foundation, New York, some years ago, and also to other unsigned notes and translations of works on Northwest Coast ethnography, art and oral traditions by Marius Barbeau and others in the Georges Duthuit Fonds now in the Kandinsky Library. Some of these bear handwritten annotations attributable to Duthuit. At this stage of research, these materials, taken together, suggest that Duthuit was planning a publication on Northwest Coast ceremony and art, for which Riopelle would have provided illustrations; these were never executed.

7. Georges Duthuit, "Le don indien sur la Côte Nord-Ouest de l'Amérique (Colombie britannique)," *Labyrinthe*, no. 18 (April 1946), p. 9; repr. in *Représentation et présence: Premiers écrits et travaux, 1923-1952* (Paris: Flammarion, 1974), p. 316. See excerpt translated by Marie Mauzé, "Surrealists and the New York Avant-garde, 1920–60," in *Native Art of the Northwest Coast: A History of Changing Ideas*, eds. Charlotte Townsend-Gault, Jennifer Kramer and Ki-ke-in (Vancouver: UBC Press, 2013), p. 290.

8. Ibid.

9. Pieces owned by Duthuit, Breton, Lebel and Waldberg (**25**) were included in the exhibition *Le Masque*. On the *Masterpieces* exhibition, see Diana Nemiroff, "Modernism, Nationalism and Beyond: A Critical History of Exhibitions of First Nations Art," in *Land, Spirit, Power: First Nations at the National Gallery of Canada*, exh. cat., Diana Nemiroff, Charlotte Townsend-Gault and Robert Houle (Ottawa: National Gallery of Canada, 1992); and Ruth B. Phillips, "Modes of Inclusion: Indigenous Art at the National Gallery of Canada and the Art Gallery of Ontario," in R. B. Phillips, *Museum Pieces: Toward the Indigenization of Canadian Museums* (Montreal: McGill-Queen's University Press, 2011), pp. 254–259.

"I don't take anything *from* Nature. I move *into* Nature"
—Jean Paul Riopelle, 1995

It would have been impossible for any modern artist in post-World War II Paris *not* to have encountered the powerful primitivist currents of the French art world. The tenets of modernist aesthetic primitivism had emerged in their most influential iteration at the turn of the twentieth century among avant-garde artists in Paris, who were searching for a vitality and sincerity they felt had been lost in Western art.[1] They saw in African, Oceanic and North American Indigenous arts expressions of an ability to live in harmony with the rhythms of nature that had been lost to Western artists through the multiple alienations of the modernized world.

During the 1920s, modernist primitivism gained new dimensions through the Surrealist movement led by the writer André Breton. When Breton and others fled Paris for New York City during World War II, they gained access to the more extensive collections of Indigenous North American arts on display in the city's ethnographic museums than were available in Paris. Masks, totem poles, drums and rattles from the Arctic and the Northwest Coast held a particular attraction, because their shamanistic iconography and performative dimensions gave visual form to concepts of transformation central to the Surrealist affirmation of dreams, the subconscious and non-rational reality. When these artists, critics and intellectuals returned to Paris after the war, they brought back not only their sense of connection with Northwest Coast and Arctic arts, but also many examples they had found in curio shops or acquired, via intermediaries, from New York's Museum of the American Indian itself.[2]

Riopelle settled in Paris only a couple of years later, in 1947. He was drawn into Breton's circle almost immediately, and formed a close and enduring friendship with the art historian, critic and collector Georges Duthuit. Duthuit was in New York in 1939 and remained there throughout the war, frequenting the Northwest Coast Hall of the American Museum of Natural History with Claude Lévi-Strauss and other French exiles. He also acquired examples of Arctic and Northwest Coast carvings, many of them large and imposing.[3] Duthuit shared with Riopelle not only his knowledge of the anthropological literature on Northwest Coast arts and cultures, but also his collections. The artist's daughter Yseult Riopelle recalls that during her childhood in the mid-1950s, "Georges Duthuit would lend us masks, regularly exchanging them for different ones"[4] (**188**). One mask, she further recalled, was "used in the winter ceremonial of the Kwakiutls [Kwakwaka'wakw] of the northwest Pacific Coast, known as the Hamshamtses";[5] open, the mask represents a raven and closed, an anthropomorphic being with a bird beak that Duthuit had identified as "l'homme corbeau" (**187**), or "raven man."

Duthuit's collection was an enduring touchstone for Riopelle, even when the objects were not in his home. Tucked into a copy of George Swinton's 1972 text *Sculpture of the Eskimo*, owned by Riopelle, was a set of twenty photographs probably given to him by Duthuit. Nine of these show Indigenous objects, many from Duthuit's collection. As we will see, masks and other pieces from this collection would later appear in Riopelle's prints and drawings of the 1970s. A folder labelled "Riopelle / for book / Indian Stories" found by Yseult Riopelle suggests the further intriguing possibility that the seeds of the prints and drawings Riopelle would make in the 1970s had been planted twenty years earlier, when he was planning to collaborate on a publication with Duthuit.[6]

Some of the same images had already appeared as illustrations to the essay "Le don indien" on the Northwest Coast potlatch and its arts Duthuit published in the journal *Labyrinthe* in 1946 (**192**), in which he melded ethnographic analyses with richly poetic flights of prose expressive of Surrealist understandings. He imagined, for example, a masked dancer performing "in a realm where dream and reality, and the familiar and the mysterious meet, the transformation of animal into man and man into spirit."[7] As we will also see, this evocation of the performative context of Northwest Coast masquerades seems to foretell images Riopelle would draw three decades later in the medium of silverpoint. A further comment is also particularly striking: Duthuit wrote that "for he who can see by looking and hear by listening, the drum and the rattle and the frenzied gesticulations may unite, beyond the ravaged flesh and the wounded will, the disconnected forces of his universe made of waves and foliage."[8] Duthuit's verbal imagery bears an uncanny resemblance to the compositional structure Riopelle invented three decades later, in which Northwest Coast masks and rattles are incorporated into a ground of fallen leaves. The artist's interest was sustained for the next two decades. In Paris, he visited the Musée de l'Homme with his family, and saw special exhibitions, such as *Le masque* at the Musée Guimet in 1959–60 and *Masterpieces of Indian and Eskimo Art from Canada* in 1968, which was co-organized by the National Museum of Man (now the Canadian Museum of History) in Ottawa and the Société des amis du Musée de l'Homme in Paris.[9] Riopelle also continued to acquire books on Arctic and Northwest Coast arts; on the evidence of his graphic work, he must have acquired his copy of Claude Lévi-Strauss' *La voie des masques* (**190**) soon after it was published in 1975.

Two questions immediately emerge from even so brief an account. The first has to do with the period of gestation between Riopelle's initial contact with Duthuit and other enthusiasts of Northwest Coast arts and the appearances of recognizable references to these arts in the artist's prints and drawings made more than two decades later. Although Riopelle had referred to Indigenous ritual and art in the titles of a number of his works as early as 1956, his imagery was most often non-representational. Why then do these references become not only figurative, but also strikingly explicit in their references to their ethnographic sources in the 1970s? Second, how might we understand the reproduction of Northwest Coast arts by a Quebec artist during the 1970s in light of the debates around colonial and settler practices of appropriation that were soon to erupt and that remain contested within contemporary projects of institutional decolonization?

In order to suggest answers to these questions, we need to look more closely at the three distinct groups of prints and drawings Riopelle made during the mid-1970s in which Northwest Coast arts appear; they take the form both of direct and more allusive citations of examples the artist had found in books and articles. The two largest groups are a set of silverpoint drawings made in 1977 and the *Lied à Émile Nelligan*, an album of sixteen lithographic prints created that same year to mark the 100th anniversary of the birth of one of Quebec's most beloved poets.[10] The third category of works with Northwest Coast imagery consists of four coloured lithographs made about 1979.

We will argue that such an examination shows that Riopelle's references to these and other Indigenous arts are tied to his lifelong desire to "move *into* Nature"—as he phrased it— through his art, and also to his evolving sense of identification as a Canadian who felt an affinity with North America's Indigenous peoples. We will also urge considering the issue of appropriation as a problematic whose terms have shifted over time, and which therefore needs to be understood not only from a contemporary perspective, but also in specific historical contexts.

THE SILVERPOINT DRAWINGS

In the silverpoint technique, the artist uses a silver stylus to make images on a prepared gesso surface.[11] The silver lines oxidize quickly, resulting in a monochromatic drawing, and the images that emerge from the shimmering surface are subtle, elusive and visually fleeting. It is a technique that favours a personal and intimate process of recording. Of the twenty-one known silverpoint drawings Riopelle made at this time, over half incorporate Northwest Coast Indigenous images, most of which are derived from illustrations in *La voie des masques* and from the loose photographs found in Riopelle's copy of George Swinton's book. Interestingly, many of these images had also been reproduced in Duthuit's 1946 *Labyrinthe* essay, discussed above. Among the drawings based on carvings reproduced both in Duthuit's publication and in the loose photographs are *Masque de la Côte Ouest* (197), *Potlach* (206), *Autre masque* (203) and *Suite II* (202).

Other images draw on diverse sources, such as a small Tlingit bone charm representing a wolf (218) given to Riopelle by Duthuit, and may also derive from illustrations in the catalogue of the 1968 Musée de l'Homme *Masterpieces* exhibition.[12] In these silverpoint drawings Riopelle uses various hatching techniques to create layered images. In some instances, the Indigenous objects are presented in a clear manner and the sources are relatively easy to identify. For example, in *Costume du côté de Kitimat* he has referenced the photograph of a "Kwakiutl" chief in full regalia as seen in a photograph reproduced in Franz Boas' classic ethnography and, later, in an article by Surrealist writer Wolfgang Paalen (26).[13] In other works, such as *Wolf* (217), hatching covers the entire picture space, overlaying and obscuring the Northwest Coast imagery. In *Bombée* (189), Riopelle has introduced other techniques into the drawing, using spray paint (which the artist called "peinture à la bombe") to incorporate a direct print made from a leaf placed at the bottom of the composition. Within a few years, the use of spray paint would become more prevalent in his work, particularly from the mid-1980s until he stopped working in 1992.[14] Riopelle's efforts to understand not only Northwest Coast arts, but also silverpoint and its relationship to other media, imbue these graphic works with a sense of experimentation. The visual language he worked out in the silverpoint drawings—the use of hatching, the Indigenous references and the gestural qualities—would be carried over to the other groups of Northwest Coast-inspired work.

10. The total number of silverpoint drawings Riopelle made is not known with certainty. There are twenty-one extant, and we know that he included twenty-five others in the initial edition of the *Lied*, although none of these has been located. Since Riopelle was exploring a medium new to him, it is highly likely that he made a great many more.

11. See Gilles Daigneault, "Riopelle and Printmaking, an Encounter" in *Jean Paul Riopelle: Catalogue raisonné des estampes*, ed. Yseult Riopelle (Montreal: Hibou Press; Moudon, Switzerland: Acatos, 2005), p. 42.

12. Riopelle attended this exhibition, which was also shown at the National Gallery of Canada in 1968–69. See Phillips, "Modes of Inclusion," pp. 253–259, and Nemiroff, "Modernism, Nationalism, and Beyond."

13. Kitimat is located in the territories of the Haisla people, who were not distinguished from the "Kwakiutl" [Kwakwaka'wakw]—in the early twentieth century. See Franz Boas, "The Social Organization and the Secret Societies of the Kwakiutl Indians," in the *Report of the United States National Museum for 1895* (Washington, D. C.; Government Printing Office, 1897) pp. 309–738. *Kwakiutl Indians*, pl. 47, "Lao- 'laxa dancer"; and Wolfgang Paalen, "Totem Art," *DYN*, Amerindian number, no 4–5 (1943).

14. René LeMoigne, Riopelle's regular printer, told Yseult Riopelle that the leaf was first used in 1967: see *Catalogue raisonné des estampes*, p. 113.

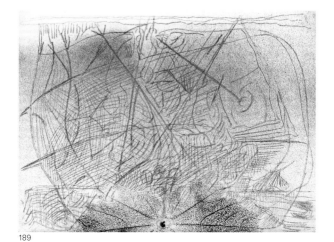

189

189
Jean Paul Riopelle
Bombée
About 1977
Silverpoint and ink on paper

190
Covers of vols. 1 and 2 of Claude Lévi-Strauss, *La voie des masques: les sentiers de la création* (1975)

191
Film still from *Behind the Mask* (1973)

Claude-Lévi Strauss is shown talking about a *Xwexwe* mask (244) during a lecture at the Museum of Anthropology at the University of British Columbia.

190a

b

190 | Most of the classical anthropological literature on the Northwest Coast had been written in English and German. However, there were also two significant French-language scholars, Marius Barbeau and Claude Lévi-Strauss, and they both were to make a significant impression on Riopelle and his Parisian friends.

Lévi-Strauss was in the circle of exiles living in New York during the Vichy era. Renowned as a pioneer of structural anthropology, he applied aspects of linguistic theory to the understanding of mythology and Aboriginal belief systems. His analysis of certain Kwakwaka'wakw masks in relation to those of their neighbours, published in his monumental 1975 study *La voie des masques*, appears to have been a major source of inspiration for Riopelle, who drew some of the masks illustrated in Lévi-Strauss' monograph.

After completing his studies at Oxford and at the Sorbonne, anthropologist Marius Barbeau returned to Canada, where he found employment at what was then the National Museum of Canada (now the Canadian Museum of History, Gatineau) in Ottawa. Although much of his theoretical work has long been questioned, his numerous monographs on the art and culture of the Northwest Coast were widely read and, as the principal works in the French language on these subjects, readily accessible to Francophone readers, including Riopelle and Georges Duthuit.

Like Lévi-Strauss, Barbeau was especially drawn to the art of the Indigenous peoples speaking the languages of the Tsimshian (meaning "Inside the Skeena River") language family. Home to the Ts'msyen, Nisga'a and Gitksan peoples, this region stretches deep into the interior of northern British Columbia along the Nass and Skeena rivers, and along the coast between their two estuaries. Having a lot in common with the culture of their neighbours, they nonetheless have a distinctive form of the classical northern coastal art, characterized by a consistent concern for the portrayal of human emotion. Less hieratic and formal than that of their Haida or Tlingit neighbours, their art can at times show whimsy or humour. A long history of vigilant resistance to colonialism has led these cultures in recent years to undergo a strong cultural revival, and their legal and political struggles to assert their traditional rights continue to have a major national impact. – BHR

191

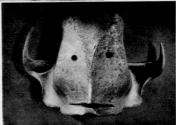

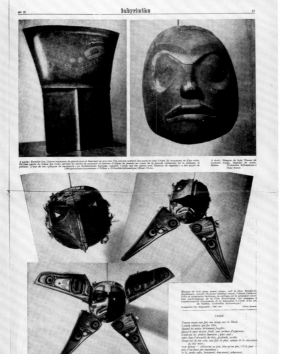

192

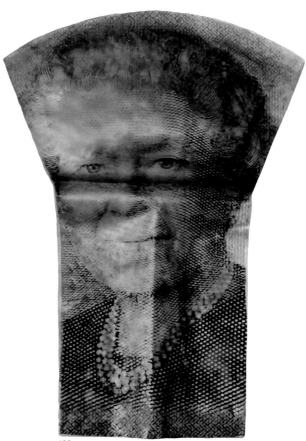

193

192
Georges Duthuit, "Le don indien sur la côte nord-ouest de l'Amérique (Colombie britannique)," *Labyrinthe*, 1946

During World War II, Georges Duthuit took refuge in New York, where he discovered North American Indigenous art. When he returned to Paris, he wrote an essay on the potlatch entitled "Le don indien." Published in the magazine *Labyrinthe* (1944–46), the essay was illustrated with works from his collection, some of which were photographed by Georges Brassaï.

193
Alison Bremner
Ceremonial Wealth
2020
Copper, acrylic, ink

The copper shield, or *tináa*, is an object of wealth and prestige among the Northwest Coast Indigenous peoples. It was brought out for display during the potlatch and represented more than just the value of the copper it was made of. Each time a copper shield was brought out at a potlatch, it accumulated value, thus becoming a sign of great material wealth. *Tináas* once held a monetary value something like that of paper money today. The *Potlatch Dollar* series was created by superimposing images of money onto copper shields.
– Alison Bremner

15. Daigneault, "Riopelle and Printmaking, an Encounter," p. 42.

16. As Nina Milner writes, Nelligan wrote the 170 poems, sonnets, rondels and prose that comprise his oeuvre in just four years. His work was influenced by Charles Baudelaire, Arthur Rimbaud and Lord Byron. See "Émile Nelligan (1879–1941)," in *Canadian Poetry Archive* (Ottawa: Library and Archives Canada), http://www.collectionscanada.gc.ca/wapp/canvers/bios/enelligan.htm (accessed April 16, 2019).

17. Robert Inverarity, *Art of the Northwest Coast Indians* (Berkeley: University of California Press Books, 1950 [1967]), pl. 51. This was one of the most widely available publications on Indigenous art of the Northwest Coast, and remained in print for decades.

18. Ibid. pl. 199.

19. Ibid., pl. 126, Tlingit, Southwest Museum of the American Indian, Los Angeles.

20. Ibid., pl. 77, Tlingit, Washington State History Museum.

21. For a classic formulation of this world view, widely shared across Indigenous North America, see A. Irving Hallowell, "Ojibwa Ontology, Behavior and World View," in *Culture in History: Essays in Honor of Paul Radin*, ed. Stanley Diamond (New York: Columbia University Press, 1960), pp. 2–25.

THE *LIED À ÉMILE NELLIGAN*

The *Lied à Émile Nelligan* (**227, 229-233, 237, 2398**) was a more self-evidently public project, although retaining the sense of personal exploration of the silverpoint drawings. It was issued as an edition of seventy-five, each album containing a facsimile of two poems by Nelligan, a manuscript of his *Motifs du récital des anges* (1899) and Riopelle's black and white lithographs. The artist also included an original silverpoint drawing in each of the initial twenty-five editions. Riopelle had been interested in Nelligan since his high-school years,[15] and his attraction to the highly evocative romanticism and symbolism of the poetry accords with his early engagement with Surrealism.[16] His series remains true to the spirit of the art song, rather than attempting a direct illustration of Nelligan's poems. Riopelle singled out two poems—*Paysage fauve* (1903) and *Sérénade triste* (1903)—as inspiration for the visual verse he dedicated to the poet. His selections reflect the intensity of his engagement with nature and the North during those years. In *Paysage fauve*, for example, Nelligan writes: "C'est l'Hiver; c'est la Mort; sur les neiges arctiques" [It is Winter; it is Death; on Arctic snow]. *Sérénade triste* begins: "Comme des larmes d'or qui de mon cœur s'égouttent / Feuilles de mes bonheurs, vous tombez toutes, toutes" [Like golden tears that drop from my heart / Leaves of my happiness, you all fall].

The two unifying elements of the *Lied* lithographs are their Indigenous references and the incorporation of leaves either traced or directly printed from real leaves. Riopelle's falling leaves demarcate the picture space, create portals to other realms and are brought together to give shape to otherworldly beings. The romantic and emotional evocation of the forest and its seasonal rhythms in Nelligan's poems freed Riopelle to make visual connections with Indigenous arts as a channel for intensifying his sense of oneness with the natural world. As we page through the sixteen prints, we are transported into a world of Riopelle's imagination, his way of understanding and being with nature.

Riopelle worked with his sources in several different ways, either translating them unaltered from photographic reproductions found in books into his prints and drawings, or reworking them into a more personal iconography of shamanistic faces, animals and animal features. The first of these approaches is illustrated by the first plate of the *Lied* (**239**), in which the artist reproduces a Kwakwaka'wakw stone pile driver (**240**) from Robert Inverarity's *Art of the Northwest Coast Indians* (**194**) and overlays it on a bed of leaves.[17] Equally faithful to its source is the rendering of the Tlingit helmet mask (**234**) from Inverarity's book that appears in Plate 12 (**233**), where it is juxtaposed with two large leaves.[18] Comparing the book illustrations and Riopelle's lithographs, we can see that he has replicated not only the objects, but also the precise angles and light/shadow balance seen in the photograph. In both of these prints, the artist's faithful reproduction of mechanical reproductions functions to maintain a distance from the

original; this strategy, we suggest, constituted a refusal of appropriation—a term that, in its usual sense, conveys the meaning of its Latin source, to "take to oneself." Rather, Riopelle's literalness in these images seems to engage the viewer as a fellow traveller in his own acts of contemplation of an "other" reality he admired and his quest for connection to it.

In contrast, Riopelle does take liberties with his sources in other lithographs from the *Lied* project, recombining forms and features with compositions of leaves and features of land and landscape. In Plate 5 (**232**), he suggests the lower half of an anthropomorphic figure with a mask-like face of his own invention. The rattles held in each hand can be identified with an *Art of the Northwest Coast Indians* illustration.[19] These images are integrated with a set of leaves shot through with light. In Plate 9 (**237**), Riopelle takes the recombination approach further. He has retained the integrity of a Tlingit bear mask (**238**) that appears in Inverarity,[20] but whereas in the previous examples Indigenous objects were clearly superimposed on background compositions of leaves, here, the mask is fully enmeshed with them. Additionally, shapes suggestive of the eye-forms seen on many Northwest Coast masks appear at the bases of several of the leaves. In such drawings, we see Riopelle approaching, via Indigenous arts, the fusion of nature and culture he sought.

In the largest group of prints—eight out of sixteen— the Indigenous sources have been still further deconstructed. In Plate 7, a line whose contour resembles the pile driver illustrated in the first plate connects four leaves, which are animated by eyes suggestive of mask-like forms or mythical beings that may ultimately derive from unidentifiable Indigenous sources. In Plate 4, masks emerge from the land forms that comprise the background, but in such a subtle way that they are easily missed at first glance. In this image, the artist's vision of land imbued with spiritual presence comes very close to Indigenous world views that recognize personhood as a multitude of non-human entities.[21]

About 1979, Riopelle made four colour lithographs in which he returned one more time to the Northwest Coast motifs and gestural lines of the *Lied* and the silverpoint drawings. In two of the most remarkable, he reproduces the two mask types at the heart of the structural analysis of Northwest Coast mythology and mask traditions presented in Lévi-Strauss' *La voie des masques*. In one of these lithographs, entitled *Sorciers* (**241**), Riopelle represents two mask-like faces similar to the mask shown on the book's cover (**190**). In a second print, entitled *Masques* (**242**), he reproduces a "Kwakiutl Xwexwe" [Kwakwaka'wakw Xwixwi] and a "Kwakiutl Dzonokwa" [Kwakwaka'wakw Dzonoqua] exactly as they appear in the two colour plates that face each other in the book (**243, 244**). Riopelle pays homage to the greatness of the Northwest Coast artistic traditions, but also to the anthropologist's influential study of relationships of opposition and complementarity in myth, ritual and art. In the first print, the artist obscures the right-hand image with layers of hatch marks, while in the second, he shows the two images clearly.[22]

NATURE AND RETURN

As we noted earlier, it is striking that Riopelle's longstanding interest in Northwest Coast art did not find full, figurative expression in his own art until the 1970s—three decades after references to totem poles and other objects had appeared in the work of Jackson Pollock, Barnett Newman and other artists of the New York avant-garde who were drawn to Northwest Coast and other Indigenous North American arts.[23] The biographical context in which Riopelle's images make their appearance offers clues to the conjunction of interests and desires that brought them into being; it is not an accident that they emerged during the decade when the artist was re-engaging with his identity as a Canadian through renewed contact with its northern lands, animals and Indigenous cultures. Riopelle's trip to northern Quebec in 1972 had led to his *Rois de Thulé* series, and its visual references to masks worn by Inuit seal hunters set a precedent for the incorporation of Northwest Coast masks and objects into his work. These appear a few years later, following his more frequent and extended trips to Quebec and his establishment of a temporary studio on the Île-aux-Oies in the Saint Lawrence River in 1976.

Although Riopelle made the graphic works discussed earlier in Paris, for him, both the focus on the pre-eminent Quebec poet and use of leaves established a connection to the place of his birth. Leaves—which had been sent to him from Canada—made their first appearance in the *Feuilles* series of lithographs from 1967.[24] His return to the leaf motif in the *Lied* could thus be read as something of a nod to Canada, but also—since it is highly likely that the leaves he used in the 1970s were from Paris rather than Canada[25]—as a bridge between Canada and Paris,

the two worlds he straddled. Breton had assigned Riopelle the persona of "trapper" soon after his arrival in Paris, distinguishing him from other artists working in Paris at the time, and Riopelle came increasingly to embrace this identity through his love of travelling and hunting in the North. Beyond this geocultural specificity, however, lies a more universal quest that remains tied to his modernist formation and its central primitivist concerns. As we have stressed, his fusions of the natural (the leaves and animal-like creatures) with the human (the masks and faces) point to the intensity of his desire to translate into his art the harmony with nature he experienced on the land. His visual homage to Nelligan called forth atypical moments of literalness and self-revelation. Although self-portraits do not figure prominently in Riopelle's art,[26] the face that appears in the central bottom leaf of Plate 7, could, we suggest, be his own. Its contours are partially delineated by the veins of a leaf, and the long nose, full mouth and angular chin strikingly resemble the artist's own features. Moreover, a 1989 self-portrait shares the angle of the chin and the shape of the nose seen in the face in *Lied à Émile Nelligan*, Plate 7. Riopelle often spoke of becoming nature; has he, in Plate 7, become the leaf?[27]

APPROPRIATION AS A DIALOGIC STRATEGY

Less than a decade after Riopelle produced these works, the issue of appropriation erupted into the space of public debate when New York's Museum of Modern Art's celebratory exhibition *Primitivism and Twentieth-century Art: Affinities of the Tribal and the Modern* opened in 1984. Critics were appalled by the show's celebration of Western artists' formal borrowings from and fantasies of interpretation around non-Western arts, and by the lack of acknowledgement of the meanings these works have held for their original makers and their descendants, meanings that were easily accessible in a growing corpus of scholarly studies.[28] Further debates and controversies were sparked by a series of exhibitions that followed swiftly on the heels of the Museum of Modern Art's show: *Art/Artifact* at the Center for African Art in New York (1988), *The Spirit Sings: Artistic Traditions of Canada's First Peoples* at the Glenbow Museum in Calgary (1988), and *Magiciens de la terre* at the Centre Pompidou in Paris (1989).[29]

These debates are well rehearsed in the literature and do not need to be summarized here. We note them, rather, to point to the relative quietude of the 1970s, a decade during which such contestations remained largely latent. As we have seen, Riopelle's interests and knowledge were informed by a modernist engagement with ethnography and Surrealism, and were infused with a deep admiration for Indigenous peoples' cultural insights into the relationships between human beings, animals and the "natural" world. As he told Gilbert Érouart in a 1995 interview, "Abstract: 'abstraction,' 'to abstract,' 'to extract from.' 'to derive from' . . . My approach is the exact opposite. I don't take anything *from* Nature, I move *into* Nature."[30] Even more telling, perhaps,

22. Lévi-Strauss analyzes Kwakwaka'wakw and Salish traditions, but while the Salish Sxwayxwey mask is culturally sensitive and should not be exhibited or its image reproduced, the Kwakwaka'wakw have not designated their version of this mask in this way.

23. See W. Jackson Rushing, *Native American Art and the New York Avant-garde: A History of Cultural Primitivism* (Austin, Texas: University of Texas Press, 1995), and Barnett Newman, "Northwest Coast Indian Painting" (1946), reproduced in *Primitivism and Twentieth-century Art: A Documentary History*, ed. Jack Flam (Berkeley: University of California Press, 2003), pp. 282–283.

24. Daigneault, "Riopelle and Printmaking, an Encounter," p. 22.

25. The shape of the leaves used in the *Lied* are reminiscent of the foliage found on the Turkish hazel, linden, empress and London plane trees. All four trees are commonly seen on the streets of Paris.

26. There have been two self-portraits, one in 1945, and the second, a unique enhanced lithograph, from 1989.

27. Riopelle, "I Belong to the Island," in Gilbert Érouart, *Riopelle in Conversation* (Concord, Ontario: House of Anansi, 1995), p. 25.

28. On these debates, see, for example, James Clifford, "Histories of the Tribal and the Modern," in *The Predicament of Culture: Twentieth-century Ethnography, Literature, and Art* (Cambridge, Massachusetts: Harvard University Press, 1988); Hal Foster, "The 'Primitive' Unconscious of Modern Art, or White Skin Black Masks," in *Recodings: Art, Spectacle, Cultural Politics* (Seattle, Washington: Bay Press, 1985); and Thomas McEvilley, "Doctor, Lawyer, Indian Chief," in *Art and Otherness: Crisis in Cultural Identity* (Kingston, New York: McPherson and Company, 1992), pp. 27–56.

29. On these three exhibitions, see, for example: Susan Vogel ed., *Art/Artifact: African Art in Anthropology Collections* (New York: Center for African Art, 1988); Ruth B. Phillips, "Moment of Truth: *The Spirit Sings* as Critical Event and the Exhibition inside It," in *Museum Pieces: Toward the Indigenization of Canadian Museums*, pp. 48–70; and on *Magiciens de la terre* see *Third Text*, the special issue *Magiciens de la terre* (1989), and Annie Cohen Solal, *Magiciens de la terre : Retour sur une exposition légendaire* (Paris: Centre Pompidou, 2014).

30. Érouart, *Riopelle in Conversation*, p. 25.

194
Cover of Robert Bruce Inverarity, *Art of the Northwest Coast Indians* (1950)

To create his album of lithographs *Lied à Émile Nelligan* (1977–79), Riopelle mainly drew from the illustrations in American anthropologist Robert Bruce Inverarity's book *Art of the Northwest Coast Indians* (1950). He chose works by the Kwakwaka'wakw and Tlingit, depicting them rather faithfully.

31. Ibid., p. 24.

32. United Nations Declaration on the Rights of Indigenous Peoples (UNDRIP), Article 31.1, https://www.un.org/development/desa/indigenouspeoples/declaration-on-the-rights-of-indigenous-peoples.html.

33. Arnd Schneider, "On 'Appropriation.' A Critical Reappraisal of the Concept and Its Application in Global Art Practices," *Social Anthropology*, vol. 11, no. 2 (2003), pp. 215–229.

34. Ibid., p. 223.

35. Guy Sioui Durand, *Jean-Paul Riopelle : l'art d'un trappeur supérieur. Indianité* (Sainte-Foy, Quebec: Éditions GID, 2003), p. 21.

36. Guy Sioui Durand, *Les très riches heures de Jean-Paul Riopelle* (Trois-Rivières, Quebec: Éditions d'art Le Sabord, 2000), p. 9.

37. See Aaron Glass, "History and Critique of the 'Renaissance' Discourse," in *Native Art of the Northwest Coast: A History of Changing Ideas,* eds. Charlotte Townsend-Gault, Jennifer Kramer and Ki-ke-in (Vancouver: University of British Columbia Press, 2014), pp. 487–517; David Summers, "What Is a Renaissance?," in *Bill Reid and Beyond: Expanding on Modern Native Art,* eds. Karen Duffek and Charlotte Townsend-Gault (Vancouver: Douglas and McIntyre, 2004), pp. 133–154.

38. Carpenter, "Introduction," pp. 9–29.

39. Holm and Reid, *A Dialogue on Form and Freedom,* p. 46.

40. Judith Ostrowitz, "Democratization and Northwest Coast Art in the Modern Period: Native Emissaries, Non-Native Connoisseurship and Consumption," in *Native Art of the Northwest Coast,* p. 469.

is another statement made during the same conversation about the relationship of hunting to the movement into Nature. To be a successful hunter, "You make yourself into an animal, an animal with horns on its head that would break off branches if you were moving about . . . You want to hunt a moose? You have to be a moose."[31] Again, the parallel with Indigenous understandings of animal/human relationships is striking.

Appropriation has remained a much-debated issue in the age of globalization, but the terms in which it is discussed have continued to shift. The United Nations Declaration on the Rights of Indigenous Peoples (UNDRIP) affirms the right of Indigenous peoples to "maintain, control, protect and develop their intellectual property over . . . cultural heritage, traditional knowledge, and traditional cultural expressions."[32] Yet "cultural property" remains a broad term that invites further definition. Conversely, the *lack* of clear definition impedes ongoing debates about appropriation. Although fully acknowledging the legacies of theft and misuse that have occurred through the radical power imbalances of colonialism, anthropologist Arnd Schneider urges that we reject "rigid notions of cultures at both ends of the continuum between 'origin' and 'copy' [that] leave 'appropriation' in a straitjacket of cultural essentialism."[33] He instead argues for a transformative possibility through which the respectful "taking to oneself" of a foreign cultural idea or image can become a productive tool of understanding. He urges that "the way forward, is to conceptualize appropriation as one of the principal practices underlying any culture contact or exchange, and therefore underlying any dialogical situation of 'understanding' each 'other.'"[34]

Riopelle's prints and drawings of the 1970s open such a dialogue, mediated, in the absence of direct contact with Northwest Coast artists, through photographs of artworks and ethnographic texts left by earlier generations. Such a view has been eloquently stated by Wendat scholar, curator and critic Guy Sioui Durand. He recognizes in Riopelle's work an ethical commitment to the reciprocal relationship of humans and the natural world that parallels that of Indigenous people: "It is by exploring the wide open spaces, the rivers and the forests as a 'hunter, fisherman and navigator' that the artist makes himself one with them."[35] Through his imagery of animals and Indigenous arts, Sioui Durand writes, Riopelle achieved an "osmosis of identity between the artist's world view and that of Indigenous peoples."[36]

The best test for the nature of the appropriation that Riopelle enacts in his prints and drawings of the mid-1970s is, we urge, to be found in a comparison with discourses and practices developing on the Northwest Coast during that decade. The 1970s is a key period in the renewal of ancestral artistic traditions undertaken by Northwest Coast artists who engaged in a sustained conversation with a close-knit group of non-Indigenous curators, critics and art historians. Riopelle does not seem to have been aware of this "Northwest Coast Renaissance," as it was termed at the time.[37] Yet the dialogue he established

with Northwest Coast arts through the manipulations and structuring of Northwest Coast imagery in his prints and drawings more closely recalls this collaborative project of re-visioning than it does the avant-garde modernists' engagements with African and Oceanic art earlier in the century.

A contemporaneous exchange between Haida artist Bill Reid and settler art historian Bill Holm further illuminates this kind of cross-cultural dialogue. Focusing on formal approaches rather than on imagery and meaning, it was conducted in the publication that accompanied the 1975 *Form and Freedom* exhibition at Rice University in Houston, Texas. In his introductory essay, anthropologist Edward Carpenter credited the important role played by the French Surrealist exiles in reclassifying Northwest Coast carvings as works of fine art rather than ethnographic specimens.[38] In the main text, Reid and Holm examined together the examples of historic art presented in the exhibition. Picking up a dagger whose intricately carved hilt depicts a bear's head with a human figure emerging from the top, Reid said: "This, for me, really has it all together. One of the great joys I've gotten out of the Northwest Coast is the feeling I have that these people looked at the world in a very different way than we do. They weren't bound by the silly feeling that it's impossible for two figures to occupy the same space at the same time. So we have this human figure, plus a bear's head or whatever, coexisting in space and time."[39] Judith Ostrowitz has argued that Reid and Holm "practised the unobstructed 'gaze' that the scholarship of the period had invited outsiders to develop and apply."[40] A world away in Paris, thinking himself back to his native land through his contemplation of Northwest Coast Indigenous art, Riopelle shared this gaze, and recognized the same impossible but possible transformation through which two bodies could occupy the same space. In graphic works he made in the 1970s, he realized the dialogic possibilities of appropriation—and its transformative potential.

ART OF THE NORTHWEST COAST INDIANS
ROBERT BRUCE INVERARITY

195

196

195
"Pyre and graves of the family
of the Cacique An-kau at Port
Mulgrave, 1792"
Ill. in *Alrededor al mundo
por las corbetas Descubierta
y Atrevida al mando de
los Capitanes de Navio Don
Alejandro Malaspina y Don
José de Bustamante y Guerra,
desde 1789 a 1794* (1885)

In 2019, a group of pictures
was found in a copy of George
Swinton's *Sculpture of the
Eskimo* that once belonged
to Riopelle. In addition to
photographs of Northwest Coast
masks and objects, there were
illustrations from anthropology
books (**195, 196, 198, 204, 205,
208–210, 222, 225, 226**). Many,
if not all, of the works depicted
were in the collection of
Georges Duthuit, who could
have drawn the artist's attention
to them with a view to illustrating
the co-publication they
were planning. In 1977, Riopelle
based many silverpoint drawings
on these images.

196
Ceremonial plate
(Canadian Northwest Coast,
Kwakwaka'wakw)
Ill. in Georges Duthuit,
"Le don indien sur la côte nord-
ouest de l'Amérique (Colombie
britannique)," *Labyrinthe* (1946)

197
Jean Paul Riopelle
Masque de la côte Ouest
1977
Silverpoint on paper

197 | In this series of drawings, Riopelle takes up
silverpoint, an old technique rarely used today.
On a surface treated with gesso or gouache (formerly
with bone ash), a silver point is used to mark the
surface with fine, delicate lines. Initially grey toned,
the metal particles left on the paper turn into rich
brown hues over time. The great colourist Riopelle
produced works of a striking chromatic sobriety
with this technique. – **AR**

198
Kwakwaka'wakw
Transformation mask
formerly in the
collection of Georges
Duthuit (detail)
N.d.

199
Jean Paul Riopelle
Sorcier II
1977
Silverpoint on paper

199

200 | This contemporary transformation mask by Heiltsuk artist Shawn Hunt uses mixed-reality technology, which exemplifies how open Indigenous cultures have always been to new materials and technologies. In pre-contact time, First Nations were inveterate traders, and through intermarriage and complex diplomatic relations, exchanges of artistic styles and typologies, dances, songs and ceremonial practices occurred. It is effectively impossible at this remove to determine the origin of certain types of objects found throughout the region. Following the arrival of Europeans, the quick assimilation of new materials—such as California haliotis shell, machine-woven textiles, European glass beads and sheet copper—into the distinctive and innovative Indigenous cultural forms, shows a unique cultural resilience, even in the era of tragic devastating population loss from foreign diseases. Today, new digital technologies and media, such as manga and installation art, are being transformed by the Indigenous artists of these strong and proud cultures. – BHR

200 | The Heiltsuk visual culture has always been highly adaptable. In the past, artists quickly and effortlessly embraced new technology and ideas, and used them to convey our history and our stories to the next generation. I have always strived for progression in my work, whether it be in terms of design, material or concept. I am interested in the intersection of the ancient and modern, the future and the past. Most often, masks are seen in museums or in galleries. In these places, they function as sculptures, but that was not what they were created for. They are meant to be worn and performed, and then put away when not in use. My intent with *Transformation Mask* was to allow the non-Indigenous viewer/participant to experience the wearing of a Heiltsuk mask. The idea is that in wearing the mask the viewer might gain some insight and a deeper understanding as to what these masks meant to us and our communities. The technology also allows me to simulate a kind of spiritual experience or vision that one may have from performing a mask while in a ceremonial context. My hope is that the work challenges the viewers' expectations of what Heiltsuk art looks like, and to have them gain a deeper understanding of the complexities of our culture. – SH

201 | The Kwakwaka'wakw people are not one Nation, but rather "the people who speak Kwak'wala." They comprise seventeen distinct Nations, occupying the northeast quadrant of Vancouver Island and the adjacent mainland, that share not only language but also culture. Nineteenth-century anthropologists mistakenly called them the Kwakiutl, a term that unfortunately persists in popular usage.

In 1883–85, Canada's Indian Act, originally adopted in 1876, was amended to read: "Every Indian or other person who engages in or assists in celebrating the Indian festival known as the "Potlatch" or in the Indian dance known as the "Tamanawas" is guilty of a misdemeanor, and shall be liable to imprisonment." Potlatch is a word meaning "to give" in the Chinook trade jargon that was used along the West Coast. The oral culture of the region's First Nations required that transactions, such as the inheritance of cultural or physical property, land use, and transference of title among other things, needed to be widely witnessed, ideally by neutral parties. Usually held in the winter months, elaborate feasts to which outsiders were invited were occasions during which host communities would display the cultural prerogatives and associated rights of their hereditary elites to visiting witnesses. Guests from other clan houses or visitors from other communities would witness theatrical performances, listen to oratory and receive gifts from their hosts in splendid performances of patronage.

Potlatch ceremonies were deeply troubling to colonial administrators and missionaries, who sought to suppress what they felt was conspicuous extravagance as well as a focus on traditional cultural values. Most famously, in 1921 the RCMP and local Indian agents arrested the Kwakwaka'wakw Chief Dan Cranmer and his guests following a potlatch in Mimkwamlis (Village Island). Participants were jailed and their masks and regalia were confiscated and distributed by the federal government to various museum collections. Many of these objects have now been returned to the U'mista Cultural Centre in Yalis (Alert Bay), Cranmer's home community.

In addition to the potlatch itself, the Indian Act banned what it referred to, by another Chinook term, as Tamanawa. These performances were an important feature of traditional T'seka winter ceremonies, which involved supernatural forces and initiation rituals. For the Kwakwaka'wakw, one of the most important of these was the Hamatsa, a secret society into which male adolescents were initiated. Following a period of time in which they fasted and were isolated deep in the forest, they were brought back to their clan house during a feast and tamed from the wild spirits by which they were possessed. During the Hamatsa ceremony, various wild mythical creatures wearing fantastic masks appeared and danced in the big house. Among these were the humanoid monsters Bak'was and Dzunu'wa, as well as several fantastic supernatural birds, Galukwama, the Crooked Beak of Heaven, and Huxwhuka, the Cannibal Bird, both associated with a powerful creature called Baxwbakwalanuksiwe, the Cannibal at the northern end of the World. Perhaps the most spectacular of the masks used in these events are the transformation masks. They first portray the form of an animal or mythical creature, and later, during the dancing at a dramatic moment emphasized by the drumming and singing, they split open to reveal a human or humanoid face within. – BHR

200
Shawn Hunt
Transformation Mask
2017
Mixed media

201
A collection of dance masks, Anglican church parish hall, Alert Bay, British Columbia 1922

The ritual ceremony of the potlatch was banned by the Canadian government from 1885 to 1951. This photograph shows some of the Kwakwaka'wakw objects offered in exchange for the release of chiefs imprisoned following the potlatch held illegally in 1921 by Chief Dan Cranmer east of Alert Bay in Mimkwamlis. The Indian Affairs agent who raided the potlatch and was responsible for the spoliation of these objects sold a number of them to George Heye, the founder of the National Museum of the American Indian, who in turn sold several pieces through the art dealer Julius Carlebach. The large transformation mask at the top centre of the photograph was purchased by Georges Duthuit. He loaned it to Riopelle in the 1950s, and the artist was to draw it in 1979. The original community is still requesting that this mask be returned.

200

201

202

203

204

205

202
Jean Paul Riopelle
Suite II
1977
Silverpoint on paper

203
Jean Paul Riopelle
Autre masque
1977
Silverpoint on paper

204
Totem at the
tomb of a shaman
(Gilford Island,
British Columbia,
Kwakwaka'wakw)
Ill. in Georges Duthuit,
"Le don indien sur la
côte nord-ouest de
l'Amérique (Colombie
britannique),"
Labyrinthe (1946)

205
Kwakwaka'wakw
Eagle crest-figure
formerly in the
collection of Georges
Duthuit
N.d.

206
Jean Paul Riopelle
Potlach
1977
Silverpoint on paper

207
Jean Paul Riopelle
Poisson
1977
Silverpoint on paper

208
Haida
Copper shield
N.d.

209
Copy of a George
Hunt photograph of
a Kwakwaka'wakw
Hamatsa initiate
wearing hemlock
boughs
1902

206

207

208

209

210

210
Copy of a Carl Günther
cabinet photograph
of Nuxalk (Bella Coola,
British Columbia)
dancers wearing
Chilkat-style blankets
and Kwakwaka'wakw
Galukwama (Crooked
Beak of Heaven) masks
About 1886

211
Jean Paul Riopelle
Mythologie
1977
Silverpoint on paper

212

213

212
Charlie George, Sr. (?)
Mask
Before 1953
Wood, cedar bark,
feather, rubber, fibre,
paint, metal, paper, plastic

213
British Columbia,
Kwakwaka'wakw
Mask
Cedar wood, paint, fibre,
leather skin, metal

214
British Columbia,
Kwakwaka'wakw,
Dzawada'enuxw
Mask
About 1911
Wood, cedar bark,
pigment, feather, leather
skin, fibre, metal

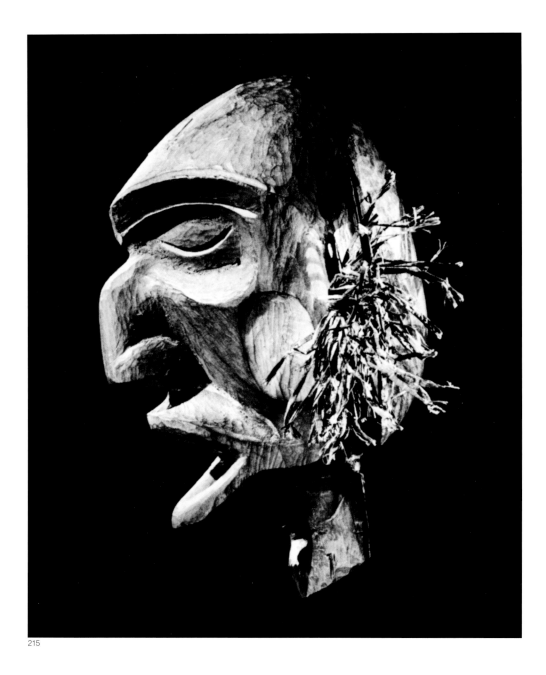

215

215
Kwakwaka'wakw
Ceremonial rattle
Ill. in Claude Lévi-
Strauss, *La voie des
masques: les sentiers
de la création*, vol. 1
(1975)

216
Jean Paul Riopelle
Sorcier III
1977
Silverpoint on paper

217

218

217
Jean Paul Riopelle
Wolf
1977
Silverpoint on paper

218
Tlingit
Bone charm
representing a wolf's
head
N.d.
Bone, horsehair (?)

219
Jean Paul Riopelle
Sorcier I
1977
Silverpoint on paper

220
Edward S. Curtis
Tsunukwalahl-Qagyuhl
N.d.
Photoengraving

Riopelle took
inspiration for his
Sorcier I from the
reproduction of Curtis'
photograph in
vol. I, p. 116, of *La voie
des masques*

219

220

221

222

223

224

225

226

227

228

227
Jean Paul Riopelle
Untitled
Pl. 15 from the album
Lied à Émile Nelligan
1977–79
Lithograph, 59/75

228
Inukshu, Povungnituk,
the Arctic, Quebec
Ill. in Fred Bruemmer,
*Seasons of the
Eskimo: A Vanishing
Way of Life* (1971)

229
Jean Paul Riopelle
Untitled
Pl. 16 from the album
Lied à Émile Nelligan
1977–79
Lithograph, 59/75

230
Jean Paul Riopelle
Untitled
Pl. 13 from the album
Lied à Émile Nelligan
1977–79
Lithograph, 59/75

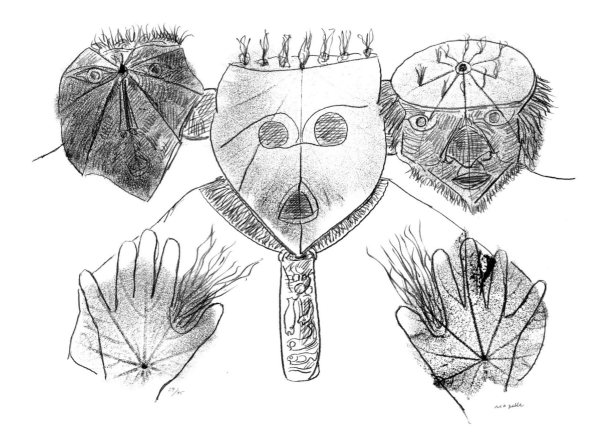

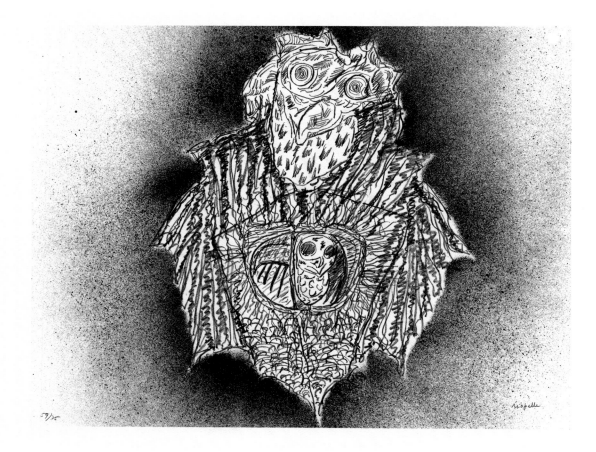

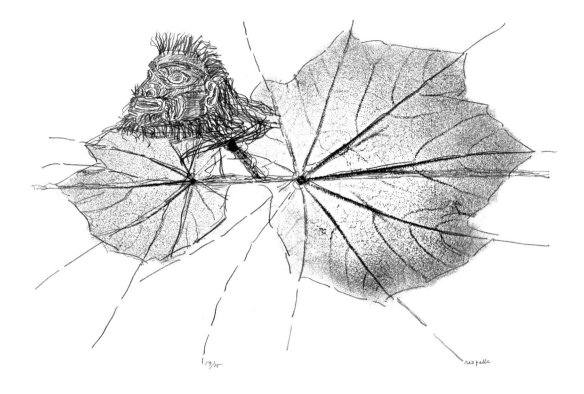

233

231
Jean Paul Riopelle
Untitled
Pl. 11 from the album
Lied à Émile Nelligan
1977–79
Lithograph, 59/75

232
Jean Paul Riopelle
Untitled
Pl. 5 from the album
Lied à Émile Nelligan
1977–79
Lithograph, 59/75

233
Jean Paul Riopelle
Untitled
Pl. 12 from the album
Lied à Émile Nelligan
1977–79
Lithograph, 59/75

234
Carved and painted
wooden helmet
embellished with hair
(probably Northwest
Coast, Alaska, Tlingit)
Ill. in Robert Bruce
Inverarity, *Art of
the Northwest Coast
Indians* (1950)

234

235

235
Northwest Coast,
Alaska, Tlingit
Rattle
19th c.
Copper, painted wood,
abalone shell, hair

236
Northwest Coast,
Alaska, Tlingit
Dagger
About 1850
Copper, abalone shell,
horn, leather

235-236 | Traders, fierce warriors, brilliant artists and deeply spiritual people, the Tlingit inhabit the deep fiords and islands of the far northern coastal region of British Columbia, the Alaskan Panhandle and adjacent Yukon areas. Masterworks of the region's tradition of the classical "formline" design, major Tlingit objects were made by professional full-time artists for the use of the community's elites. A distinctly Tlingit object type was helmets displaying clan crests or ancestors, which were worn with body armour by war leaders, most likely for ceremonial occasions rather than in battle. Similarly, elaborate weapons, such as this copper rattle with human hair and the equally rare copper knife with a Sun clan crest, would have been used to display rank and privilege on public occasions.

Copper was already a valued metal at the time of contact all along the coast, but the introduction of large sheet copper acquired in trade with Europeans increased its use. One of the unique forms in which the material was used were five-sided shields with raised T-shaped ridges, often engraved or painted with a crest animal (208); these were simply called "Coppers." They served as a kind of currency (293), and individual Coppers were well-known—they had specific names and values attached to them, for example, a certain number of blankets. – BHR

236

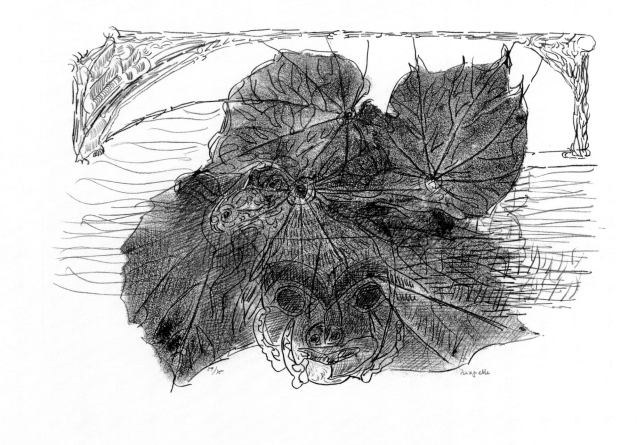

237

238

237
Jean Paul Riopelle
Untitled
Pl. 9 from the album
Lied à Émile Nelligan
1977–79
Lithograph, 59/75

238
Dance mask
representing a bear's
face (Northwest Coast
of Alaska, Tlingit)
Ill. in Robert Bruce
Inverarity, *Art of
the Northwest Coast
Indians* (1950)

239
Jean Paul Riopelle
Untitled
Pl. 1 from the album
Lied à Émile Nelligan
1977–79
Lithograph, 59/75

240
British Columbia,
Northwest Coast,
Nuxalk,
Kwakawa'wakw
Piledriver head
About 400–1800
Stone

239

240 | Widely regarded as one of the masterworks of Northwest Coast carving, this highly sculptural representation of a dogfish head, a crest of the Eagle clan, has been frequently reproduced since it was acquired in 1950 by the American collector of avant-garde art Walter Arensberg. Despite its sculptural form, it is not a ritual or ceremonial object, but rather a tool known as a piledriver, which is used to pound stakes that secure salmon nets and weirs in a river bed. Brilliantly ergonomic, the deep-set eyes and corresponding grooves on the reverse, which can be seen as gills, serve as grips to facilitate the pounding action. – BHR

240

16/75

241

241
Jean Paul Riopelle
Sorciers
1979
Lithograph, 16/75

242
Jean Paul Riopelle
Masques
1979
Lithograph, 13/75

The lithograph *Masques* of 1979 is based on double-page illustrations in Claude Lévi-Strauss' book *La voie des masques* (1975). (**190**) It features two Kwakwaka'wakw objects—a *Xwexwe* mask and a *Dzunukwa* mask—contrasted in the author's study. Housed in the Museum of Anthropology at the University of British Columbia, they were the subject of a talk given by the anthropologist and ethnologist in 1973, which was filmed by the National Film Board (**191**).

13/75

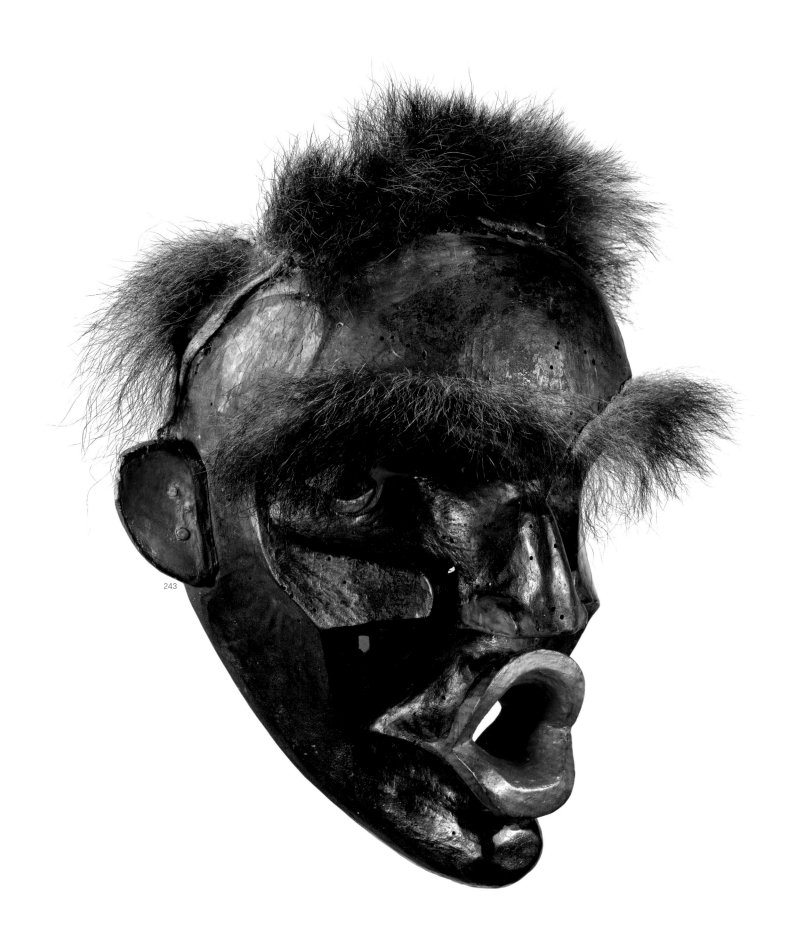

243

243
British Columbia,
Kwakwaka'wakw, Kwagu'l
Mask
Before 1900
Wood, metal, root, bear
skin, graphite mineral
and cinnabar mineral

244
Willie Seaweed
(Kwakwaka'wakw,
Mamalilikala)
Xwexwe mask
Before 1952
Wood, paint, cotton fibre

244

TERRITORI
SHARED:

INTERVIEW
CHAMPLA

BY ANDRÉANNE ROY

ES

WITH

IN

CHAREST

Many people know of radiologist Dr. Champlain Charest because of his famous Bistro à Champlain in Sainte-Marguerite-du-Lac-Masson and the extraordinary wine collection he assembled there. A great friend of Jean Paul Riopelle from 1968 until the artist's death, he shares here his memories of the man. Dr. Charest has been an ardent collector of Riopelle's work and that of many other artists, including Joan Mitchell, Joan Miró, Sam Francis and Diego Giacometti. He has also made a number of major donations of artworks to various Quebec institutions. The following interview offers a glimpse of this remarkable man and his deep friendship with Riopelle.

ANDRÉANNE ROY – Tell us about your introduction to art. I understand there were particular art lovers and collectors who had a decisive influence on you, among them André Légaré and Gérard Beaulieu. How did they help shape the development of your interest in the visual arts and in collecting?

CHAMPLAIN CHAREST – Dr. André Légaré, who I worked with at the Saint-Luc Hospital, had paintings in his home, mostly by Borduas and Riopelle. It was he who began taking me to museums and in 1964 encouraged me to purchase my first painting, a Marc-Aurèle Fortin. I was impressed by how cultured he was. He had studied in Paris and learned to appreciate art, wine, cheese. He had become quite knowledgeable, which set him apart somewhat. Later, I caught up with him. I met Riopelle before him, through Gérard Beaulieu.

I was lucky enough to meet Gérard Beaulieu here, in Estérel. We were both municipal councillors. During meetings, while the others were discussing the town of Estérel, we would talk about painting, sculpture, and so on. And Gérard bought paintings; he had works by Riopelle, Hurtubise, McEwen, Chadwick. He liked McEwen a lot, and he *adored* Riopelle. One day, he said to me: "I'm going to see Riopelle, come and meet him." I knew his work, I was aware of his importance as a man, as a painter. So I went with Gérard to meet him in Paris, before going on to Sweden to learn a radiology technique.

A.R. – Perhaps you could speak about this initial encounter with Riopelle. I believe it was then that you acquired your first work by him?

C.C. – In Paris, in 1968, my first meeting with Riopelle took place at his studio in Vanves. He was wearing a white shirt covered in paint, and his shoes were also full of spatters. As always, he had a cigarette in his hand. There were some recent paintings in the studio, but mostly collages. I saw works that interested me. I didn't go with the idea of buying, but I spotted several things I liked, including one that appealed to me especially and that I later won in an arm-wrestling contest. I thought it resembled the map of Canada, but it was actually a landscape featuring a goose hunt. It was called *Cape tournante* (**143**). But I saw something else in it. I asked Riopelle if it was for sale, but he didn't answer. Gérard Beaulieu jabbed me with his elbow, as though to say: "He's a great artist, don't do that."

We arranged to meet that evening, in a bistro in Montparnasse called the Rosebud. We drank black velvets. When the restaurant was closing, Jean Paul said to me: "Are you strong? The painting you wanted to buy today, I'll arm wrestle you for it." I had nothing to lose, he didn't ask for anything in return. He said: "If you win, the painting's yours." We went into the alley behind the Rosebud. We lay down on our bellies, at 2 o'clock in the morning, and we wrestled for the painting I'd wanted to buy. He didn't let me win easily.

The next day, we decided to pay a visit to the Maeght gallery. I saw a Riopelle in the office of [Daniel] Lelong, who was director at the time. It was entitled *Sainte Marguerite* (**145**), which is an island off the south coast of France. I lived in Sainte-Marguerite, Quebec, so I said to Lelong: "I'll buy that painting." It didn't feel right to have won a painting for nothing! That was how my first encounter with Jean Paul concluded.

A.R. – What impression did you have of him at the time? Did you sense that the two of you might become friends?

C.C. – I got the same impression I always got afterwards: that I had met someone truly superior. I was a little overwhelmed. He had his head a bit in the clouds; I was more down to earth, being in medicine. I was happy to have met someone different from me. He was a great man.

A week later he phoned me, saying: "It's Riopelle, I'm at the airport, come and pick me up." I wasn't expecting it at all! I picked him up, and we went to hunt snow geese at the Club Soumande in Cap Tourmente. And from that point on, whenever he came to Quebec, he stayed at my place—it was his home away from home. He became part of my life. So we had a studio built in Estérel, on a piece of land next to mine. This was in 1974, six years after we first met. He would come to hunt once or twice a year. We went goose hunting, mainly, and sometimes fishing. I had a plane, and we took several trips up North. In Europe, he told people it was his plane!

245

245
Champlain Charest, Réjane Saint Pierre Charest, Riopelle and an Air France stewardess
Early 1970s

246
Jean Paul Riopelle
La Bolduc
1964
Oil on canvas

A.R. – The year 1974 was a key year in your journey together. It was also then that you both became members of the private hunting club at Île-aux-Oies. This region would play a major part in Riopelle's life and work. Was it you who introduced him to the area?

C.C. – For a period of three or four years we'd go hunting on the boat owned by the Lachance family, and they'd take us from Montmagny to the island. In the evening, we'd return to harbour and sleep on the boat. It was there we had the idea of becoming members of the hunting club at Île-aux-Oies. It's a great place!

Once, when we were fishing at the Vieux poste de Mistassini camp, which belongs to Indigenous people, we met an old school friend who was a member of the club, and he said: "Maybe there'd be room for you at Île-aux-Oies." He sponsored us, and that was it! Riopelle and I became members. His name probably helped. Every fall we'd go goose hunting. Since 1974, I've never missed an autumn trip to the island.

A.R. – Canada's Far North was another important place in Riopelle's art and life. In the 1970s, you and he made several trips there, notably to Pangnirtung, on Baffin Island. What prompted your first trips?

C.C. – The first year we visited Pangnirtung, in 1969, we went with Theo Waddington, the gallery owner and collector of Inuit art. He went there to buy whalebone sculptures, among other things. The first trips took place in 1969 and 1971. After, we went on fishing trips among the ice floes, full of small icebergs. They were so beautiful, the ice floes, as they rose and fell with the tide! True monuments. We'd go in the summer, and when they broke apart in the heat of the sun, it was like a thunderclap. Jean Paul loved it! We fished among the ice floes alongside Inuit.

For several years we had an Inuit guide named Jaco Kunilusie. We went to Pangnirtung because Jaco was there. We slept at his place. He had children who spoke English. He didn't speak a word, but we managed to communicate. We were also lucky to know the Inuit pilot Johnny May, and to fly with him. We used to go fishing with him around Kuujjuaq, in Nunavik. There are several deltas in that area, several rivers that flow into Ungava Bay: that's where we would go fishing. And he was a fantastic friend—Jean Paul knew him very well.

A.R. – These hunting and fishing trips, both in the boreal zone and to the Far North, had a definite influence on Riopelle's production. It could be said that you contributed, in a roundabout way, by taking all those trips with the artist and having him accompany you in your seaplane. Riopelle actually portrayed you in the print entitled *Le call* (**119c**), from the *Parler de corde* series. Does this work refer to a particular event?

C.C. – The events surrounding *Le call* took place one hundred kilometres north of Sainte-Anne-des-Lacs, on a hunting ground where Riopelle and I used to go, the Club L'Andalousie. One fine morning I was calling a moose that was in the lake in front of us. Riopelle was behind me, and he'd brought his sketchbook, which was rare. He was sitting down, listening to me talking to the moose. And the moose replied several times. This was what Jean Paul dreamed of, more than anything! It wasn't the gunshot that was important to him, it was the situation, what happened during the hunt. And Jean Paul made a sketch of me, which I wasn't aware of at the time. Three quarters of an hour later, we saw the moose come closer, and we shot it at a distance of about a hundred metres.

There's also a story behind the painting called *Le brûlé* (**248**), which I still own. It was at the same place, a few years later. There'd been a fire at the Club L'Andalousie about six, seven, maybe eight years before. The forest had burned down, but it was beginning to grow back. There were lots of little saplings, poplars and aspens, creating colour between the areas of burnt wood, which is captured in the painting. Moose love feeding off this new growth. And on that occasion I shot a moose across the scorched area.

A.R. – I'd like to talk about the many donations of works by Riopelle you've made with your fellow radiologists. Am I right in thinking that your goal was not only to give back to society but also to help disseminate Riopelle's work?

C.C. – We made many donations, mostly of works by Riopelle. We were keen to promote the work of our friend. When Riopelle came here, he shared every aspect of my life; he came to the hospital, he sat down with my colleagues. It was an honour to introduce them to Riopelle. We all knew each other, and he was part of our lives. All my colleagues would go to the Maeght gallery to buy Riopelles.

There was the donation of *La Bolduc* (**246**) to the Place des Arts. It was my colleague André Légaré who had seen the painting at the [Pierre] Matisse gallery in New York. We'd decided to give it to the Place des Arts because of the connection to music. Jean Paul liked La Bolduc so much, he was in awe of her! There was also the donation of *Iceberg V* (**185**) to Jeunesses Musicales Canada. The director at the time, Gilles Lefebvre, was a close friend of Riopelle. If Jean Paul found someone interesting, then that person interested us too. If Jean Paul thought that someone was a person of quality, he let us know. It was also a particular encounter that led to the donation of *Piroche* (**262**) to the Université de Sherbrooke. It's a beautiful painting. We bought it from Jean Paul, and we donated it. We also gave a very fine *Untitled* (**247**) to the faculty of medicine of the Université de Montréal, where I studied.

247
Jean Paul Riopelle
Untitled
About 1958
Oil on canvas

A.R. – And let's not forget *La Joute* (**100, 101**), a major bequest to the citizens of Montreal.

C.C. – I'd seen the plaster version of *La Joute* in Riopelle's studio. We wanted to help Riopelle by presenting it on the occasion of the 1976 Olympic Games. It was a donation from me and my radiologist colleagues. We bought *La Joute* and had it cast in collaboration with the Maeght and Matisse galleries.

At the time, people always said we did it for the tax receipts. But we paid at least half the value. Museums wouldn't exist if there were no donations. It's true that the state contributes, everyone contributes—but at the same time, everyone benefits!

A.R. – Your collection of works by Riopelle has included paintings from every period. In conclusion, are there certain series or works to which you're particularly attached? What aspect of his work interests or touches you especially?

C.C. – What I liked most about Riopelle was his way of evolving over time, as he grew older and his knowledge increased. At the beginning, I didn't know much about abstract art. When I saw Riopelle's early paintings, what I found especially beautiful was the way the colours were arranged to create the forms.

Still today, I look at his works and I ask myself: "What was he trying to do in this painting?" I always wonder: "What was his starting point?" I know that Riopelle always started from something: there was always a substratum to what he produced. Riopelle always began with forms that he liked. That's why, as I see it, Riopelle is not an abstract painter. He's an abstract painter if you don't study his technique and his thinking. He reproduced nature, but he magnified or minimized it. And this magnification and minimization made recognition difficult for someone not familiar with these things.

And he ended up with things that are easily identifiable, although there's always something a bit unexpected about the ducks and the geese. With Riopelle's painting, it's important to look not just at the image, but instead at all of it—in other words, to understand how the work was made, what the circumstances were. It's a lengthy undertaking, learning just what Jean Paul was trying to do in his paintings. That's the beauty of his work, and it's not necessarily obvious. I've been lucky enough to grow old surrounded by these things.

248
Jean Paul Riopelle
Le brûlé (triptych)
1974
Oil on canvas

248

248 | The title *Le brûlé* refers to an area of forest decimated by fire. When vegetation rises from the ashes, these areas become particularly attractive to deer in search of food. In addition, the title invokes the story of a moose hunt that, as recounted by Champlain Charest, took place in a fire-barren area around Mont-Laurier. The triptych, painted in Estérel, presents a network of thick black markings that may suggest, through the work's composition and palette, the contrast of charred tree trunks against a background of burgeoning flora. As the artist stated that nature constitutes a "unique reference" for him, these abstract landscapes seem to be allusions to his experience and his subjective vision, rather than faithful representations of nature. – AR

249

252

250

254   255

251

249
Riopelle at work in
the studio at Île-aux-Oies
1990

250
Inside the studio at
Île-aux-Oies
1990

251
Riopelle and the hunting
guide Gilles Gagné
1990

252
Paul Rebeyrolle, unknown,
Stanley Cosgrove (?),
Riopelle, unknown,
Champlain Charest,
Jacques Lamy and René
Gagnon
About 1974–75

253
Champlain Charest and
Riopelle
1970s

254
Champlain Charest at
Île-aux-Oies
Early 2000s

255
Claude Duthuit photograph
of Paul Rebeyrolle,
René Gagnon, Riopelle,
Stanley Cosgrove (?) and
Champlain Charest
About 1974–75

256
Film still showing Riopelle
(about 1981) at Île-aux-Oies
from Riopelle (1982)

257
Champlain Charest hunting
Late 1980s–early 1990s

258
Film still showing
Champlain Charest and
his float plane (1970s) from
Marie Saint Pierre se révèle
(2016)

259
Riopelle and Champlain
Charest
1970s

260
Vincent Corriveau and
Riopelle
1970s

1. Gilbert Érouart, *Riopelle in Conversation* (Concord, Ontario: House of Anansi, 1995), p. 18.

Jean Paul Riopelle's life came to a close in the Isle-aux-Grues archipelago. A life of creativity in which the territories and countries he chose were at the core of his identity. Just where does territory end in the imagination? Where does nature begin? Why does a person decide one day to go live in a particular place, return there or settle there permanently? The same questions arise in regard to art and creation. For Riopelle, these areas would forever be intertwined.

It is common knowledge that, with literature and the visual arts, in order to find yourself, you must go elsewhere. Taking some distance from one's centre, oneself, is invaluable for an artist. Then one day, Riopelle returned to his native country. The North beckoned. A friend helped.

The North was already a poeticized place before Riopelle. Ever since Robert Flaherty's 1922 documentary *Nanook of the North*, Europeans had been fascinated by the "Eskimos," as the inhabitants of the Arctic were then called. This fascination coincided with a growing awareness of a culture, an art, and has persisted from generation to generation until this day.

Jean Paul Riopelle and his friend Champlain Charest went to the North for the first time in 1969, with the art dealer Theo Waddington. Champlain was a radiologist in Montreal. A year earlier, in November 1968, the doctor had been introduced to the painter in Paris by a collector friend. Champlain Charest, then thirty-five, was becoming interested in art and took up collecting. Jean Paul Riopelle was forty-five.

Much is owed to Champlain, certainly more than history has given him credit for until now. There is no doubt that he played a major role in Jean Paul's embracing of the territories he did after the two met.

—

Champlain Charest won a painting by Jean Paul Riopelle in an arm-wrestling match against the artist in the streets of Paris when they first met. Their meeting would prove significant for both of them on various fronts. They immediately became fast friends. Champlain had the calibre of a nation-builder. A force of nature.

The two men forged ties that extended beyond art, including engagement with territory. On several occasions, up until the Île-aux-Oies adventure, that territory was the North. Of the Isle-aux-Grues archipelago, where Jean Paul would reside until his last days, he said, "It's paradise., The most beautiful thing in the world."[1] Champlain and Jean Paul became members and co-owners of the Île-aux-Oies hunt club in 1974. As we know, the Île would be of paramount importance in the painter's work.

Furthermore, in 1974 Jean Paul built his studio and Canadian pied-à-terre adjacent to Champlain's Estérel property. The building's wood cladding came from an old barn that Champlain and his father had taken apart in Sainte-Hélène-de-Kamouraska.

That same year, the two friends bought a heritage property they wanted to protect, the general store in the village of Sainte-Marguerite-du-Lac-Masson, and turned it into a fine dining restaurant. Champlain Charest's wine collection was to become one of the most notable in the world. Gastronomy had not yet taken hold in Quebec at that time; terroir-based cuisine only existed in country kitchens. Everyone who went to Bistro à Champlain in Sainte-Marguerite-du-Lac-Masson left more "educated"—on wine and art—by this man who was ever concerned with awakening others to the beauty the world has to offer.

Champlain was born on a family farm in Kamouraska. He learned to get by on meagre means. Aspiring beyond the everyday became essential. He has spoken of this throughout his life, without going to great lengths, being the man he is. Dozens of Riopelles hung on the Bistro's walls. And all conversation began and took place over a bottle of wine, a painting, caribou meat, mushrooms, crab, goose, cheese.

Champlain and Jean Paul mirrored each other. They had found each other. The two men inhabited the same territory. On his migratory path, Jean Paul soon made his way back to his country. Hardly any stretch of road in Quebec had been asphalted before 1965. An effort had been made for Expo 67. In a vast nation where nature enjoyed more rights than its inhabitants—a nation struggling to get out from under the yoke of a Church and a paternalistic state it had been trying to separate since Jean Lesage—artists had led the charge. Twenty years earlier, Jean Paul had signed Paul-Émile Borduas' *Refus global*, which denounced the moral fetters and social chains that a people were striving to throw off. The two men actively took part, each in his own way, in the shaping of a nation that they were born into and that was on the road to modernity.

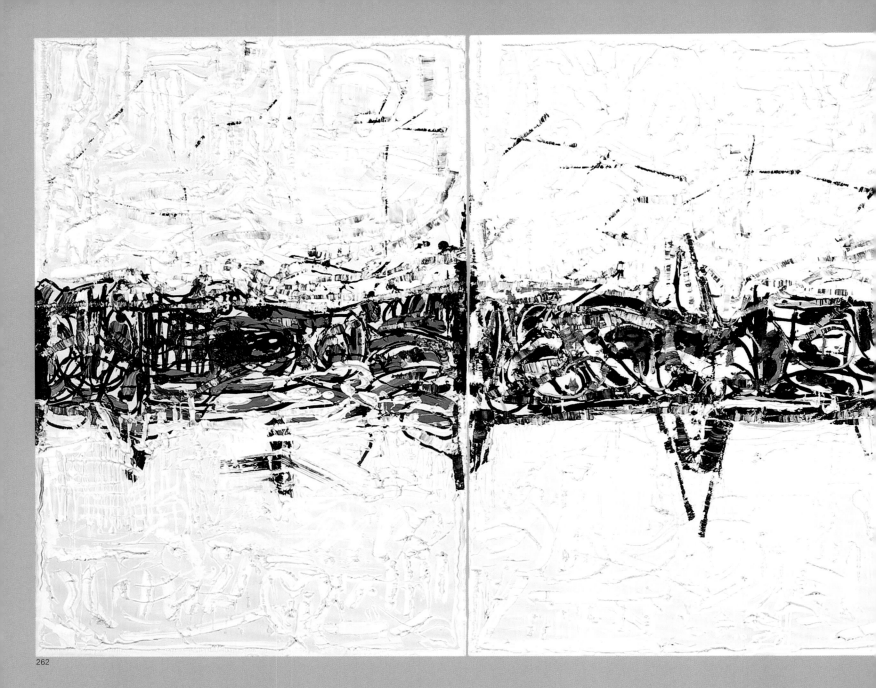

262

262 | The painting *Piroche* shows the inspiration Riopelle found in Île-aux-Oies as of 1976. A member of a private hunting club there, the artist developed a strong attachment to the place and to the goose, which travels far and wide. Feathered creatures hold a special place in his bestiary— a few years earlier, Riopelle had been interested particularly in owls. The artist henceforward found a symbolic kinship with the goose, a migratory bird whose life is in sync with the changing seasons. *Piroche* is an abstract work that nevertheless suggests the movement of the animal in flight. It renders the dynamic motion of the goose's flapping wings and trajectory through space in a horizontal composition whose central motif stands out against a white, highly textured ground, recalling a northern landscape. – **AR**

262
Jean Paul Riopelle
Piroche (quadriptych)
1976
Oil on canvas

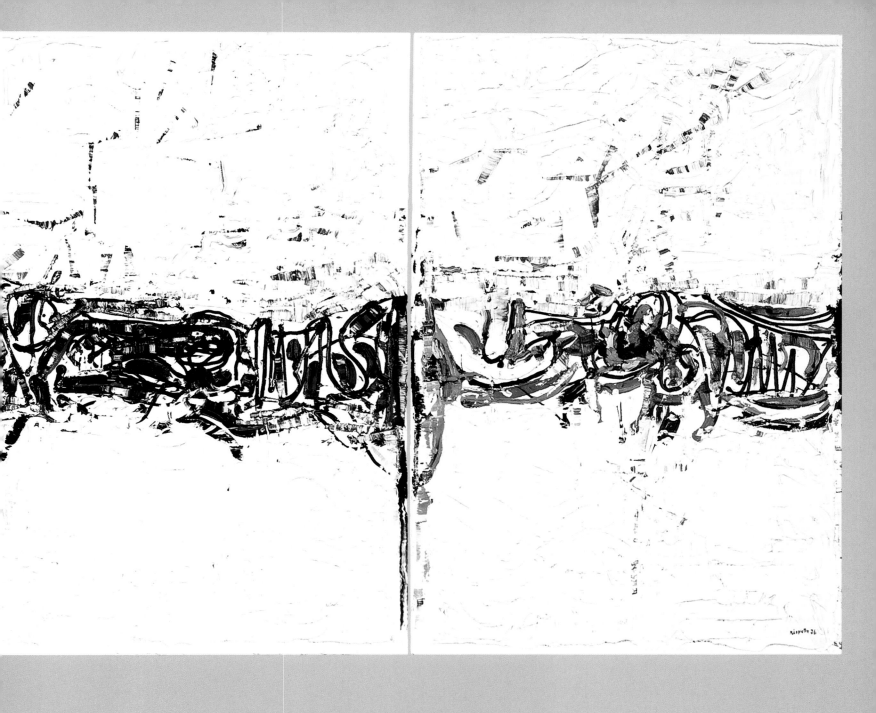

Friend Champlain, the son of a farmer, became a doctor in the big city, completing his studies by day while earning a living as a Port of Montreal longshoreman by night. Between 1931, the year he was born, and his meeting Jean Paul for the first time in Paris, the man was permeated by a revolution of ideas ranging from day-to-day survival to a love of art. He delved into medicine, flying, the land, wine, and yet another desire: to render service. An imperative.

What goes into the fabric of a friendship? Where do the invisible ties that attach us to others set out from? Jean Paul established himself in France, Champlain in Quebec. The two first shared their respective territories by visiting each other on various occasions. Then the day came when they would together share their worlds: the Bistro, the call of the North and the Île-aux-Oies.

THE RETURN

Their first trip to the Far North was organized by the British gallery owner Theo Waddington. He was interested in Inuit art. He wanted to go see and acquire "Eskimo" sculpture. Jean Paul and Champlain went with him. The three men arrived in Pangnirtung, Nunavut. In those days, the 2,359-kilometre journey was more like an expedition.

After that, the two friends went to the North a number of times to fish and hunt. In 1977, Claude Duthuit, the son of art historian and collector Georges Duthuit, was also visiting. The hunting was good. This is what books and historians emphasize, through photographs and writings, about these repeated trips. Unfortunately, the more time passes, the more the effect of a wilderness world on the artist tends to be glorified and crystallized—in error and for the wrong reasons.

Salmon, Arctic char, birds and caribou were just an excuse to go and probe this realm; the delving done was within. Artists need a context to come into their own (always).

Jean Paul sought the sacred and found it there. The doctor admired his friend's instincts. Art fascinated Champlain Charest, who took sustenance from its ineffable beauty. Jean Paul Riopelle had always tried to approach enchantment; by wanting to render service, Champlain took advantage of the privilege. The two men needed the land.

Champlain admired his friend and would do anything to assist.

008.91

On an aircraft's flight instruments, 008.91 degrees designates the bearing required to reach Pangnirtung from Montreal. It is calculated by taking into account the geographic North and the magnetic North. The bearing points to a destination, but does not indicate the point of arrival. A navigational setting has no end point. The two men went regularly to Nunavik and to Nunavut. Their migration. We all need a direction in order to move forward. Art provides one, especially when it leads to nature. In Jean Paul's case, nature led to the art.

Jean Paul and Champlain made Inuit friends. These people take on life in those latitudes with pride. This pride bears consideration here, because people who achieve self-sufficiency on their land are ultimately respected. We will encounter this connection again with Jean Paul, in the Isle-aux-Grues archipelago.

Lands that are remote, harsh and isolated are indescribably beautiful to an artist. A catalyst for artistic ambitions. A unique revelation of self. It is understandable that Jean Paul and Champlain would have wanted to encompass and embrace such places. And why Jean Paul would have wanted to paint them.

Quebec's North is also a land of enormous freedom, and the reserve and respect experienced there negates the South's fantasies of survival. Such lands are not to be talked about, they are to be lived in. Attempts to describe them are mere conceits, more or less successful. Art is human. The country, still relatively untamed, is at the margins of a cultural humanity that begins to take shape. One could certainly explore its light, its colours, the distant horizon that delineates it, the people who live there, its resources and the feelings of deference and the sublime that such places awaken in those who venture there; such places remain invincible. Jean Paul attempted to express them, to express himself, through the places he chose to settle in, in order to understand time.

263
Jean Paul Riopelle
Oies
1980–83
Mixed media on lithographs mounted on canvas

264
Jean Paul Riopelle
La Loi c'est l'oye
1972–83
Lithographs with highlights, mixed media on paper (trial proofs for the album "Cap Tourmente," 1983, and "Suite," 1972) mounted on canvas

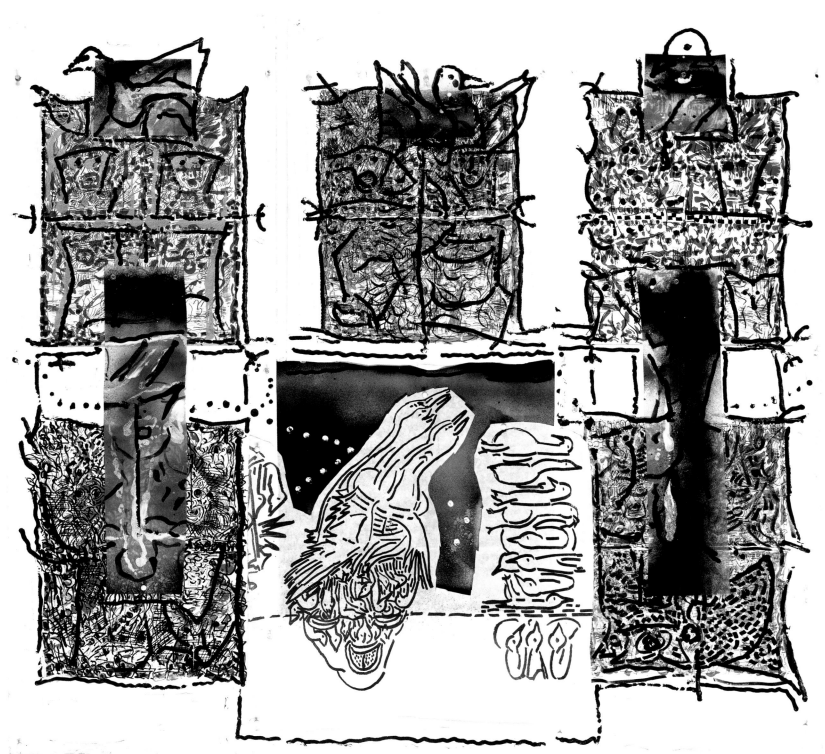

The call is larger than life. On the one hand we yield, and on the other we seek to understand through the supernatural quality of art—its sole purpose. We are fascinated by the migration of caribou and birds. They travel to another place over and over again in order to survive. In a century that hails technology and the breaking down of borders, we must not be surprised by the distant murmur of these autonomous, untamed domains. We sense that in this murmur, Jean Paul also found echoes of his own voice. Of this sacred notion. One has to connect with the ground to speak of life.

In this country, nordicity is the stuff of dreams. It has come into fashion. Yet what arrests our attention is its immutability. Anyone who has had the privilege of going there understands that the romanticism associated with it has been co-opted by the purveyors of meaning, the Whites from the South who have based books, films, artworks and exhibitions on it. Because we are left without answers vis-à-vis the lands that define us. And nobody can ignore the questions raised. Sometimes, it is through art that we try to find answers. And it is to this impossible end that Jean Paul was drawn. As the contemporary world becomes increasingly global, nature henceforward functions in the opposite way: it leads back to self, to isolation. For an artist, this is all that matters.

The two friends went to Nunavik and to Nunavut to fish among the drifting ice floes, which they hunted down in a rowboat. Sea fish follow the huge blocks of ice that float and melt in the salted seawater. When the ice cracks, a thunderous noise erupts. One can imagine the wondrous scene. Jean Paul recorded such moments in his *Icebergs* series of 1977 (**178-181, 185**).

The artist found inspiration in this place. This place as pole. An inevitable migration. In light of this, Jean Paul's territories marked a change of orientation in his work. The painter was inspired by the places he experienced. We "recognize" the place and time. Once Jean Paul settled in the Isle-aux-Grues archipelago, that country haunted his entire output, through the 1980s and up until *L'hommage à Rosa Luxemburg* in 1992.

Yet again, it was Champlain who helped set up Jean Paul's studios in the houses of the Isle. The friend who forced fate. "He changed my life because to me he was the most extraordinary man I had ever met,"[2] Champlain would say of his friend.

To set up Jean Paul on the Isle made perfect sense.

—

Their friendship was built on needs and generosity, and on the shared idea of occupying territory. Champlain bought his first aircraft in 1972. The two men were at still greater liberty to push their limits and go to the Isle "when it was time." Champlain said in a recent interview that Riopelle had insisted on the mode of transportation for their first trips: aviation. It was by taking to the air that they made their way to Nunavik, Nunavut and the Isle, that they got to grips with the country. They were in love with flying.

I have wondered whether, in their explorations, travels, reflections and conversations, the journey itself wasn't the main issue. According to Champlain, his friend Jean Paul would talk non-stop when they flew. We had a different image of the artist. Jean Paul, in trying to gain a hold on things, had to put words to them. Perhaps painting had its limits?

Jean Paul embarked on trips because he wanted to see the icebergs, the coast, the caribou, the mountains, the moose and the trout, as well as eat fish, hunt geese and paint them, along with the horizon and the sunsets. This from a visceral and inexhaustible need to describe everything. And Champlain would make it happen.

Even when life is skilfully described, parts remain missing. You have to live it. And that is what the two friends did. Intensely. Then, one day, Jean Paul felt the need to take root and settle down. He chose to do so in the Isle-aux-Grues archipelago.

THE ISLE

Champlain said of his friendship with Jean Paul, "It's the most beautiful thing in my life, after love and family."[3]

I will not go poking behind the scenes; what matters most is that they were men, and even if regret may have clouded their relationship, ultimately the fondest of memories prevailed. All the way up until the last trip, in 1999, to Lake Bérard (near Leaf River, in Nunavik). A slowed down Jean Paul, wheelchair-bound and accompanied by an aide, felt it was important to be there. Three years later, he passed away. One does not give up one's territories. They continue to exist without one. The best works are not necessarily the most significant in a whole body of work. For artists, in creative silence, what is publicly celebrated is light years away from their inner revelations.

The Île-aux-Oies is a rocky island forming part of the Appalachian Mountains. Located in the Isle-aux-Grues archipelago, it is connected to the Isle-aux-Grues itself by wetlands. Home to North America's largest intertidal marshes, it is a truly unique place. At once the centre of the world and nowhere. A stopover on the migratory path

2. Champlain Charest, "Riopelle, mon ami," *Vie des Arts*, vol. 46, no. 187 (2002), pp. 34–35.

3. Champlain Charest interviewed by Marc Séguin, August 23, 2019.

of the snow goose and other waterfowl in the spring and the fall since time immemorial. A stopover necessary for survival, between the Arctic region to the North, where they go to breed, and the South, where they spend the winter. They are just passing through.

The Île-aux-Oies lies on a fault, which is something that delighted Jean Paul. Was it because it is doomed to disappear or because of its telluric nature? Its geography, wilderness state and inhabitants (especially the hunting guide Gilles Gagné) convinced Jean Paul to take up residence there. From 1976 to his last painting in 1992, *L'Hommage à Rosa Luxemburg*. The territory was painted. For a painter, a studio is a promise of love.

Anybody who spends time on Île-aux-Oies will grasp and experience the feeling of humility inspired by nature and the raw force that gives it life. Without any doubt whatsoever, it was the poetry of this land that prompted Jean Paul to put down roots and live there for more than a decade. Something about the place is beyond real.

Jean Paul first went there to hunt. He observed and admired the beauty of the geese in the fall. One day, he decided to paint them. He settled into a house on the Isle, the Prairies hautes, and set up a makeshift studio in the living room. Hunting and geese were to become pretexts for art at the service of another grand nature: painting. Later, he moved into a different house, misnamed La mairie (this town hall's real name was Le repaire). Riopelle had stopped migrating.

The Île-aux-Oies had given Jean Paul another life. Larger than life. Limitless. Because of its millennial age. Because of friendship. Because of hunting, that "sacred violence." Because the Isle distorts time with its beauty. Because it is foundational to this New France. Because the artist was an animist. And because roots are truths.

This territory also marks migrations, including those all-too human migrations of which the geese that move from the Arctic to the South, year after year, are a metaphor. We all search for our territories. Jean Paul chose to live his last days on the Isle-aux-Grues.

—

On fall evenings, because I live in the house where he painted *Rosa*, I can see a few kilometres away, beyond the magnificent marshes, the lights of the Manoir MacPherson-Le Moine on Isle-aux-Grues, where his migration ended: in the territory of the goose.

—

We artists learn early on to keep quiet and smile at those who do the "knowing" on our behalf. Historians and curators become the keepers of a world that is to some degree their own invention. For the artist—and I can't stress this enough—the points of reference lie elsewhere. They're different. Silent.

Although at first separated by an ocean, Champlain and Jean Paul were united to the end by their native land. Their relationship was built upon a territory. Men of the earth. The admiration of roots knows no end. Some firmly rooted men are capable of marvelling at others. Jean Paul, even after twenty-five years spent far from his origin, never became "uprooted." He came back home to settle in, with the help of a friend, to reconnect with a land of instinct.

I repeat, the trips have been overly poeticized. What we need to exist is a place. Some places are cursed with beauty. Such as painting or the Île-aux-Oies. It is by means of an emotional intelligence—like art—that those who inhabit these places survive; because it requires an unnameable algorithm, born of doubt and courage, to occupy them. Such as going into the studio with the intention of presenting oneself—oneself and us. The notion of territory has been all but neglected in the works of Jean Paul. Territory is a work of art. Of perfect humility.

The story that concerns us here is that of an artist who could be filled with wonder. His works are signs of respect, and some are marks of a friendship. It is also the story of two men who loved each other.

No matter how hard we try, we do not inhabit the places that define us, they inhabit us. Sometimes, signs remain that show we were just passing through.

265a

b

265
Jean Paul Riopelle
a. *Mi-Carême* (recto)
b. *Merry go round* (verso)
1990
Mixed media on panel

266
Jean Paul Riopelle
a. *Matinée au cap Tourmente (Les faisans dans la volière)* (recto)
b. *L'oie hélico* (verso)
1990
Mixed media on panel

267
Jean Paul Riopelle
Untitled (recto/verso)
1990
Mixed media on wood

268
Jean Paul Riopelle
a. *Hommage à Duchamp* (recto)
b. *Hommage à Maurice Richard* (verso)
1990
Acrylic, oil, fluorescent paint, silver metallic paint, gold metallic paint with metal sequins on plywood

266a

b

265

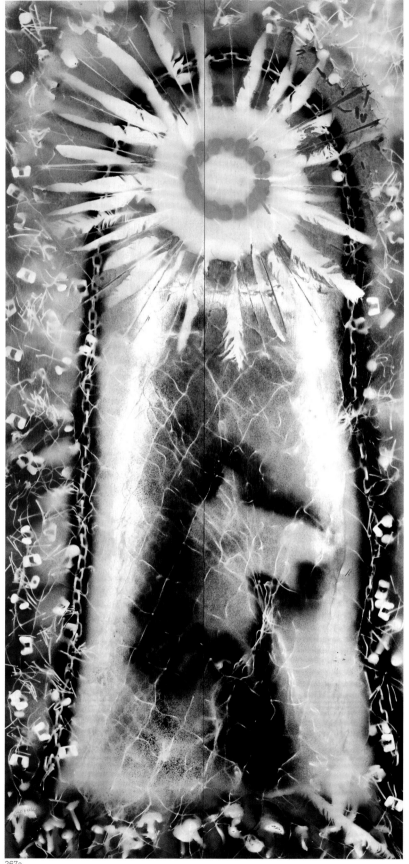

267a

b

268a

b

CHRONOLOGY

Andréanne Roy, Bruce H. Russell,
Louis Gagnon, in association
with Ruth B. Phillips and Jacques
Des Rochers

1914

Oxford-educated ethnographer Marius Barbeau, an employee of the National Museum of Canada since 1911, conducts three months of fieldwork in Lax Kw'alaams (Port Simpson), in northern British Columbia. In the decades to come, he continues working among the Tsimshianic-speaking peoples (Tsimshian, Gitksan and Nisga'a) and other First Nations of the Northwest Coast. Barbeau will publish a number of lengthly studies on the art and culture of these peoples, which remain useful despite errors and now discredited theoretical contentions.

1919

Frederick Cleveland Morgan begins collecting Northwest Coast objects for the collection of the Montreal Art Association (now the Montreal Museum of Fine Arts), initially in collaboration with the Canadian Handicrafts Guild, of which he is president. Morgan will later purchase additional objects from the estate of Louis Comfort Tiffany and from the same New York dealers from whom the Surrealist exiles acquired North American Indigenous works.

1921

Kwakwaka'wakw 'Namgis hereditary chief Dan Cranmer holds the largest potlatch on record on the northwest coast of British Columbia. With the collusion of the local Indian Agent, the RCMP arrests forty-five people at Mimkwamlis, on Village Island. They are given the choice of either surrendering their potlatch regalia—to prevent them from holding future potlatches—or going to jail. Twenty-two people choose to go to jail. The objects surrendered to the Crown are distributed to Canadian and foreign museums; some are subsequently deaccessioned and acquired by private collectors, including the French Surrealists exiled in New York.

1883

Canada's Parliament passes an amendment to the Indian Act banning the potlatch and the Sun Dance of the Plains peoples. This becomes law on January 1, 1885.

1912

In accordance with an application made by Quebec to the federal government in November 1907, the province's territory is extended to include the district of Ungava.

1883 · 1912 · 1914 · 1919 · 1921 · 1923 · 1926 · 1927 · 1936 · 1943-46

1923

Jean Paul Riopelle is born on October 7 on De Lorimier Avenue in Montreal.

He was to develop an attachment to nature during his adolescent years as a Boy Scout: His Troop Leader said of Riopelle, nicknamed "Taureau-la-liberté" [Free-will Bull], that he liked being a Scout because, above all, he loves nature—with a passion.

1936

Riopelle begins taking drawing lessons with Henri Bisson, who works in an academic painting style; he studied under him until 1943. Riopelle said: "We disliked modern painting. What we wanted was to copy nature."[1]

Riopelle attends a talk given by Archibald "Grey Owl" Belaney. He develops a fascination for this conservationist and author of many books who had pretended to be Indigenous.

1943–46

Riopelle studies at the École du meuble, between 1943 and 1946, where he meets Paul-Émile Borduas and other students who will form the Automatiste group.

During World War II, the Automatistes are introduced to the work of André Bréton, who will visit Quebec in 1944, travelling to Gaspésie and the Laurentians.

In 1945, Riopelle turns to Automatiste abstraction in his pictorial explorations.

Riopelle travels to France for the first time in 1946. He returns determined to settle there: "I've decided that it's in Ile-de-France, where the light is loveliest, that I will live."[2] He and his wife, Françoise Riopelle, move there definitively on December 28.

1947

Riopelle meets Pierre Loeb, who will become his principal dealer from 1952 to 1956. Through him, Riopelle becomes acquainted with some of the Surrealists who collected non-Western art—in particular Indigenous North American art—including André Breton, Robert Lebel and Isabelle Waldberg. They had discovered Inuit and Northwest Coast art during their time in New York during World War II, and were introduced to Indigenous art on their visits to the American Museum of Natural History; they acquired works from the New York art dealer Julius Carlebach.

In June, Riopelle joins the Surrealists in signing the *Rupture inaugurale* manifesto, written by Henri Pastoureau.

In August, he takes part in the exhibition *Le surréalisme en 1947. Exposition internationale du surréalisme*, presented by Breton and Marcel Duchamp at the Maeght gallery in Paris.

1926
Between 1926 and 1941, Northwest Coast objects can be seen in Montreal at McGill University's Ethnological Museum, located in the Strathcona Building. F. Cleveland Morgan arranges for objects from the Art Association to be transferred to this museum on an interim basis. This collection will eventually be transferred to the McCord Museum.

1927
Marius Barbeau organizes the *Exhibition of Canadian West Coast Art*, showcasing Indigenous objects alongside artworks by artists of settler origin inspired by their travels in the region. The exhibition is shown at the National Gallery of Canada, the Art Gallery of Toronto and the Montreal Art Association.

1948
Artist James Archibald Houston makes his first trip to Port Harrison (now Inukjuak), on the east coast of Hudson Bay. Houston plays a vital role by encouraging the Inuit to develop and market the artworks (carvings and later prints) for which they will become famous. It was in the community of Inukjuak that in 1920–21 Robert Flaherty shot his film *Nanook of the North*.

1949
In the fall, James Houston is instrumental in organizing the first annual exhibition-sale of Inuit art and crafts held at the Canadian Handicrafts Guild on Peel Street, in Montreal. The event is a major success: according to reports of the time, almost everything sells in three days.

The MMFA's first director, Robert Tyler Davis, publishes *Native Arts of the Pacific Northwest from the Rasmussen Collection of the Portland Art Museum*. Davis had been director of the Portland museum before coming to Montreal in 1947.

1951
Prohibition of the potlatch is quietly dropped during a routine updating of the Indian Act, without Indigenous communities being informed.

1953
Kwakwaka'wakw chief and master carver Mungo Martin builds a traditional big house adjacent to the British Columbia Provincial Museum in Victoria. To celebrate its inauguration, he hosts the first legal potlatch in sixty-seven years.

F. Cleveland Morgan purchases three Inuit sculptures from the Canadian Handicrafts Guild that are the first such objects to enter the MMFA's collection. His view that Inuit carvings are works of art is considered innovative at the time.

1947 1948 1948 1949 1949 1951 1951 1952 1953 1953

1948
Riopelle strikes up a friendship with Georges Duthuit, Henri Matisse's son-in-law. The historian of Byzantine art and contemporary art critic is also a collector of North American Indigenous art.

On August 9, Riopelle and the Automatistes sign the *Refus global* manifesto in Montreal; the cover bears one of his watercolours.

1949
Following the February 5 publication in *Le Devoir* of Pierre Gauvreau's essay "Cadenas et Indiens: une protestation," Riopelle writes in a letter to the artists Madeleine Arbour and Pierre Gauvreau of his support for the Wendat Jules Sioui, who is charged with seditious conspiracy, describing him as "a figure . . . of great interest." He declares, "We find ourselves on the side of the bullies because we are non-coloured, non-smelling, visa-carrying people . . . We need to make it known that we will not play a part in this struggle (in this case, the matter of a minority people, a most worthy cause)."[3]

His first solo show in Paris, *Riopelle à la Dragonne*, is held at the Nina Dausset gallery. The catalogue presents "an aside" between Élisa Breton, André Breton and Benjamin Péret. André Breton therein stresses the artist's Canadian character: "For me, it's the art of a *superior trapper* . . . The Indians, if they were here to see, would find themselves at home again."[4] Henceforward, Parisian critics start pointing out the "Americanicity" of the artist, in other words, his supposedly "savage" nature.

1951
Solo show at Paul Facchetti's Studio, presented by Michel Tapié: Georges Duthuit takes an interest as an art critic in Riopelle's work at that time.

1952
In an attempt to help Riopelle financially Georges Duthuit tries to sell two Tlingit objects around this time. Finding no buyer, Riopelle keeps the objects.

The exhibition *Jean Paul Riopelle – Isabelle Waldberg: peintures, gouaches et objets* is held at the Henriette Niepce gallery in Paris. Robert Lebel writes his essay "Essuie-glace" to accompany the exhibition.

Georges Duthuit publishes "A Painter of Awakening, Jean-Paul Riopelle," translated by Samuel Beckett, in *Canadian Art*.

1953
Georges Duthuit publishes, in *Premier bilan de l'art actuel 1937-1953*, the essay "Les animateurs de silence," which talks about the work of Riopelle, Sam Francis, Pierre Tal-Coat and Bram van Velde.

1954

Publication of the booklet *Canadian Eskimo Art* by the Department of Northern Affairs and National Resources. According to the brief overview of Canadian Inuit art provided in the forty-page publication, "this primitive art persists, original, creative and virile." The booklet appears in both of Canada's official languages (the French edition comes out in 1955) and will be republished numerous times over the next two decades.

1956

People of the Potlatch, the first Canadian exhibition devoted entirely to Northwest Coast Indigenous objects in a fine arts context, is presented at the Vancouver Art Gallery. In 1967, the same institution organizes the more ambitious *Arts of the Raven*.

1957–58

James Houston introduces the Inuit to the art of printmaking and sets up a print workshop at Kinngait (Cape Dorset), in Nunavut.

1958

Founding of the Skeena Treasure House Museum in Hazelton, British Columbia, the first component in what would develop into the 'Ksan Historical Village and living museum of the Gitksan people. The complex, completed in 1970, will include the Gitanmaax School of Northwest Coast Indian Art, attended by many leaders of the artistic revival that begins in the 1960s and spreads throughout the Northwest Coast.

1959

Creation in George River (now Kangiqsualujjuaq), Nunavik, of the first Inuit cooperative, succeeded the following year by the one in Puvirnituq (Povungnituk).

Alaska becomes an American state, which has an impact on the Yup'ik and other Indigenous peoples of the American Far North.

1961

Founding of the National Indian Council to represent Indigenous peoples of Canada, which inaugurates a new era of advocacy and self-governance for Canada's First Nations.

1962

Anthropologist Bernard Saladin d'Anglure publishes an article entitled "Discovery of Petroglyphs near Wakeham Bay" (*The Arctic Circular*), which describes his visit to the petroglyph site at Qajartalik, in mid-June 1961.

1965

Art historian and artist George Swinton publishes the classic *Eskimo Sculpture/Sculpture esquimaude*, the first attempt to present a broad survey of contemporary Inuit art. It takes an original approach, using a regional review to distinguish the production of Canada's Inuit. It also explores the historical origins of this artistic tradition by examining its links to earlier northern cultures, such as those of the Dorset and Thule peoples.

 1954 1954 1955 1956 1956 1957 1958 1959 1960 1961 1962 1963 1964

1954

Georges Duthuit and Riopelle plan to co-publish a book on Northwest Coast Indigenous art and cultures; they hold on dearly to the plan until 1959.

On February 19, Riopelle writes to the anthropologist Marius Barbeau. From their correspondence, which was to continue with the latter's son-in-law, the sociologist Marcel Rioux, we learn that the two men had met and talked about the possibility of collaborating on the book about Northwest Coast art that Riopelle had been planning with Georges Duthuit. An exhibition in Paris is also forecast: Duthuit and Riopelle both recognize "the need to have this art better known in France."

Pierre Gauvreau publishes his article "Réflexions sur l'art indien" in the *Journal musical canadien*, in which he stresses the importance of Indigenous art.

First solo exhibition at the Pierre Matisse gallery in New York. The catalogue reprints, with some minor changes, Georges Duthuit's essay "A Painter of Awakening, Jean-Paul Riopelle."

Riopelle travels to Austria, where he finds in the glaciers he sees a new source of colour and formal inspiration.

Mid-1950s

Georges Duthuit lends Riopelle some Northwest Coast works, including a large Kwakwaka'wakw transformation mask.

1955

A solo exhibition is held at the Rive Droite gallery in Paris; Georges Duthuit writes an essay for the catalogue. In a letter written by Riopelle to Duthuit in December, we learn that the artist planned to exhibit Indigenous masks and objects from British Columbia belonging to the collector. He abandons the idea for reasons of preventive conservation.

Inspired by Surrealist collections, Riopelle executes gouaches with titles making reference to "Eskimo" masks.

1956

The exhibition *Jean Paul Riopelle, Paintings, Gouaches, Watercolours* is held at Gimpel Fils in London. Riopelle discovers the Inuit art collection of Charles Gimpel.

Riopelle begins work on a series of gouaches with titles referring to the Gitksan people of Northern British Columbia. He possibly learns about this culture through the writings of the Surrealist Kurt Seligmann and of the anthropologist Marius Barbeau.

1960

Riopelle visits the exhibition *Le masque*, held at the Musée Guimet in Paris. The show of non-Western art displays masks from various collections of some Surrealists, including André Breton, Robert Lebel, Georges Duthuit and Isabelle Waldberg.

Riopelle spends more than a year in East Hampton, Long Island, where he executes some works with titles referring to the Indigenous presence in the area (*Two Shinnebock Whalers*, *The Great Sachem*).

1963

Riopelle executes *Point de rencontre — Quintette*, commissioned for Pearson Airport, Toronto.

1966
Presentation at the Musée du Québec of *Esquimaux, peuple du Québec*, the first major exhibition in Quebec of the provincial collection of Inuit art assembled by geographer Michel Brochu.

1967
The Canadian government's Ministry of Indian Affairs and Northern Development begins assembling what will become an outstanding collection of contemporary First Nations and Inuit art.

The Indians of Canada Pavilion at Expo 67, in Montreal, showcases the heritage of First Nations and Inuit people to international visitors. It is the first comprehensive, Indigenous-curated exhibition devoted to Indigenous history, art and culture. The name given to the inverted pyramid that forms the Canada Pavilion, Katimavik, is an Inuit word meaning "gathering place."

James Houston publishes *Eskimo Prints*. This first bilingual survey of Inuit printmaking will long be seen as the complement to George Swinton's *Eskimo Sculpture/Sculpture esquimaude*.

Foundation of Ilagiisaq, the Fédération des coopératives du Nouveau-Québec, whose various operations and services include the role of wholesaler overseeing distribution of the art of the Inuit of Nunavik.

Establishment of the Canadian Eskimo Arts Council, which assumes an independent consultative role. Its mandate is to assess the aesthetic rather than the commercial value of the drawings submitted to it. The aim is to select high-quality works suitable for reproduction in print editions for the annual collection of the Inuit cooperatives involved in printmaking. The controversial body would be dissolved in 1989.

1969
Unveiling of Prime Minister Pierre Elliott Trudeau's White Paper proposing abolition of the Indian Act, reserves and any special status for Canada's First Nations. Although Indigenous Canadians had always fought against colonialist federal legislation, the assimilationist alternative proposed by the government meets with widespread resistance.

1970
Citizens Plus—known as the "Red Paper"—a response to the White Paper, is issued by the Indian Association of Alberta and adopted by the National Indian Brotherhood. It rejects the federal White Paper, affirming Indigenous land rights and demanding that past agreements between Canada and the First Nations be honoured.

1971
The Alaska Native Claims Settlement Act is signed into law.

The James Bay region of northern Quebec becomes a political battleground as the provincial government and the James Bay Cree face off over a hydroelectric mega-project, originally planned on the assumption that the Cree have no rights to the land.

1965 1966 1966 1967 1968 1969 1969 1970 1970 1971 1971 1972

1964
Riopelle takes part in the group exhibition *Surréalisme : sources – histoire – affinités*, presented by Patrick Waldberg at the Charpentier gallery. There, Surrealist works are displayed along with non-Western artworks, among them Northwest Coast and Arctic pieces.

Riopelle travels to Superbagnères, France, for a Christmas vacation in the mountains. Having injured a knee, he makes the most of it by making sketches of the Pyrenees from his bedroom.

1966
Riopelle begins exhibiting regularly with the Maeght gallery in Paris.

1968
Riopelle meets Dr. Champlain Charest and his wife, Réjane, in Paris. Fast becoming friends, largely through their shared passion for hunting and fishing, Champlain Charest and Riopelle go hunting in the fall to Cap Tourmente, Quebec. The artist then begins to travel to Canada more often to engage in such activities with Charest.

1969
Riopelle visits the exhibition *Chefs-d'œuvre des arts indiens et esquimaux au Canada*, held at the Musée de l'Homme in Paris.

Riopelle takes his first trip to Pangnirtung (Baffin Island), Nunavut, on the initiative of gallery owner Theo Waddington, who is going there to acquire Inuit sculpture. Champlain Charest goes also.

Riopelle begins a series of sculptures, some of which will make up *La Joute*, a sculptural group including numerous owls, the "Indian" figure and the artist's first depictions of Inuit string games.

1970
For the exhibition *Une fête en Cimmérie. Les Esquimaux vus par Henri Matisse*, held at the Canadian Cultural Centre in Paris, Riopelle co-authors a text with the writer and historian Pierre Schneider. Matisse's series of Inuit portraits will become a source of inspiration for Riopelle in the execution of his future *Rois de Thulé* series.

1971
Riopelle travels a second time to Pangnirtung, Nunavut, with Theo Waddington and Champlain Charest.

Riopelle begins the *Jeux de ficelles* series of acrylics on paper, which is markedly influenced by the book *Les jeux de ficelle des Arviligjuarmiut* by the anthropologist Guy Mary-Rousselière.

1972
Riopelle visits the exhibition *Sculpture of the Inuit: Masterworks of the Canadian Arctic*, held at the Grand Palais in Paris. He attends the opening to meet the Inuit artists. He may have made the acquaintance of the sculptors Michael Amarook and John Kaunak at the event.

The Canadian Cultural Centre in Paris showcases the Arctic and Inuit in its programming of films and lectures, which Riopelle may have attended.

In the fall, Riopelle joins others, including Champlain Charest, on a big hunting trip to eastern James Bay and to Hudson Bay.

1973
French anthropologist Claude Lévi-Strauss visits British Columbia for the first time, lecturing at the University of British Columbia, in Vancouver, and visiting museum collections in the region. His research leads to publication of *La voie des masques* (1975), which will directly inspire a number of Riopelle's drawings.

The Professional Native Indian Artists Incorporation, a coalition of primarily Woodlands artists, is founded in Winnipeg by Odawa-Potawatomi painter Daphne Odjig.

From March 23 to April 22, the international travelling exhibition *Sculpture of the Inuit: Masterworks of the Canadian Arctic* is on view at the Montreal Museum of Fine Arts.

1974
After nearly five decades of Kwakwaka'wakw activism, the National Museum of Man (now the Canadian Museum of History, Gatineau) agrees to return its portion of the objects acquired illegally from attendees at Dan Cranmer's 1921 potlatch to descendants living at Alert Bay and Cape Mudge. The U'mista Cultural Centre will open in 1980 to display these objects in an innovative installation that pioneers Indigenous museology in the region and opens the way for further repatriations of items held in other major institutions.

1975
Signing on November 11 of the James Bay and Northern Quebec Agreement, now considered the first modern treaty negotiated between Canada's governments and its Indigenous peoples. Aside from providing for financial compensation, it accords political and administrative autonomy and grants exclusive rights and uses to the Inuit and the Cree (and later to the Naskapi) in two distinct categories of land in exchange for their ancestral rights and the right to develop natural resources, such as rivers, mines and forests, throughout the vast ancestral territories of the Nord-du-Québec region.

1980
Alaska clan leaders, traditional scholars and elders found the Sealaska Heritage Institute, a non-profit foundation aimed at perpetuating and enhancing Indigenous cultures of the state of Alaska.

1982
Prime Minister Pierre Elliott Trudeau patriates Canada's federal constitution, in the face of opposition from Indigenous Canadians. Many Indigenous communities feel that they had established treaties with the British Crown and that these legal relationships should remain outside the domain of the federal government.

Chiefs of Canada's Indigenous communities hold their first assembly as the Assembly of First Nations (AFN) in Penticton, British Columbia.

1986
Following a referendum held among the communities of Nouveau-Québec, the population adopts the name of Nunavik ("the place where we live" in Inuktitut) as the new official toponym of this territory situated north of the 55th parallel, beyond the treeline.

1973 1973 1974 1974 1975 1975 1976 1977 1980 1981-83 1982 1985 1986

1973
After his trip to James Bay and Hudson Bay the previous fall, Riopelle paints a group of works with references to the North.

Fuelled by his trips and by numerous sources of northern and Inuit inspiration, Riopelle executes the *Rois de Thulé* series.

1974
Riopelle has a house/studio built for himself in Estérel, on a property next to the one of his friend Dr. Champlain Charest. The building's shape is inspired by old barns. He begins to produce several works referencing the landscapes of the Laurentians, including the *Sainte-Marguerite* series (1974–75).

Riopelle and Champlain Charest become members of a private hunting club on Ile-aux-Oies in the Isle-aux-Grues Archipelago.

Riopelle and Champlain Charest buy the former general store at Sainte-Marguerite-du-Lac-Masson, to save the heritage building, and open a restaurant there, the *Va-nu-pieds*. Champlain Charest would take over the restaurant, which would later become the *Bistro à Champlain*.

About 1974–75
Riopelle and Champlain Charest take fishing trips to Mistassini's "Camp du Vieux-Poste," where the Cree work as guides.

1975
In 1975 or 1976, Riopelle and Champlain Charest go fishing on the Akilasakalluq River (George River), Nunavik.

In 1975 and 1976, Riopelle paints a series of oils on canvas bearing titles inspired by Indigenous place names and beginning with the letter "M." The letter "K" was chosen previously for a series of works on paper. This may mean that the artist used an Indigenous dictionary to find titles for his works.

1976
La Joute is installed in Montreal's Olympic Park.

Riopelle executes a first series of drawings with the goose as subject, which he would explore as a theme until 1992. The abundance of geese in his oeuvre can be explained in light of his interest in the territories of the North and in migration.

1977
In June, Riopelle returns once more to Pangnirtung, along with Champlain Charest and Claude Duthuit (Georges Duthuit's son). Their Inuit guide is named Jaco Kunilusie. Back from his trip, he paints the *Icebergs* series in his studio in Estérel, then in Saint-Cyr-en-Arthies, France.

In France, Riopelle executes a series of silverpoint drawings of numerous Indigenous works of the Northwest Coast. These are based on photographs Georges Duthuit gave him and on illustrations in certain anthropological publications.

Riopelle begins the *Lied à Émile Nelligan* series of lithographs, after having worked on silverpoint drawings, in which motifs of leaves, owls and Indigenous objects are intermingled.

1988

Opening of *The Spirit Sings*, an exhibition organized by the Glenbow Museum as part of the Calgary Olympics cultural program. An international boycott organized by supporters of the Lubicon Cree land claim results in protests from Indigenous communities and their supporters across Canada, raising a wider range of issues concerning Indigenous museum collections, their display and interpretive authority.

The Musée de la civilisation in Quebec City, founded in 1984, opens to the public.

1989

The Canadian Museum of Civilization (now the Canadian Museum of History), opens in Hull (now Gatineau).

The federal Task Force on Museums and First Peoples is initiated in response to the boycott of *The Spirit Sings* exhibition held the previous year.

1990

A proposed golf course expansion and condo development on unceded land near Oka, Quebec, which includes a traditional burial ground, leads to an armed confrontation between the Mohawk of Kanesatake and the Sûreté du Québec. The Oka Crisis triggers a new phase of activism among First Nations across Canada.

1992

In the year of the Columbus Quincentenary, two landmark travelling exhibitions of Canadian Indigenous art open: *Land, Spirit, Power: First Nations at the National Gallery of Canada,* and *Indigena: Contemporary Native Perspectives in Canadian Art*, an entirely Indigenous-curated exhibition organized by the Canadian Museum of Civilization (now the Canadian Museum of History).

Turning the Page, the report of the Task Force on Museums and First Peoples, is accepted by the Assembly of First Nations and the Canadian Museums Association. It establishes new guidelines for partnership between museums and Indigenous peoples, repatriation, the handling of sacred objects and other issues.

1996

Commissioned by the municipality of Kangiqsujuaq, the Avataq Cultural Institute embarks in July on its first archaeological project, involving the study and conservation of the petroglyph site at Qajartalik, which will be added to UNESCO's tentative list of Canadian world heritage sites in 2018.

1997

The Supreme Court of Canada's Delgamuukw decision affirms that Aboriginal title to land is an ancestral right. It admits as evidence the oral traditions related by Gitksan and Wet'suwet'en elders and advances the land claims of Northwest Coast First Nations, practically none of whom had surrendered lands by signing treaties.

1999

On April 1 the Northwest Territories are divided in two to create Nunavut, which means "our land" in the Inuit language of Inuktitut.

1988 1989 1990 **1990** 1992 **1995** 1996 1997 1999 **1999** **2000** **2002**

1981–83

Riopelle executes his first lithographs with white geese. He uses trial proofs as a support for lithographs with heightening and litho-collages.

Riopelle's technique changes considerably, mainly through his introduction of new materials into his practice.

1985

Riopelle executes three series of lithographs on flies, inspired by the work of his friend Paul Marier, who made artificial fishing flies and was a fly-fishing champion.

1990

Riopelle moves back to Canada definitively.

1995

He buys the Manoir Macpherson on Isle-aux-Grues, and lives between there and Estérel the rest of his life.

1999

Riopelle visits the Great North one last time with his friend Champlain Charest. They go to Kuugaaluk River (Leaf River), Nunavik.

2000

In support of the founding of the Maison amérindienne, Mont Saint-Hilaire, Riopelle donates various Indigenous objects from his collection, notably the canoe made by the great Atikamekw canoe maker César Newashish that the artist had acquired in the 1970s.

2002

Jean Paul Riopelle dies on March 12 on Isle-aux-Grues.

1. Pierre Schneider, ed., *Jean-Paul Riopelle. Peinture, 1946-1977*, exh. cat. (Paris: Musée nationale d'art moderne, Centre Georges Pompidou; Quebec City: Musée du Québec; Montreal: Musée d'art contemporain, 1981), pp. 11–12.

2. Ibid.

3. Letter from Riopelle to Madeleine Arbour and Pierre Gauvreau, Bois-Colombes, France, February 17, 1949, The Montreal Museum of Fine Arts Library, fonds Madeleine Arbour.

4. Breton, André et al., "Aparté," in *Riopelle à La Dragonne*, exh. cat. (Paris: Galerie Nina Dausset, 1949).

SELECTED BIBLIOGRAPHY

ARCHIVES

Archives Catalogue raisonné Jean Paul Riopelle, Montreal

Archives Champlain Charest, Sainte-Marguerite-du-Lac-Masson

Archives Huguette Vachon, Sainte-Marguerite-du-Lac-Masson

Archives Isabelle Waldberg, Paris

Archives Yseult Riopelle, Montreal

Artexte, Montreal
Dossier Jean Paul Riopelle

Bibliothèque Kandinsky – Centre Pompidou, Paris
Fonds Georges Duthuit

Canadian Museum of History, Gatineau
Fonds Marcel Rioux

Joan Mitchell Foundation, New York

Library and Archives Canada, Ottawa
Fonds Basil Zarov
Fonds Hélène de Billy

The Montreal Museum of Fine Arts
Fonds Jean Paul Riopelle
Fonds Madeleine Arbour

Musée d'art contemporain de Montréal
Dossier Jean Paul Riopelle

Musée national des beaux-arts du Québec, Quebec City
Fonds Jean Paul Riopelle

National Gallery of Canada, Ottawa
Dossier Jean Paul Riopelle

GENERAL WORKS

Arsenault, Daniel, Louis Gagnon, Daniel Gendron and Claude Pinard. "Kiinatuqarvik: A Multidisciplinary Archaeological Project on Dorset Petroglyphs and Human Occupation in the Kangirsujuaq Area." In Patricia. D. Sutherland, ed. *Contributions to the Study of the Dorset Palaeo-Eskimos*. Gatineau: Canadian Museum of Civilization, 2005, pp. 105–120.

Ashley, Clifford W. *The Ashley Book of Knots: Every Practical Knot—What It Looks Like, Who Uses It, Where It Comes From, and How to Tie It*. New York: Bantam Doubleday Dell, 1944.

Auster, Paul. "Lumières nordiques. La peinture de Jean-Paul Riopelle." In *Le carnet rouge, suivi de L'art de la faim*. Arles: Actes sud, 1992, pp. 223–229.

Barbeau, Marius. *Haida Myths Illustrated in Argillite Carvings*. Ottawa: Department of Ressources and Development, National Parks Branch, National Museum of Canada, 1953.

_____. *The Downfall of Temlaham*. Ills. by A.Y. Jackson, Edwin H. Holgate, W. Langdon Kihn, Emily Carr and Annie D. Savage. Toronto: The Macmillan Company of Canada, 1928.

_____. *Totem Poles of the Gitksan, Upper Skeena River, British Columbia*. Ottawa: F. A. Acland, Printer to the King's Most Excellent Majesty, 1929.

Billy, Hélène de. *Riopelle*. Montreal: Art Global, 1996.

Boas, Franz. *Sixth Annual Report of the Bureau of Ethnology: The Central Eskimo*. Washington, D.C.: Smithsonian Institution, 1888.

_____. "The Social Organization and the Secret Societies of the Kwakiutl Indians." In *Report of the United States National Museum for 1895*. Washington, D.C.: Government Printing Office, 1897, pp. 309–738.

Borm, Jan and Daniel Chartier, eds. *Le froid. Adaptation, production, effets, représentations*. Quebec City: Presses de l'Université du Québec, 2018.

Bosredon, Bernard. *Les titres des tableaux : une pragmatique de l'identification*. Paris: Presses universitaires de France, 1977.

Breton, André. *Le surréalisme et la peinture : 1928-1965*. Paris: Gallimard, rev. ed. 1965.

Brunet-Weinmann, Monique. "Riopelle, l'élan d'Amérique." *Colòquio Artes*. 2nd series, no. 56 (March 1983), pp. 5–15.

Chartier, Daniel. *Qu'est-ce que l'imaginaire du Nord? Principes éthiques*. Montreal: Imaginaire-Nord / Harstad, Norway: Arctic Arts Summit, 2018.

Chartier, Daniel and Jean Désy. *La nordicité du Québec, entretiens avec Louis-Edmond Hamelin*. Quebec City: Presses de l'Université du Québec, 2014.

Clifford, James. "Histories of the Tribal and the Modern." In *The Predicament of Culture: Twentieth-century Ethnography, Literature, and Art*. Cambridge, Massachusetts: Harvard University Press, 1988, pp. 189–214.

Cohen Solal, Annie. *Magiciens de la terre : retour sur une exposition légendaire*. Paris: Musée national d'art moderne, Centre Pompidou, 2014.

Collection Robert Lebel : vente. Paris: Drouot-Richelieu (December 4, 2006).

Duchemin-Pelletier, Florence. *"Les sculptures ne sont pas uniquement des sculptures." Réception de l'art inuit contemporain en France des années 1950 à nos jours*. Doctoral thesis in Art History, Université Paris Ouest Nanterre la Défense, 2014, vols. 1 and 2.

Duffek, Karen and Charlotte Townsend-Gault. *Bill Reid and Beyond: Expanding on Modern Native Art*. Vancouver: University of British Columbia Press, 2004.

Duthuit, Georges. "Les animateurs du silence." In Robert Lebel, ed. *Premier bilan de l'art actuel 1937-1953*. Paris: Soleil noir, 1953, pp. 111–117.

_____. *Représentation et présence. Premiers écrits et travaux (1923-1952)*. Paris: Flammarion, 1974.

Eco, Umberto. *Apostille au Nom de la rose*. Paris: Grasset, 1985.

Érouart, Gilbert. *Riopelle in Conversation, with an interview by Fernand Seguin*. Concord, Ontario: House of Anansi, 1995.

Foster, Hal. "The 'Primitive' Unconscious of Modern Art, or White Skin Black Masks." In *Recodings: Art, Spectacle, Cultural Politics*. Seattle: Bay Press, 1985, pp. 181–210.

Gagnon, Daniel. *Riopelle, grandeur nature*. Montreal: Fides, 1988.

Gagnon, François-Marc. *Chronique du mouvement automatiste québécois 1941-1954*. Montreal: Lanctôt Éditeur, 1999.

Gell, Alfred. *Art and Agency: An Anthropological Theory*. Oxford: Clarendon Press, 1998.

Genette, Gérard. *Seuils*. Paris: Éditions du Seuil, 1987.

Gingras, Sylvain, Sonia Lirette and Claude Gilbert. *Le Club Triton : l'histoire du plus prestigieux club de chasse et pêche au Québec*. Quebec City: Les Éditions Rapide Blancs, 1989.

Goldwater, Robert. *Primitivism in Modern Art*. Cambridge, Massachusetts: Harvard University Press, [1938] 1986.

Hallowell, Alfred Irving. "Ojibwa Ontology, Behavior and World View." In Stanley Diamond, ed. *Culture in History: Essays in Honor of Paul Radin*. New York: Columbia University Press, 1960, pp. 2–25.

Hardenberg, Mari. *Trends and Ontology of Artistic Practices of the Dorset Culture 800 B.C.–1300 A.D.* Doctoral thesis, Copenhagen University, Department of Prehistoric Archaeology, Faculty of Humanities, 2013.

Havard, Gilles. *Histoire des coureurs de bois : Amérique du Nord, 1600-1840*. Paris: Les Indes savantes, 2016.

Heinich, Nathalie. *La gloire de Van Gogh : essai d'anthropologie de l'admiration*. Paris: Éditions de Minuit, 1991.

Hess, Thomas B. *Derrière le miroir*. no. 232. Paris: Maeght, 1979.

Hessel, Ingo. *Inuit Art: An Introduction*. London: British Museum Press, 1998.

Igloliorte, Heather. "Arctic Culture/Global Indigeneity." In Lynda Jessup, Erin Morton, and Kristy Robertson, eds. *Negotiations in a Vacant Lot: Studying the Visual in Canada*. Montreal: McGill-Queen's University Press, 2014.

Inuit Heritage Trust. *Inuit Contact and Colonization*. 2008, http://www.inuitcontact.ca.

Inverarity, Robert. *Art of the Northwest Coast Indians*. Berkeley: University of California Press Books, 1950.

Jenness, Diamond. *Report of the Canadian Arctic Expedition, 1913–18*, vol. 13, *Eskimo Folk-lore. Part B: Eskimo String Figures Southern Party, 1913–16*. Ottawa: F. A. Acland Printer to the King's Most Excellent Majesty, 1924.

Koninck, Marie-Charlotte, ed. *Territoires. Le Québec : habitat, ressources et imaginaire*. Quebec City: Éditions Multimondes, 2007.

Labrusse, Rémi. "Le muséoclaste." *Cahiers du MNAM* (special issue 2015), pp. 14–16 and 21–44.

Lagerlöf, Selma. *The Wonderful Adventures of Nils*. New York: Harper, 1907.

Lévi-Strauss, Claude. *La voie des masques : les sentiers de la création*. Geneva: Skira, 1975 vols. 1 and 2.

Lopez, Barry. *Rêves arctiques : imagination et désir dans le paysage arctique*. Paris: Albin Michel, 1987.

Malaurie, Jean. *Les derniers rois de Thulé*. Paris: Plon, 1955.

Mary-Rousselière, Guy. *Les jeux de ficelle des Arviligjuarmiut*. Bulletin 233. Ottawa: National Museums of Canada, 1969.

McEvilley, Thomas. "Doctor, Lawyer, Indian Chief." In *Art and Otherness: Crisis in Cultural Identity*. Kingston, New York: McPherson and Company, 1992, pp. 27–56.

McGhee, Robert. *Ancient People of the Arctic*. Vancouver: University of British Columbia Press / Canadian Museum of Civilization, 1996.

Michaud, François-Xavier, ed. *Terres de Trickster : contes des Premières Nations*. Montreal: Possibles Éditions, 2014.

Newman, Barnett. "Northwest Coast Indian Painting" [1946]. In Jack Flam, ed. *Primitivism and Twentieth-century Art: A Documentary History*. Berkeley: University of California Press, 2003, pp. 282–283.

Onfray, Michel. *Esthétique du pôle Nord*. Paris: Grasset, 2002.

Phillips, Ruth B. *Museum Pieces: Toward the Indigenization of Canadian Museums*. Montreal: McGill Queen's University Press, 2011.

Gontran de Poncins. *Kablouna*. Paris: Delamain et Boutelleau, 1947.

Rasmussen, Knud. *Across Arctic America: Narrative of the Fifth Thule Expedition*. New York; London: G. P. Putnam's Sons, 1927.

_____. *Intellectual Culture of the Iglulik Eskimos*, vol. 7, no. 1. Copenhagen: Gyldendalske Boghandel, 1929.

_____. *The Netsilik Eskimos: Social Life and Spiritual Culture*, vol. 8, nos. 1–2, Copenhagen: Gyldendalske Boghandel, 1931.

Riopelle, Yseult, ed. *Jean Paul Riopelle. Catalogue raisonné*, vols. 1 (1939–1953)–2 (1954–1959). Montreal: Hibou Éditeurs, 1999 and 2004.

_____, ed. *Jean Paul Riopelle : Catalogue raisonné des estampes*. Montreal: Hibou Éditeur / Moudon, Switzerland: Acatos, 2005.

Riopelle, Yseult and Gilles Daigneault, eds. *Riopelle. Mémoires d'ateliers*. Montreal: Catalogue raisonné de Jean Paul Riopelle, 2010.

Riopelle, Yseult and Tanguy Riopelle, eds. *Jean Paul Riopelle. Catalogue raisonné*, vols. 3 (1960–1965)–4 (1966–1971). Montreal: Hibou Éditeurs, 2009 and 2014.

Robert, Guy. *Riopelle, chasseur d'images*. Montreal: Édition France-Amérique, 1981.

_____. *Riopelle ou la poétique du geste*. Montreal: Éditions de l'Homme, 1970.

Rushing, W. Jackson. *Native American Art and the New York Avant-garde: A History of Cultural Primitivism*. Austin, Texas: University of Texas Press, 1995.

Savard, Rémi. *Carcajou à l'aurore du monde : fragments écrits d'une encyclopédie orale innue*. Montreal: Recherches amérindiennes au Québec, 2016.

Schneider, Pierre. *Riopelle : signes mêlés*. Paris: Maeght / Montreal: Leméac, 1972.

_____. *Riopelle : parler de corde*. Paris: Maeght, 1972.

Sherman, Daniel. *French Primitivism and the Ends of Empire, 1945–1975*. Chicago: University of Chicago Press, 2011.

Sioui Durand, Guy. *Jean Paul Riopelle : l'art d'un trappeur supérieur. Indianité*. Sainte-Foy: Les Éditions GID, 2003.

_____. *Les très riches heures de Jean-Paul Riopelle*. Trois-Rivières: Éditions d'art Le Sabord, 2000.

_____. "Un Wendat à la recherche de l'art, ou le souffle activiste d'un Tsie8ei." In Louis-Jacques Dorais and Jonathan Lainey, eds. *Wendat et Wyandot d'hier et d'aujourd'hui / Wendat and Wyandot Then and Now / Eonywa'ndiynonhratehkwih chia' ekwää'tatehkwih : actes du premier Congrès d'études wendat et wyandot, Wendake, Québec, 13 au 16 juin 2012*. Wendake: Éditions Hannenorak, 2013, pp. 51–63.

Taçon, Paul S. C. "Stylistic Relationship between the Wakeham Bay Petroglyphs of the Canadian Arctic and Dorset Portable Art." In Paul Bahn and Michel Lorblanchet, eds. *Rock Art Studies: The Post-stylistic Era, or Where Do We Go from Here?* Oxford: Oxbow Books, 1993, pp. 151–162.

Townsend-Gault, Charlotte, Jennifer Kramer and Ki-ke-in, eds. *Native Art of the Northwest Coast: A History of Changing Ideas*. Vancouver: University of British Columbia Press, 2013.

Van Raalte, Sharon. *Sculpture/Inuit: An Odyssey. Sculpture of the Inuit, Masterworks of the Canadian Arctic: Report* [1975]. Ottawa: Department of Indian and Northern Affairs, Social Development Division, 1975.

Vaugeois, Denis, Louise Tardivel and Louise Côté. *L'indien généreux : ce que le monde doit aux Amériques*. Montreal: Boréal, 1992.

Viau, René. *Jean-Paul Riopelle : la traversée du paysage. Écrits sur le peintre et sur son œuvre*. Montreal: Leméac, 2002.

Viau, René, Jean-Louis Prat and Pierre-Jean Meurisse. *Riopelle : laves émaillées*. Toulouse: Art'poche, 1992.

Vigneault, Louise. *Espace artistique et modèle pionnier : Tom Thomson et Jean-Paul Riopelle*. Montreal: Hurtubise, 2011.

_____. *Identité et modernité dans l'art du Québec : Borduas, Sullivan, Riopelle*. Montreal: Hurtubise, 2002.

EXHIBITION CATALOGUES

L'art indien aux États-Unis. Paris: Centre culturel américain, 1958.

Art primitif : Amérique du Nord. Paris: Galerie Jacques Kerchache, 1965.

Arts primitifs dans les ateliers d'artistes. Paris: Société des amis du Musée de l'Homme, 1967.

Auster, Paul. "Introduction." In *Jean-Paul Riopelle: Paintings from 1974, Pastels from 1975*. New York: Pierre Matisse Gallery, 1975.

Blais, Simon. *Jean Paul Riopelle : Pastel*. Montreal: Éditions Simon Blais, 2004.

_____. *Riopelle, tigre de papier : œuvres sur papier 1953-1989*. Laval: Les 400 coups, 1997.

Blanchard, Pascal, Gilles Boëtsch and Nanette Jacomijn Snoep, eds. *Exhibition. L'invention du sauvage*. Paris: Arles Sud / Musée du quai Branly - Jacques Chirac, 2011.

Bordier, Roger, ed. *Riopelle, œuvres 1966-1977*. Paris: Maeght, 1991.

Breton, Elisa, André Breton and Benjamin Péret. "Aparté" in *Riopelle à La Dragonne*. Paris: Galerie Nina Dausset, 1949.

Chefs-d'œuvre des arts indiens et esquimaux du Canada. Paris: Société des amis du Musée de l'Homme, 1969.

Chefs-d'œuvre du Musée de l'Homme. Paris: Caisse nationale des monuments historiques, 1965.

Duffy, Helen. "Jean-Paul Riopelle." In *Les Laurentides : peintres et paysages*. Edited by Mela Constantinidi. Toronto: Art Gallery of Ontario, 1977.

Dupin, Jacques. *Riopelle 74*. Paris: Maeght, 1974.

Duthuit, Georges. *Riopelle*. New York: Pierre Matisse Gallery, 1953.

Duthuit, Georges, et al. *Riopelle: Paintings, Pastels, Assemblages*. New York: Pierre Matisse Gallery, 1969.

Érouart, Gilbert and Michel Noël. *Signes premiers : Riopelle, Kijno, Chi Teh Chun*. Quebec City: Le Loup de Gouttière, 1994.

Hess, Thomas B. *Riopelle: Paintings from 1970–1973 and the Le Roi de Thulé Series, 1973*. New York: Pierre Matisse Gallery, 1974.

Holm, Bill and William Reid. *A Dialogue on Form and Freedom: Northwest Coast Indian Art*. Houston: Institute for the Arts, Rice University, 1975.

Jean-Paul Riopelle. Ottawa: National Gallery of Canada, 1963.

Jean-Paul Riopelle. Montreal: The Montreal Museum of Fine Arts, 1991.

Labrusse, Rémi, Claude Duthuit et al. *Autour de Claude Duthuit*. Arles: Actes Sud, 2003.

Lamarche, Bernard. *Riopelle. Impressions sans fin*. Quebec City: Musée national des beaux-arts du Québec, 2005.

Martin, Jean-Hubert, ed. *Magiciens de la terre*. Paris: Musée national d'art moderne, Centre Pompidou, 1989.

Michaud, Yves. *Jean-Paul Riopelle : les années 1960*. Paris: Didier Imbert Fine Art, 1994.

Mooney, Sean and Chuna McIntyre. *Yua. Henri Matisse and the Inner Arctic Spirit*. Phoenix: Heard Museum, 2018.

Nemiroff, Diana, Charlotte Townsend-Gault and Robert Houle, eds. *Land, Spirit, Power: First Nations at the National Gallery of Canada*. Ottawa: National Gallery of Canada, 1992.

Poinsot, Jean-Marc. *Quand l'œuvre a lieu : l'art exposé et ses récits autorisés*. Geneva: Musée d'art moderne et contemporain / Villeurbanne: Institut d'art contemporain, 1999.

Riopelle : ficelles et autres jeux. Paris: Centre culturel canadien, 1972.

Riopelle: First American Exhibition. New York: Pierre Matisse Gallery, 1954.

Riopelle, Jean Paul. *Riopelle*. Paris: Galerie Rive Droite, 1954.

Riopelle, Yseult, ed. *Riopelle : les migrations du bestiaire. Une retrospective*. Montreal: Kétoupa Édition, 2014.

———, ed. *Riopelle au Cap Tourmente : de la nature à l'atelier*. Montreal: Kétoupa Édition, 2016.

Routledge, Marie and Ingo Hessel. "Contemporary Inuit Sculpture: An Approach to the Medium, the Artists, and Their Work." In *In the Shadow of the Sun: Perspectives on Contemporary Native Art*. Hull: Canadian Museum of Civilization, 1993, pp. 443–478.

Schneider, Pierre, ed. *Jean-Paul Riopelle. Peinture, 1946-1977*. Paris: Musée national d'art moderne, Centre Pompidou / Quebec City: Musée du Québec / Montreal: Musée d'art contemporain, 1981.

Sioui, Georges E. "La découverte de l'Américité." In *Indigena. Perspectives autochtones contemporaines*. Edited by Gerald McMaster and Lee-Ann Marin. Hull: Canadian Museum of Civilization, 1992, pp. 59–70.

Szymusiak, Dominique et al. *Les Esquimaux vus par Matisse. Georges Duthuit : Une fête en Cimmérie*. Paris: Hazan / Le Cateau-Cambrésis: Musée départemental Matisse, 2010.

Waldberg, Patrick. *Le surréalisme : sources – histoire – affinités*. Paris: Galerie Charpentier, 1964. Vogel, Susan, ed. *Art/artifact: African Art in Anthropology Collections*. New York: Center for African Art, 1988.

Waldberg, Isabelle and Patrick Waldberg, *Un amour acéphale, correspondance 1940-1949*. Paris: Éditions de la Différence, 1992.

Waldberg, Michel, ed. *Riopelle vu par. . .* Paris: Centre culturel de Paris, 2004.

Wallen, Lynn Age. *The Face of Dance: Yup'ik Eskimo Masks from Alaska*. Calgary: Glenbow Museum, 1990.

NEWSPAPERS AND PERIODICALS

Arsenault, Daniel. "The Aesthetic Power of Ancient Dorset Images at Qajartalik, A Unique Petroglyph Site in the Canadian Arctic." *Boletín del Museo Chileno de Arte Precolombino*, vol. 18, no. 2 (2013), pp. 19–32.

Auster, Paul. "Lumière boréale." *Derrière le miroir*, no. 218. Paris: Maeght, 1976.

Barbeau, Marius. *Totem Poles: According to Crests and Topics*. Bulletin no. 119, vol. 1, Ottawa: National Museum of Canada, 1950.

Bernatchez, Raymond. "La vie, la mort, rien d'autre." *La Presse*, March 14, 2002.

Bordier, Roger. "Les lieux et les rêves de Riopelle." *Cimaise*, no. 140 (January–February 1979), pp. 9–20.

Bouyeure, Claude. "Entretien avec Jean-Paul Riopelle." *Les lettres françaises*, no. 1236 (June 12–18, 1968), p. 28.

Breton, André. "Note sur les masques à transformation de la côte pacifique Nord-Ouest." *Neuf*, no. 1 (1950), pp. 40–41.

Bruemmer, Fred. "The Petroglyphs of Hudson Strait." *The Beaver*, vol. 304, no. 1 (Summer 1973), pp. 33–35.

Caron, Claudine and Caroline Traube, eds. "*Cahiers de la société québécoise de recherche en musique*," vol. 14, no. 1 (May 2013).

Couture, Francine. "La mise en légende de Riopelle ou l'héroïsation d'un artiste moderne." *Canadian Aesthetics Journal / Revue canadienne d'esthétique*, vol. 7 (Fall 2002), https://www.uqtr.ca/AE/Vol_7/libres/couture.html.

Debray, Cécile and Rémi Labrusse. "Dossier Georges Duthuit." *Les Cahiers du Musée national d'art moderne* (special edition). Paris: Centre Pompidou, 2015.

Duchemin-Pelletier, Florence. "Un silence éloquent. Du désintérêt des surréalistes pour l'art inuit contemporain." *Histoire de l'art*, no. 75 (2014), pp. 111–122.

Duthuit, Georges. "A Painter of Awakening: Jean-Paul Riopelle." *Canadian Art*, vol. 10, no.1 (1952), pp. 24–27.

———. "Le don indien sur la côte nord-ouest de l'Amérique (Colombie britannique)." *Labyrinthe*, no. 18 (April 1946), pp. 9–11.

Éluard, Paul. "La nuit est à une dimension." *Cahiers d'art*, nos. 5–6 (1935), pp. 99–101.

"The Eskimo World." *artscanada*, nos. 162–163 (December 1971–January 1972).

Gagnon, François-Marc. "En mémoire de Jean-Paul Riopelle 1923-2002. Riopelle, Heidegger et les animaux." *Journal of Canadian Art History / Annales d'histoire de l'art canadien*, vol. 23, nos. 1–2 (2002), pp. 90–107.

Galy-Carles, Henry. "Les ficelles et autres jeux de Jean-Paul Riopelle." *Vie des Arts*, no. 88 (Fall 1972), pp. 56–59.

Gauvreau, Pierre. "Réflexions sur l'art indien." *Journal musical canadien* (December 1954), p. 6.

Gombrich, Ernst. "Image and Word in Twentieth-century Art." *Word and Image*, vol. 1, no. 3 (July–September 1985), pp. 213–241.

Greenwood, Michael. "Riopelle Icebergs." *Canadian Art*, vol. 36, no. 1 (May–June 1979), p. 50.

Harris, Lawren. "Revelation of Art in Canada." *The Canadian Theosophist*, vol. 7, no. 5 (July 1926), pp. 85–88.

Kleist, Mari. "Anthropomorphic Images of the Late Dorset Culture." *North Atlantic Archaeology Journal*, vol. 5 (2018), pp. 1–25.

Lamy, Laurent. "Un peintre québécois connu dans le monde entier : Riopelle." *Forces*, no. 28 (July 1974), pp. 38–48.

Mauss, Marcel. "Essai sur le don. Forme et raison de l'échange dans les sociétés archaïques." *L'Année sociologique*, vol. 1 (1923–24), pp. 30–186.

Mauzé, Marie. "Odes à l'art de la côte Nord-Ouest. Surréalisme et ethnographie." *Gradhiva*, no. 26 (2017), pp. 180–209.

Michel, Jacques. "Riopelle sur un iceberg." *Le Monde*, February 9, 1979.

Paalen, Wolfgang. *DYN*, no. 2 (July–August 1942).

———. *DYN, The Amerindian Number*, nos. 4–5 (1943).

Rioux, Marcel. "Exposition canadienne à Paris." *Notre temps* (July 12, 1947), p. 5.

Saladin d'Anglure, Bernard. "Découverte de pétroglyphes à Qajartalik sur l'île de Qikertaaluk." *North/Nord*, vol. 9, no. 6 (1962), pp. 34–39.

Schneider, Arnd. "On 'Appropriation.' A Critical Reappraisal of the Concept and Its Application in Global Art Practices." *Social Anthropology*, vol. 11, no. 2 (June 2003), pp. 215–229.

Schneider, Pierre. "Riopelle, les humeurs du Blanc." *L'Express* (February 17–23, 1979), p. 43.

Sioui Durand, Guy. "L'onderah." *Inter Art Actuel*, no. 122 (Winter 2016), pp. 4–19.

———. "Le ré-ensauvagement par l'art. Le vieil Indien, les pommes rouges et les Chasseurs-Chamanes-Guerriers." *Captures*, vol. 3, no. 1 (May 2018), www.revuecaptures.org/node/1927

Swinton, George. "Prehistoric Dorset Art: The Magico-religious Basis." *The Beaver*, vol. 298 (Fall 1967), pp. 32–47.

Taylor, William E., Jr. "Prehistoric Dorset Art: The Silent Echoes of Culture." *The Beaver*, vol. 298 (Fall 1967), pp. 32–47.

Viau, Guy. "Six peintres canadiens. Reconnaissance de l'espace." *Notre temps* (July 12, 1947), p. 5.

Viau, René. "Chez Jean-Paul Riopelle. Un atelier qui s'inspire des granges québécoises." *Décormag* (May 1977).

Vigneault, Louise. "Riopelle et la quête ludique de l'autre." *Journal of Canadian Art History / Annales d'histoire de l'art canadien*, vol. 18, no. 2 (1997), p. 92.

Warnod, Jeanine. "Les icebergs de Riopelle." *Le Figaro*, March 2, 1979.

269
Jean Paul Riopelle
Maple
1977
Oil on canvas

269

LIST OF ILLUSTRATIONS

The titles of Jean Paul Riopelle's works listed herein are the original ones given by the artist.

1
Denise Colomb
Paris 1902 – Paris 2004
Jean Paul Riopelle, Jacques Germain, Maria Elena Vieira da Silva, Pierre Loeb, Georges Mathieu and Zao Wou-ki
1953, print 2020
Black and white photograph
Archives Yseult Riopelle

2
Georges Duthuit in his University Street studio in Paris with Riopelle's *Untitled* (1954) and Northwest Coast Indigenous objects in his collection
N.d.
Black and white photograph
Musée national d'art moderne – Centre de création industrielle, Centre Pompidou, Paris
Fonds Georges Duthuit, don de Barbara Duthuit, 2015
Inv. BK 17910 DUTH 159

3
Jean Paul Riopelle
Montreal 1923 – L'Isle-aux-Grues 2002
Hochelaga
1947
Oil on canvas
60 x 73 cm
Power Corporation of Canada Collection
Inv. 1987.041.1

4
Jean Paul Riopelle
Montreal 1923 – L'Isle-aux-Grues 2002
La roue (Cold Dog – Indian Summer)
1954–55
Oil on canvas
250 x 331 cm
The Montreal Museum of Fine Arts, purchase, with a special grant from the Government of Quebec
Inv. 2001.163

5
Jean Paul Riopelle
Montreal 1923 – L'Isle-aux-Grues 2002
Un coin de pays
1962
Oil on canvas
200 x 200 cm
The Global Affairs Canada – Visual Art Collection, Ottawa

6
Jean Paul Riopelle
Montreal 1923 – L'Isle-aux-Grues 2002
Paysage d'autrefois
1977
Oil on canvas
131 x 97 cm
Collection of Michael Audain and Yoshiko Karasawa

7
Éliane Excoffier
Born in Saint-Jérôme, Quebec, in 1971
Paysage, Île-aux-Oies
2003
Black and white photograph
Collection of the artist

8
Marcel Masse, Riopelle, unknown, Clément Richard, and Bernard and Louise Lamarre at Château-Musée de Vallauris in France for the opening of the exhibition *Jean-Paul Riopelle : laves émaillées, terres, peintures*
1985
Black and white photograph
Archives Yseult Riopelle

9
Éliane Excoffier
Born in Saint-Jérôme, Quebec, in 1971
Goose Hunting, Hiding in a Corn Field, Île-aux-Oies (from l. to r.: Marc Séguin, his son, Marc-Émile, and the hunting guide Gilles Gagné)
2003
Black and white photograph
Collection of the artist

10
Claude Duthuit photograph of Paul Rebeyrolle, Riopelle, Jacques Lamy and Champlain Charest on a fishing trip
About 1975, print 2020
Black and white photograph
Archives Yseult Riopelle

11
Jean Paul Riopelle
Montreal 1923 – L'Isle-aux-Grues 2002
Point de rencontre – Quintette
(polyptych)
1963
Oil on canvas
428 x 564 cm (5 panels)
Centre national des arts plastiques, Paris
Inv. FNAC 90069

12
Duane Linklater
Born in Moose Factory, Ontario, in 1976
A Gift from Doreen
2016–19
Hand-dyed canvas, teepee canvas, blueberry extract, grommets, nails
274 x 686 x 312 cm (various dimensions)
The Montreal Museum of Fine Arts, in process of acquisition
Inv. 20.2020

13
Jean Paul Riopelle
Montreal 1923 – L'Isle-aux-Grues 2002
Les masques (triptych)
1964
Oil on canvas
195 x 357 cm
Musée national des beaux-arts du Québec, achat grâce aux revenus générés par les activités commerciales du Musée et à une contribution de Loto-Québec
Inv. 2002.25

14
Claude Duthuit photograph of Riopelle in Pangnirtung, Nunavut (detail)
July 1977
Black and white photograph
Archives Yseult Riopelle

15
Basil Zarov
Montreal 1905 (?) – Toronto 1998
Jean Paul Riopelle outside of the Studio at Sainte-Marguerite-du-Lac-Masson with "La Défaite" in the Distance
About 1976
Black and white photograph
Library and Archives Canada, Ottawa

16
Beau Dick
Alert Bay, British Columbia, 1955 – Vancouver 2017
Weather Spirit
N.d.
Wood, leather, twigs, paint
106 x 91.4 x 60.9 cm
Collection of David Allison and Chris Nicholson, Vancouver

17
Tlingit
Human-face mask
About 1900 (?)
Animal skull
12 x 10 x 5 cm
Private collection

18
Georges Duthuit in his University Street studio in Paris with Riopelle's *Untitled* (1954–55) and a Northwest Coast mask
N.d.
Black and white photograph
Musée national d'art moderne – Centre de création industrielle, Centre Pompidou, Paris
Inv. BK 17910 DUTH 159

19
Jean Paul Riopelle
Montreal 1923 – L'Isle-aux-Grues 2002
Le roi de Thulé
1973
Painted wood
25 x 20 cm
Collection of Huguette Vachon

20
Jean Paul Riopelle
Montreal 1923 – L'Isle-aux-Grues 2002
Untitled (Bûche)
1973
Painted wood
H. 45 cm
Private collection

21
Letter from Gabriel Illouz to Yseult Riopelle
October 16, 1991
Archives Yseult Riopelle

22
Advertisement for the Julius Carlebach gallery in New York
In *VVV*, nos. 2–3 (1943)
The Montreal Museum of Fine Arts Library

23
"Aparté," by Elisa Breton, André Breton and Benjamin Péret, in *Riopelle à La Dragonne*, exh. cat. (Paris: Galerie Nina Dausset, 1949)
Archives Yseult Riopelle

24
Cover of Jean Paul Riopelle, *Riopelle*, exh. cat. (Paris: Galerie Rive Droite, 1954)
Archives Yseult Riopelle

25
"Pl. XIV. Masque de chaman à accessoires. Eskimo de l'Alaska"
Ill. in *Le masque, Paris*, exh. cat. (Paris: Éditions des Musées nationaux, 1959)
Archives Yseult Riopelle

26
Cover of the "Amerindian Number" of Wolfgang Paalen's *DYN*, nos. 4–5 (1943)
McGill University, Humanities and Social Sciences Library, Montreal

27
Letter from Riopelle to Georges Duthuit
Vanves, 1954
Musée national d'art moderne – Centre de création industrielle, Centre Pompidou, Paris
Fonds Georges Duthuit, don de Barbara Duthuit, 2015
Inv. BK 17910 DUTH 55-70

28
Letter from Riopelle to Marius Barbeau
February 19, 1954
Canadian Museum of History, Gatineau

29
Hélène Adant
Russia 1903 – France 1985
Georges Duthuit in His University Street Studio in Paris with Jean Paul Riopelle's "Untitled" (1954) and Yup'ik Masks in His Collection
N.d.
Black and white photograph
Musée national d'art moderne – Centre de création industrielle, Centre Pompidou, Paris
Fonds Georges Duthuit, don de Barbara Duthuit, 2015
Inv. BK 17910 DUTH 159

30
Georges Duthuit with a Yup'ik mask in his collection (attributed to Ikamrailnguq, about 1900)
N.d.
Black and white photograph
Musée national d'art moderne – Centre de création industrielle, Centre Pompidou, Paris
Fonds Georges Duthuit, don de Barbara Duthuit, 2015
Inv. BK 17910 DUTH 159

31
Georges Duthuit in front of a Kwakwaka'wakw transformation mask in his collection
N.d.
Black and white photograph
Musée national d'art moderne – Centre de création industrielle, Centre Pompidou, Paris
Fonds Georges Duthuit, don de Barbara Duthuit, 2015
Inv. BK 17910 DUTH 159

32
Paul Éluard
Saint-Denis, France, 1895 – Charenton-le-Pont, France 1952
"Le monde au temps des surréalistes"
Ill. in *Variétés* (1929), pp. 26–27
National Gallery of Australia, Canberra

33
Kurt Seligmann
Basel 1900 – Sugar Loaf, New York, 1962
Manuscript describing the location and circumstances of the acquisition of the Kaiget totem pole
Canadian Museum of History, Gatineau

34
Henri Tracol
Paris 1909 – (?) 1997
Main entrance of Musée de l'Homme, Paris, with a totem pole (Kaiget Totem Pole)
About 1939
Black and white photograph mounted on cardboard
Musée du quai Branly - Jacques Chirac, Paris

35
Marius Barbeau standing by a mantel with a reduced totem pole
About 1940
Black and white photograph
Canadian Museum of History, Gatineau

36
Cover of Marius Barbeau, *Haida Myths Illustrated in Argillite Carvings* (Ottawa: Department of Resources and Development, National Parks Branch, National Museum of Canada, Ottawa, 1953)
The Montreal Museum of Fine Arts Library

37
Cover of Marius Barbeau, *Totem Poles of the Gitksan: Upper Skeena River, British Columbia* (Ottawa: F. A. Acland, 1929)
The Montreal Museum of Fine Arts Library

38
Cover of Marius Barbeau, *The Downfall of Temlaham,* ills. by A. Y. Jackson, Edwin H. Holgate, W. Langdon Kihn, Emily Carr and Annie D. Savage (Toronto: The Macmillan Company of Canada, 1928)
The Montreal Museum of Fine Arts Library

39
Cover of Marcel Evrard, ed., *Chefs d'œuvre des arts indiens et esquimaux du Canada / Masterpieces of Indian and Eskimo Art from Canada* (Paris: Société des amis du Musée de l'Homme, 1969)
The Montreal Museum of Fine Arts Library

40
Cover of Georges Duthuit, *Une fête en Cimmérie* (Paris: Éditions Mourlot, 1964)
25 x 19.5 cm (each)
Global Affairs Canada – Visual Art Collection, Ottawa

41
Cover of Jean Malaurie, *Les derniers rois de Thulé. Une année parmi les Eskimos polaires du Groenland* (Paris: Plon, 1955)
The Montreal Museum of Fine Arts Library

42
Exhibition poster for *Sculpture/Inuit : chefs-d'œuvre de l'Arctique canadien (Sculpture of the Inuit: Masterworks of the Canadian Arctic)* held at Galeries nationales du Grand Palais, Paris, February 11–April 2, 1972
60 x 41 cm
The Montreal Museum of Fine Arts, purchase

43
Jean Paul Riopelle
Montreal 1923 – L'Isle-aux-Grues 2002
Untitled
1947
Watercolour and ink on paper
24.2 x 31.2 cm
Collection of Michael Hackett-Hale

44
Kay Sage
Albany, New York, 1898 – Woodbury, Connecticut, 1963
Copy of a design for a tarot card
(verso of **46**)
About 1946
Ink on paper
17.5 x 12.6 cm
Private collection

45
Kay Sage
Albany, New York, 1898 – Woodbury, Connecticut, 1963
Design for a tarot card
1941
Gouache, brush, pen and India ink on paper
23.5 x 13.5 cm
Private collection, courtesy of Kay Sage Catalogue Raisonné

46
Jean Paul Riopelle
Montreal 1923 – L'Isle-aux-Grues 2002
Untitled (recto of **44**)
1946
Watercolour and ink on paper
17.5 x 12.6 cm
Private collection

47
Film still from *L'invention du monde : les surréalistes et le cinéma* (1952)
Script and direction by Michel Zimbacca and Jean-Louis Bédouin
The Montreal Museum of Fine Arts Library

48
Southwest Alaska, Yup'ik
Mask
About 1910
Driftwood, baleen, feathers, paint, cotton twine
49 x 39 cm
National Museum of the American Indian, Smithsonian Institution, Washington, D.C.
Inv. 12/910

49
Southern shores of Kuskokwim Bay, Goodnews Bay, Yup'ik
Mask representing a fish
Early 20th c.
Painted wood, feathers
H. 48 cm
Musée du quai Branly - Jacques Chirac, Paris, achat de l'État en 1999

50
Lower Yukon, Alaska, Yup'ik
Mask
Early 20th c.
Wood, driftwood, spruce root, pigment, watercolour, nails, cotton thread, rattan (?)
59 x 57 x 12.5 cm
Glenbow Museum, Calgary
Inv. AB 1134

51
Lower Yukon, Alaska, Yup'ik
Mask
Early 20th c.
Wood, driftwood, spruce root, rattan (?), feathers, pigment, watercolour, cotton thread, nails, glue
60 x 55 x 13 cm
Glenbow Museum, Calgary
Inv. AB 1131

52
Hooper Bay region of southwest Alaska, Yup'ik
Mask
Early 20th c.
Wood, driftwood, spruce root, pigment, watercolour, nails, cotton thread
73 x 71.4 x 15 cm
Glenbow Museum, Calgary
Inv. AB 1129

53
Sabine Weiss
Born in Saint-Gingolph, Switzerland, in 1924
André Breton at Home in France with His Art Collection
About 1960
Black and white photograph
Archive Photos/Getty Images

54
Attributed to Ikamrailnguq
Napaskiap Village, Kuskokwim River, Central Alaska, Yup'ik
Dance mask representing *Tunutellgem Yua* (Arctic loon spirit), formerly in the collection of Georges Duthuit
About 1900
Wood, feathers, pigment and vegetable fibres
84 x 60 x 57 cm
Private collection

55
Set of pages from Robert Lebel's sketchbook of drawings of Yup'ik masks
Ill. in *Collection Robert Lebel: vente*, Paris: Drout-Richelieu, December 4, 2006
1942–46
Ink, graphite and coloured pencil drawings on paper in a cardboard-bound sketchbook
13 x 20.5 x 1.3 cm
Musée du quai Branly - Jacques Chirac, Paris
Inv. 70.2007.11.1

56
Jean Paul Riopelle
Montreal 1923 – L'Isle-aux-Grues 2002
Masque esquimau
1955
Gouache on paper
49.5 x 65 cm
Private collection, Montreal

57
Jean Paul Riopelle
Montreal 1923 – L'Isle-aux-Grues 2002
Masque eskimo
1955
Gouache on paper
103 x 75.5 cm
Private collection

58
Jean Paul Riopelle
Montreal 1923 – L'Isle-aux-Grues 2002
Eskimo Mask
1955
Gouache on paper
75.6 x 106.7 cm
Brooklyn Museum, Caroline A. L. Pratt Fund
Inv. 59.98

59
Jean Paul Riopelle
Montreal 1923 – L'Isle-aux-Grues 2002
Masque esquimau
1955
Gouache on paper
73.6 x 104.1 cm
Albright-Knox Art Gallery, Buffalo, gift of Seymour H. Knox, Jr., 1957
Inv. K1956:12

60
Jean Paul Riopelle
Montreal 1923 – L'Isle-aux-Grues 2002
Sous le mythe de Gitksan no 4
1956
Gouache on paper
74 x 105 cm
Private collection, Paris

61
Jean Paul Riopelle
Montreal 1923 – L'Isle-aux-Grues 2002
Sous le mythe de Gitksan no 3
1956
Gouache on paper
73.7 x 106.8 cm
Vancouver Art Gallery, gift of J. Ron Longstaffe
Inv. 80.53

62
Jean Paul Riopelle
Montreal 1923 – L'Isle-aux-Grues 2002
Sous le mythe de Gitksan no 2
1956
Gouache on paper
76 x 106 cm
Private collection

63
Jean Paul Riopelle
Montreal 1923 – L'Isle-aux-Grues 2002
Sous le mythe de Gitksan no 8
1956
Gouache on paper
50 x 65 cm
Private collection

64
Jean Paul Riopelle
Montreal 1923 – L'Isle-aux-Grues 2002
Sous le mythe de Gitksan nº 10
1956
Gouache on paper
50 x 65 cm
Private collection, France

65
Jean Paul Riopelle
Montreal 1923 – L'Isle-aux-Grues 2002
Gitksan
1959
Oil on paper mounted on canvas
108 x 75 cm
Private collection

66
Jean Paul Riopelle
Montreal 1923 – L'Isle-aux-Grues 2002
Un autre Gitksan
1957
Gouache on paper
107 x 75 cm
Private collection, Montreal

67
British Columbia, unidentified origin
Human-face mask with clan crest
markings
About 1800–50
Painted wood
21.6 x 17.3 cm
The Montreal Museum of Fine Arts,
anonymous gift
Inv. 1984.Ab.1

68
Gitksan (?)
Mask
1920–25
Wood, paint, metal
24.2 x 20.5 x 13.1 cm
McCord Museum, Montreal, gift of
Edwin Holgate
Inv. M973.85.2

69
Northwest Coast, Alaska, Tlingit
Ladle
About 1870
Mountain-sheep horn, abalone shell,
copper
47 x 13.7 x 19.5 cm
The Montreal Museum of Fine Arts,
purchase, gift of F. Cleveland Morgan
Inv. 1950.51.Ab.2

70
Northwest Coast, British Columbia,
Tsimshian or Gitksan
Soul catcher
Early 19th c.
Bone, abalone shell, paint
3.6 x 18.3 x 2.7 cm
The Montreal Museum of Fine Arts,
purchase, gift of F. Cleveland Morgan
Inv. 1950.51.Ab.1

71
Northwest Coast, British Columbia,
Tsimshian
Amhalayt (frontlet)
About 1880
Painted wood, abalone shell
20.2 x 18.8 cm
The Montreal Museum of Fine Arts,
purchase, gift of F. Cleveland Morgan
Inv. 1958.Ab.1

72
Jean Paul Riopelle
Montreal 1923 – L'Isle-aux-Grues 2002
Les rois de Thulé
1973
Mixed media on paper
64 x 49.5 cm
Collection of the Charest family

73
Jean Paul Riopelle
Montreal 1923 – L'Isle-aux-Grues 2002
Untitled
From the series *Rois de Thulé*
1973
Acrylic, gouache and charcoal on paper
65 x 50 cm
Musée national des beaux-arts du Québec.
Don
Inv. 2007.21

74
Jean Paul Riopelle
Montreal 1923 – L'Isle-aux-Grues 2002
Les rois de Thulé
1973
Mixed media on paper
65.4 x 50.2 cm
Private collection

75
Jean Paul Riopelle
Montreal 1923 – L'Isle-aux-Grues 2002
Les rois de Thulé
N.d.
Mixed media on paper
65.4 x 50.2 cm
Collection of Galerie Simon Blais, Montreal

76
Jean Paul Riopelle
Montreal 1923 – L'Isle-aux-Grues 2002
Les rois de Thulé
1973
Mixed media on paper
65.5 x 50 cm
Private collection

77
Jean Paul Riopelle
Montreal 1923 – L'Isle-aux-Grues 2002
Les rois de Thulé VII
1973
Gouache on paper
65.5 x 50 cm
Private collection, France

78
Jean Paul Riopelle
Montreal 1923 – L'Isle-aux-Grues 2002
Blizzard Sylvestre
1953
Oil on board
170.5 x 254.7 cm
The Museum of Modern Art, New York,
gift of Mr. and Mrs. Ralph F. Colin, 1954
Inv. 26.1954

79
Riopelle photograph of *Apparition –
Triceratos automatique*
(1947–48, H. 24 cm)
N.d.
Black and white photograph
Archives Yseult Riopelle

80
Riopelle photograph of *Hommage
à Sade*
(1947–48, H. 34 cm)
N.d.
Black and white photograph
Archives Yseult Riopelle

81
Jean Lespérance (?) photograph
of Françoise and Riopelle on a ski trip
About 1946
Black and white photograph
Archives Yseult Riopelle

82
Sylvie Riopelle photograph of Riopelle
at Superbagnères, Pyrenees
December 1964, print 2020
Black and white photograph
Archives Yseult Riopelle

83
Basil Zarov
Montreal 1905 (?) – Toronto 1998
*Bernard Morisset, Riopelle and
Madeleine Arbour outside the Studio
at Sainte-Marguerite-du-Lac-Masson*
About 1977
Black and white photograph
Library and Archives Canada, Ottawa

84
Jean Paul Riopelle
Montreal 1923 – L'Isle-aux-Grues 2002
Autriche
1954
Oil on canvas
193 x 300 cm
Private collection

85
Jean Paul Riopelle
Montreal 1923 – L'Isle-aux-Grues 2002
Autriche III
1954
Oil on canvas
200 x 300.7 cm
Montreal Museum of Fine Arts, purchase,
Horsley and Annie Townsend Bequest
1963.1395

86
Jean Paul Riopelle
Montreal 1923 – L'Isle-aux-Grues 2002
Blizzard
1954
Oil on canvas
89 x 116 cm
Private collection, Montreal

87
Jean Paul Riopelle
Montreal 1923 – L'Isle-aux-Grues 2002
Blizzard
1954
Oil on canvas
95.5 x 125 cm
Collection of Michael Audain and Yoshiko
Karasawa

88
Jean Paul Riopelle
Montreal 1923 – L'Isle-aux-Grues 2002
Regel
1957
Oil on canvas
72.5 x 92 cm
The Montreal Museum of Fine Arts,
gift of Dr. Sean B. Murphy
Inv. 2013.80

89
Jean Paul Riopelle
Montreal 1923 – L'Isle-aux-Grues 2002
Lumière du Nord
1957
Oil on canvas
45.7 x 54.9 cm
Private collection

90
Jean Paul Riopelle
Montreal 1923 – L'Isle-aux-Grues 2002
Avalanche
1957
Oil on canvas
200 x 300 cm
Power Corporation of Canada Collection

91
Jean Paul Riopelle
Montreal 1923 – L'Isle-aux-Grues 2002
L'Indien
1969–70, cast about 1971
Bronze
Michelucci Foundry, Italy
175 x 51 x 51 cm
Private collection

92
Jean Paul Riopelle (photo Bruno
Massenet, 1995)
Ill. in Huguette Vachon et al., *Jean Paul
Riopelle : les traces de l'envol* (Gatineau:
Galerie Montcalm, 2003), p. 68
Black and white photograph
The Montreal Museum of Fine Arts Library

93
Basil Zarov
Montreal 1905 (?) – Toronto 1998
*Jean Paul Riopelle outside of
the Studio at Sainte-Marguerite-du-
Lac-Masson*
About 1976
Black and white photograph
Library and Archives Canada, Ottawa

94
Basil Zarov
Montreal 1905 (?) – Toronto 1998
*Jean Paul Riopelle with "Hibou-pelle"
(1969–70) outside of the Studio at
Sainte-Marguerite-du-Lac-Masson*
About 1976
Black and white photograph
Library and Archives Canada, Ottawa

95
Riopelle and Cécile Newashish
About 1992
Colour photograph
Collection of Cécile Newashish

96
Claude Kistabish, Roger Echaquan,
Riopelle and Cécile Newashish
About 1992
Colour photograph
Collection of Cécile Newashish

97
César Newashish working on a
bark canoe with a child watching on
N.d.
Black and white photograph
Collection of Pierre Lepage

98
Jean Paul Riopelle
Montreal 1923 – L'Isle-aux-Grues 2002
Le canot à glace
1992
Mixed media on wood
56 x 724 x 168 cm
The Montreal Museum of Fine Arts,
purchase, with a special grant from the
Government of Quebec
Inv. 2001.166

99
César Newashish
Manawan, Quebec, 1903 – Manawan
1994
Bark canoe
H. 33 cm (centre), 30 cm (ends);
W. 84 cm; L. 406 cm
La Maison amérindienne de
Mont-Saint-Hilaire

100
La Joute (plaster model) exhibited
at the Musée d'art moderne de la Ville
de Paris
1972
Black and white photograph
Archives Yseult Riopelle

101
La Joute on display outside
of the Olympic Stadium, Montreal
After 1976
Black and white photograph
Archives de la Ville de Montréal

102
Jean Paul Riopelle
Montreal 1923 – L'Isle-aux-Grues 2002
Grand duc
1970
Oil on canvas
242 x 163 cm
Private collection

103
Jean Paul Riopelle
Montreal 1923 – L'Isle-aux-Grues 2002
Hibou-masque
1973
Bronze
29 x 29 x 16 cm
Private collection, Montreal

104
Jean Paul Riopelle
Montreal 1923 – L'Isle-aux-Grues 2002
Hibou-totem
1973, cast 1986
Bronze, 3/8
Fratelli Bonvicini Foundry,
Sommacampagna, Italy
36 x 19.5 x 21 cm
The Montreal Museum of Fine Arts,
gift of Dr. Michael Kapusta
Inv. 2003.239

105
Jean Paul Riopelle
Montreal 1923 – L'Isle-aux-Grues 2002
Femme hibou
1969–70, cast about 1971
Bronze
Michelucci Foundry, Italy
114 x 46 x 46 cm
Private collection

106
Jean Paul Riopelle
Montreal 1923 – L'Isle-aux-Grues 2002
Hibou A
1969–70, cast 1976
Bronze
143 x 104 x 92 cm
Michelucci Foundry, Carrara, Italy
The Montreal Museum of Fine Arts,
gift of Sylvie Cataford and Simon Blais
2013.412

107
Jean Paul Riopelle
Montreal 1923 – L'Isle-aux-Grues 2002
Hibou-Arctique
1970
Oil on canvas
100 x 73 cm
Private collection, Montreal

108
Jean Paul Riopelle
Montreal 1923 – L'Isle-aux-Grues 2002
Hibou-Snow flake
Oil on canvas
100.3 x 72.5 cm
Private collection

109
Jean Paul Riopelle
Montreal 1923 – L'Isle-aux-Grues 2002
Hibou patriote
1970
Oil on canvas
100.3 x 72.4 cm
Private collection, courtesy Galerie
Simon Blais

110
Jean Paul Riopelle
Montreal 1923 – L'Isle-aux-Grues 2002
L'étang – Hommage à Grey Owl
1970
Oil on canvas
299.5 x 400 cm
The Montreal Museum of Fine Arts,
gift of the Canadian Imperial Bank of
Commerce
Inv. 2001.184

111
Jean Paul Riopelle
Montreal 1923 – L'Isle-aux-Grues 2002
Avatac (quadriptych)
1971
Acrylic on lithographs mounted on canvas
160 x 448 cm
Galerie Maeght, Paris

112
Film still with Michael Arvaarluk Kusugak
from *Storytelling Night* (2008)
Performance at the Alianait Arts Festival
in Iqaluit, June 21–July 1, 2008

113
Cover of Guy Mary-Rousselière, *Les
jeux de ficelle des Arviligjuarmiut,*
Bulletin 233 (Ottawa: National Gallery
of Canada, 1969)
Collection of Huguette Vachon

114
Poster for the exhibition *Riopelle :
ficelles et autres jeux* presented by
the Canadian Cultural Centre and
the Musée d'art moderne de la Ville de
Paris, June 15–October 12, 1972
Canadian Cultural Centre, Paris

115
Luke Akuptangoak
? 1940 – Gjoa Haven, Nunavut, 1987
Hands with String Game (Beluga Whale)
1978
Stone, sinew
5.8 x 9.2 x 9 cm
Winnipeg Art Gallery, the Ian Lindsay
Collection, acquired with funds from the
Volunteer Committee to the Winnipeg
Art Gallery
Inv. G-85-405

116
Noah Arpatuq Echalook
Born in 1946, at an outpost camp on
Elsie Island, north of Inukjuak
Woman Playing a String Game
1987
Dark green stone, ivory, hide
26 x 39 x 24 cm
National Gallery of Canada, Ottawa,
purchased in 1991

117
Noah Arpatuq Echalook
Born in 1946, at an outpost camp on
Elsie Island, north of Inukjuak
The String Game
1986
Soapstone, sinew
18 x 15 x 13 cm
Canadian Museum of History, Gatineau
Inv. IV-B-1945

118
Pudlo Pudlat
Camp Kamadjuak, Baffin Island, 1916 –
Cape Dorset 1992
Untitled No. 13
1976
Watercolour and coloured pencil on paper
52 x 66 cm
Collection of the Canada Council Art Bank
Inv. ABBA 77/8-0620

119
Jean Paul Riopelle
Montreal 1923 – L'Isle-aux-Grues 2002
Plates. from the album *Parler de corde*
Pl. 3, *L'Indien*
Pl. 4, *Avion à flotteurs*
Pl. 8, *Le call*
Pl. 9, *Original*
1972
Lithographs, 10/75
46 x 32.1 cm (each)
The Montreal Museum of Fine Arts,
gift of Yvon M. Tardif, M.D.
2005.173.3, .4, .8, .9

120
Jean Paul Riopelle
Montreal 1923 – L'Isle-aux-Grues 2002
Avion à flotteurs
1971
Acrylic on the lithograph (*Suite Radisson*)
mounted on canvas
159.5 x 121 cm
Collection of Stephen Angers
Inv. 2216

121
Jean Paul Riopelle
Montreal 1923 – L'Isle-aux-Grues 2002
L'esprit de la ficelle (triptych)
1971
Acrylic on lithograph mounted on canvas
160 x 360 cm
Private collection

122
Jean Paul Riopelle
Montreal 1923 – L'Isle-aux-Grues 2002
Serge et Gauguin jouant à la ficelle
(triptych)
1971
Acrylic on lithographs mounted on paper
289 x 355 cm
Private collection

123
Jean Paul Riopelle
Montreal 1923 – L'Isle-aux-Grues 2002
Ménage à trois-Pistol (triptych)
1972
Acrylic on lithographs mounted on canvas
160 x 361 cm
Private collection

124
Jean Paul Riopelle
Montreal 1923 – L'Isle-aux-Grues 2002
Paysage
1971
Acrylic on lithograph mounted on canvas
160 x 120 cm
Collection of the Charest family

125
Jean Paul Riopelle
Montreal 1923 – L'Isle-aux-Grues 2002
Tyuk (triptych)
1971
Acrylic on lithographs mounted on canvas
160 x 440 cm
Collection of Jules Maeght
Inv. BAC 2487

126
Jean Paul Riopelle
Montreal 1923 – L'Isle-aux-Grues 2002
Rois de Thulé
1973
Mixed media on paper
67 x 44 cm
Private collection, Montreal

127
Henri Matisse
Le Cateau-Cambrésis, France, 1869 –
Nice 1954
Pls. 1, 2, 3, 9, 11, 16, 18, 20 of the series
of original lithograph illustrations (31
in total) in Georges Duthuit, *Une fête
en Cimmérie* (Paris: Tériade, 1963)
1948–49
27 x 21 cm (each)
The Global Affairs Canada – Visual Art
Collection, Ottawa

128
"Qingaruvdliaq, the woman who knew
all the men's songs and prompted
them when they forgot the words"
Ill. in Knud Rasmussen, *Across Arctic
America: Narrative of the Fifth Thule
Expedition* (New York; London: G. P.
Putnam's Sons, 1927), p. 92
The Montreal Museum of Fine Arts Library

129
"Native from Pelly Bay"
Ill. in Knud Rasmussen, *Across Arctic
America: Narrative of the Fifth Thule
Expedition* (New York; London: G. P.
Putnam's Sons, 1927), p. 164
The Montreal Museum of Fine Arts Library

130
"Tatilgaq, who described the Native
Methods of Hunting"
Ill. in Knud Rasmussen, *Across Arctic
America: Narrative of the Fifth Thule
Expedition* (New York; London: G. P.
Putnam's Sons, 1927), p. 77
The Montreal Museum of Fine Arts Library

131
Dorset
Antler with carved faces
N.d.
Caribou antler
11 x 7.3 x 1.9 cm
Itsanitaq Museum, Churchill, Manitoba
Inv. C45.1-325

132
Petroglyphs at Qajartalik, Nunavik
2004
Colour photograph
Avataq Cultural Institute

133
Cover of "The Eskimo World" issue
of *artscanada*, nos. 162–163
(December 1971–January 1972)
Private collection

134
Mattiusi Iyaituk
Born in a camp near Akulivik (Cape Smith)
in 1950
A Young Hunter's First Catch (I)
1979
Soapstone, caribou antler, walrus ivory
18 x 34 x 11 cm
La Fédération des coopératives du
Nouveau-Québec

135
Jean Paul Riopelle
Montreal 1923 – L'Isle-aux-Grues 2002
Untitled
From the series *Rois de Thulé*
1973
Acrylic and gouache on paper
59 x 49.2 cm
Musée national des beaux-arts
du Québec, don
Inv. 2007.22

136
Jean Paul Riopelle
Montreal 1923 – L'Isle-aux-Grues 2002
Untitled
1973
Gouache on paper
68 x 44 cm
Collection of Isabelle Maeght
Inv. BAC 1201

137
Jean Paul Riopelle
Montreal 1923 – L'Isle-aux-Grues 2002
Les rois de Thulé
1973
Mixed media on paper
66.4 x 43 cm
Collection of Galerie Simon Blais,
Montreal

138
Jean Paul Riopelle
Montreal 1923 – L'Isle-aux-Grues 2002
Les rois de Thulé
1973
Mixed media on paper
66.5 x 43 cm
Collection of Galerie Simon Blais,
Montreal

139
Jean Paul Riopelle
Montreal 1923 – L'Isle-aux-Grues 2002
Pls. *L, O, P, W-X*
From the series of illuminated letters
L'alphabet de Thulé
About 1979
Lithographs
44 x 31 cm (each)
Private collection

140
Jean Paul Riopelle
Montreal 1923 – L'Isle-aux-Grues 2002
Fonte
1973
Oil on canvas
200 x 300 cm
Collection of Jules Maeght
Inv. BAC 3705

141
Riopelle
Colour photograph
The Montreal Museum of Fine Arts
Library

142
Riopelle
Ill. in *Jean Paul Riopelle, Jean-Julien
Bourgault*, exh. cat. (Montmagny:
Théâtre de l'oie blanche, 1991) p. 30
The Montreal Museum of Fine Arts Library

143
Jean Paul Riopelle
Montreal 1923 – L'Isle-aux-Grues 2002
Cape tournante
About 1967
Oil on canvas
81 x 116 cm
Collection of the Charest family

144
Jean Paul Riopelle
Montreal 1923 – L'Isle-aux-Grues 2002
Sucker hole à Matagami
1973
Oil on canvas
87.5 x 127.5 cm
Musée d'art de Joliette, don de Paul
Ivanier
Inv. 1984.071

145
Jean Paul Riopelle
Montreal 1923 – L'Isle-aux-Grues 2002
Sainte Marguerite
1966
Oil on canvas
89 x 116 cm
Private collection

146
Jean Paul Riopelle
Montreal 1923 – L'Isle-aux-Grues 2002
Il a neigé sur Opinaca
1973
Oil on canvas
91 x 65 cm
Private collection, Paris

147
Jean Paul Riopelle
Montreal 1923 – L'Isle-aux-Grues 2002
Baie James
1973
Oil on canvas
81 x 100 cm
Private collection

148
Jean Paul Riopelle
Montreal 1923 – L'Isle-aux-Grues 2002
D'un long voyage (triptych)
1973
Oil on canvas
162.6 x 355.6 cm
Private collection

149
Jean Paul Riopelle
Montreal 1923 – L'Isle-aux-Grues 2002
Au-delà du 52ᵉ
1973
Oil on canvas
65 x 54 cm
Private collection

150
Jean Paul Riopelle
Montreal 1923 – L'Isle-aux-Grues 2002
Fort George
1975
Oil on canvas
73 x 60 cm
Private collection

151
Jean Paul Riopelle
Montreal 1923 – L'Isle-aux-Grues 2002
Iceland
1973
Oil on canvas
97 x 130 cm
Private collection

152
Jean Paul Riopelle
Montreal 1923 – L'Isle-aux-Grues 2002
De la grande baleine (triptych)
1973
Oil on canvas
200 x 424 cm
Private collection, France

153
Riopelle standing in front of *Micmac*
(1975)
About 1976
Colour photograph
Archives Yseult Riopelle

154
Unidentified person, Riopelle, Kenny
Brien (guide) and Louis Gosselin at the
camp of Vieux poste du lac Mistassini,
north of Chibougamau
About 1975–76
Colour photograph
Archives Yseult Riopelle

155
Jean Paul Riopelle
Montreal 1923 – L'Isle-aux-Grues 2002
Micmac (diptych)
1975
Oil on canvas
300 x 400 cm
Private collection, France

156
Jean Paul Riopelle
Montreal 1923 – L'Isle-aux-Grues 2002
Tête de boule 1, 2, 3 (triptych)
1974
Oil on canvas
l. to r.: 73 x 92 cm; 100 x 81 cm; 73 x 92 cm
Private collection

157
Jean Paul Riopelle
Montreal 1923 – L'Isle-aux-Grues 2002
Muscowequan
1976
Oil on canvas
300 x 200 cm
Collection of the Charest family

158
Jean Paul Riopelle
Montreal 1923 – L'Isle-aux-Grues 2002
Lac du Nord-Est
1975
Oil on canvas
200 x 300 cm
Private collection

159
Jean Paul Riopelle
Montreal 1923 – L'Isle-aux-Grues 2002
Mascouche
1975
Oil on canvas
200 x 300 cm
Collection Lune Rouge
Inv. 2008.035

160
Jean Paul Riopelle
Montreal 1923 – L'Isle-aux-Grues 2002
Mitchikanabikong (triptych)
1975
Oil on canvas
195.5 x 391.5 cm
Musée national d'art moderne – Centre
de création industrielle, Centre Pompidou,
Paris, don de M. Aimé Maeght, 1979
AM 1979-254

161
Claude Duthuit photograph of Riopelle
in Pangnirtung, Nunavut
July 1977
Black and white photograph
Archives Yseult Riopelle

162
Claude Duthuit photograph of
Champlain Charest in Pangnirtung,
Nunavut
July 1977
Black and white photograph
Archives Yseult Riopelle

163
Jean Paul Riopelle
Montreal 1923 – L'Isle-aux-Grues 2002
Pangnirtung (triptych)
1977
Oil on canvas
200 x 560 cm
Musée national des beaux-arts du Québec,
achat grâce à une contribution spéciale
de la Société des loteries du Québec
Inv. 1997.113

164
"Eskimo Hunt on the Arctic" (postcard)
Published by L. Lennox & Co., Calgary
Sent by Riopelle to Joan Mitchell in 1977
Inscription: "La pêche et la chasse
au milieu des plus belles sculptures du
monde, grande amitiée [sic], JP."
Joan Mitchell Foundation Archives,
New York

165
"The Arctic Walrus" (postcard)
Published by L. Lennox & Co., Calgary
Sent by Riopelle to Joan Mitchell in 1977
Inscription: "Pour avoir bien chaud,
un manteau de phoque ou de morse,
grande amitiée [sic], JPR"
Joan Mitchell Foundation Archives,
New York

166
"Crater Lake N.W.T." (postcard)
Published by Leigh Brintnell
Sent by Riopelle to Joan Mitchell in 1977
Inscription: "Il eu neiger [sic] et
la pêche était bonne à 'Pangnirtung',
Grande amitiée [sic] JP"
Joan Mitchell Foundation Archives,
New York

167
"The Arctic White Whale" (postcard)
Published by L. Lennox & Co., Calgary
Sent by Riopelle to Joan Mitchell in 1977
Inscription: "Tous ici pense [sic] que
tuer le bœuf pour manger est un scandle
[sic], grande amitiée [sic] riopelle"
Joan Mitchell Foundation Archives,
New York

168
"Pangnirtung Fiord" (postcard)
Published by Leigh Brintnell
Sent by Riopelle to Joan Mitchell in 1977
Inscription: "A gauche sur la carte
vestiges d'une citée [sic], du dernier des
rois de Thulé, grande amité [sic] JP"
Joan Mitchell Foundation Archives,
New York

169
Lawren S. Harris
Brantford, Ontario, 1885 – Vancouver
1970
Icebergs, Davis Strait
1930
Oil on canvas
121.9 x 152.4 cm
McMichael Canadian Art Collection,
gift of Mr. and Mrs. H. Spencer Clark
Inv. 1971.17

170
Champlain Charest and Riopelle
standing in the centre among fellow
travellers in the Arctic
July 1977
Colour photograph
Archives Yseult Riopelle

171
Jean Paul Riopelle
Montreal 1923 – L'Isle-aux-Grues 2002
Fontaine
About 1964–77
Painted plaster and ropes
400 x 300 x 300 cm
Private collection

172
Basil Zarov
Montreal 1905 (?) – Toronto 1998
*Jean Paul Riopelle in His Studio at
Sainte-Marguerite-du-Lac-Masson*
About 1978
Black and white photograph
Library and Archives Canada, Ottawa

173
Basil Zarov
Montreal 1905 (?) – Toronto 1998
*Jean Paul Riopelle in front of the
diptych "La ligne d'eau" in His Studio
at Sainte-Marguerite-du-Lac-Masson*
1978
Black and white photograph
Library and Archives Canada, Ottawa

174
Basil Zarov
Montreal 1905 (?) – Toronto 1998
*Inside Jean Paul Riopelle's Studio
at Sainte-Marguerite-du-Lac-Masson*
1978
Black and white photograph
Library and Archives Canada, Ottawa

175
Jacqueline Hyde
Berlin 1922 – Paris 2013
*Jean Paul Riopelle's studio at Saint-
Cyr-en-Arthies, France*
1978, print 2020
Black and white photograph
Archives Yseult Riopelle

176
Jean Paul Riopelle
Montreal 1923 – L'Isle-aux-Grues 2002
Cap au nord
1977
Oil on canvas
200 x 301 cm
Collection of Huguette Vachon

177
Jean Paul Riopelle
Montreal 1923 – L'Isle-aux-Grues 2002
Soleil de minuit (Quatuor en blanc)
(quadriptych)
1977
Oil on canvas
202 x 303 cm
The Montreal Museum of Fine Arts,
purchase, with a special grant from the
Government of Quebec
Inv. 2001.164.1-4

178
Jean Paul Riopelle
Montreal 1923 – L'Isle-aux-Grues 2002
Iceberg I
1977
Oil on canvas
280 x 430 cm
Private collection, Montreal

179
Jean Paul Riopelle
Montreal 1923 – L'Isle-aux-Grues 2002
Iceberg II
1977
Oil on canvas
200 x 310 cm
Private collection

180
Jean Paul Riopelle
Montreal 1923 – L'Isle-aux-Grues 2002
Iceberg VIII
1977
Oil on canvas
195 x 130 cm
Collection of Isabelle Maeght
Inv. BAC 2528

181
Jean Paul Riopelle
Montreal 1923 – L'Isle-aux-Grues 2002
Iceberg XI
1977
Oil on canvas
130 x 97 cm
Collection Yvon M. Tardif, M.D.

182
Jean Paul Riopelle
Montreal 1923 – L'Isle-aux-Grues 2002
Au pil de son masque
1978
Oil on canvas
116 x 89 cm
Private collection

183
Jean Paul Riopelle
Montreal 1923 – L'Isle-aux-Grues 2002
Rouge esquimaux (diptych)
1977
Oil on canvas
48.5 x 77.7 cm
Private collection

184
Jean Paul Riopelle
Montreal 1923 – L'Isle-aux-Grues 2002
Inuit
1977
Oil on canvas
82 x 101 cm
Collection of Charles Dutoit, Montreal

185
Jean Paul Riopelle
Montreal 1923 – L'Isle-aux-Grues 2002
Iceberg V
1977
Oil on canvas
200 x 260 cm
Power Corporation of Canada Collection

186
Beau Dick
Alert Bay, British Columbia, 1955 –
Vancouver 2017
Ghost
2012
Wood, vegetable fibre, feathers, paint
The Montreal Museum of Fine Arts,
gift of W. Bruce C. Bailey
Inv. 2019. 225

187
Georges Duthuit in front of two
masks in his collection that he loaned
to Riopelle
About 1950, print 2020
Black and white photograph
Archives Yseult Riopelle

188
Yseult and Sylvie Riopelle in the
apartment at 88 Rue Chardon-Lagache,
Paris XVI (on the wall, a mask loaned
by Georges Duthuit and Riopelle's
Pleine saison [1954])
1954
Black and white photograph
Archives Yseult Riopelle

189
Jean Paul Riopelle
Montreal 1923 – L'Isle-aux-Grues 2002
Bombée
About 1977
Silverpoint and ink on paper
25 x 32.5 cm
Private collection

190
Covers of vols. 1 and 2 of Claude Lévi-
Strauss, *La voie des masques : les
sentiers de la création* (Geneva: Albert
Skira, 1975)
The Montreal Museum of Fine Arts
Library

191
Film still from *Behind the Mask*
(1973)
Directed by Tom Shandel
National Film Board of Canada,
Montreal

192
Georges Duthuit, "Le don indien sur la
côte nord-ouest de l'Amérique
(Colombie britannique)," *Labyrinthe*,
no. 18 (April 1946), pp. 9–11
The Montreal Museum of Fine Arts
Library

193
Alison Bremner
Born in Juneau, Alaska, 1989
Ceremonial Wealth
2020
Copper, acrylic, ink
36.8 x 24.7 cm
Collection of the artist

194
Cover of Robert Bruce Inverarity,
Art of the Northwest Coast Indians
(Berkeley: University of California
Press, 1950)
Private collection

195
"Pyre and graves of the family of the
Cacique An-kau at Port Mulgrave, 1792"
Ill. in *Alrededor al mundo por las
corbetas Descubierta y Atrevida al
mando de los Capitanes de Navio
Don Alejandro Malaspina y Don José
de Bustamante y Guerra, desde 1789
a 1794* (Madrid: Don Pedro de Novo y
Colson, 1885)
Archives Yseult Riopelle

196
Ceremonial plate (Canadian Northwest
Coast, Kwakwaka'wakw)
Ill. in Georges Duthuit, "Le don indien
sur la côte nord-ouest de l'Amérique
(Colombie britannique)," *Labyrinthe*,
no. 18 (April 1946), p. 10
Archives Yseult Riopelle

197
Jean Paul Riopelle
Montreal 1923 – L'Isle-aux-Grues 2002
Masque de la côte Ouest
1977
Silverpoint on paper
32.5 x 25 cm
Private collection

198
Kwakwaka'wakw
Transformation mask formerly in the
collection of Georges Duthuit (detail)
N.d.
Black and white photograph
Archives Yseult Riopelle

199
Jean Paul Riopelle
Montreal 1923 – L'Isle-aux-Grues 2002
Sorcier II
1977
Silverpoint on paper
32.5 x 25 cm
Private collection

200
Shawn Hunt
Born in Vancouver in 1975
Transformation Mask
2017
Mixed media
Various dimensions
Collection of the artist, courtesy
of Equinox
Gallery, Vancouver

201
A collection of dance masks,
Anglican church parish hall, Alert Bay,
British Columbia
1922
Black and white photograph
Royal BC Museum, Victoria

202
Jean Paul Riopelle
Montreal 1923 – L'Isle-aux-Grues 2002
Suite II
1977
Silverpoint on paper
32.5 x 25 cm
Collection of Huguette Vachon

203
Jean Paul Riopelle
Montreal 1923 – L'Isle-aux-Grues 2002
Autre masque
1977
Silverpoint on paper
32.5 x 25 cm
Private collection

204
Totem at the tomb of a shaman
(Gilford Island, British Columbia,
Kwakwaka'wakw)
Ill. in Georges Duthuit, "Le don indien
sur la côte nord-ouest de l'Amérique
(Colombie britannique)," *Labyrinthe*,
no. 18 (April 1946), p. 10
Archives Yseult Riopelle

205
Kwakwaka'wakw
Eagle crest-figure formerly in the
collection of Georges Duthuit
N.d.
Black and white photograph
Archives Yseult Riopelle

206
Jean Paul Riopelle
Montreal 1923 – L'Isle-aux-Grues 2002
Potlach
1977
Silverpoint on paper
32.5 x 25 cm
Private collection

207
Jean Paul Riopelle
Montreal 1923 – L'Isle-aux-Grues 2002
Poisson
1977
Silverpoint on paper
32.5 x 25 cm
Private collection

208
Haida
Copper shield
N.d.
Black and white photograph
Archives Yseult Riopelle

209
Copy of a George Hunt photograph
of a Kwakwaka'wakw Hamatsa initiate
wearing hemlock boughs
1902
Black and white photograph
Archives Yseult Riopelle

210
Copy of a Carl Günther cabinet
photograph of Nuxalk (Bella Coola,
British Columbia) dancers wearing
Chilkat-style blankets and
Kwakwaka'wakw Galukwama
(Crooked Beak of Heaven) masks
About 1886
Black and white photograph
Archives Yseult Riopelle

211
Jean Paul Riopelle
Montreal 1923 – L'Isle-aux-Grues 2002
Mythologie
1977
Silverpoint on paper
32.5 x 25 cm
Collection of Huguette Vachon

212
Charlie George, Sr. (?)
British Columbia, Kwakwaka'wakw,
Tlatlasikwala
Mask
Before 1953
Wood, cedar bark, feather, rubber, fibre,
paint, metal, paper, plastic
26.8 x 29.2 x 84.3 cm
Museum of Anthropology, Vancouver
Inv. A6268

213
British Columbia, Kwakwaka'wakw
Mask
Cedar wood, paint, fibre, leather skin, metal
25.5 x 21.9 x 79.3 cm
Museum of Anthropology, Vancouver
Inv. A5304

214
British Columbia, Kwakwaka'wakw,
Dzawada'enuxw
Mask
About 1911
Wood, cedar bark, pigment, feather,
leather skin, fibre, metal
109.3 x 29.4 x 117.8 cm
Museum of Anthropology, Vancouver
Inv. A3538

215
Kwakwaka'wakw
Ceremonial rattle
Ill. in Claude Lévi-Strauss, *La voie des
masques : les sentiers de la création*,
vol. 1 (Geneva: Albert Skira, 1975), p. 81

216
Jean Paul Riopelle
Montreal 1923 – L'Isle-aux-Grues 2002
Sorcier III
1977
Silverpoint on paper
32.5 x 25 cm
Private collection

217
Jean Paul Riopelle
Montreal 1923 – L'Isle-aux-Grues 2002
Wolf
1977
Silverpoint on paper
32.5 x 25 cm
Collection of Huguette Vachon

218
Tlingit
Bone charm representing a wolf's head
N.d.
Bone, horsehair (?)
7 x 11 x 2 cm
Private collection

219
Jean Paul Riopelle
Montreal 1923 – L'Isle-aux-Grues 2002
Sorcier I
1977
Silverpoint on paper
32.5 x 25 cm
Private collection

220
Edward S. Curtis
Whitewater, Wisconsin, 1868 –
Los Angeles 1952
Tsunukwalahl-Qagyuhl
N.d.
Photoengraving
31.8 x 24 cm
The Montreal Museum of Fine
Arts Archives

221
Jean Paul Riopelle
Montreal 1923 – L'Isle-aux-Grues 2002
Du côté de chez Marius III
1977
Silverpoint on paper
32.5 x 25 cm
Private collection

222
Haida (?)
**Mask formerly in the
collection of Georges Duthuit**
N.d.
Black and white photograph
Archives Yseult Riopelle

223
Jean Paul Riopelle
Montreal 1923 – L'Isle-aux-Grues 2002
Du côté de chez Marius IV
1977
Silverpoint on paper
32.5 x 25 cm
Private collection

224
Jean Paul Riopelle
Montreal 1923 – L'Isle-aux-Grues 2002
Dans les processions
1977
Silverpoint on paper
32.5 x 25 cm
Collection of Huguette Vachon

225
Dzonokwa
**Mask formerly in the
collection of Georges Duthuit**
N.d.
Black and white photograph
Archives Yseult Riopelle

226
Haida
Mask
Ill. in Georges Duthuit, "Le don indien
sur la côte nord-ouest de l'Amérique
(Colombie britannique)," *Labyrinthe*,
no. 18
(April 1946), p. 11
Archives Yseult Riopelle

227
Jean Paul Riopelle
Montreal 1923 – L'Isle-aux-Grues 2002
Untitled
Pl. 15 from the album *Lied à Émile Nelligan*
1977–79
Lithograph, 59/75
56.1 x 76.3 cm
The Montreal Museum of Fine Arts,
gift of Dr. Serge Boucher
Inv. 2005.174.2

228
Inukshu, Povungnituk, the Arctic, Quebec
Ill. in Fred Bruemmer, *Seasons of
the Eskimo: A Vanishing Way of Life*
(Greenwich, Connecticut: New York
Graphic Society, 1971)
Courtesy Maud Bruemmer

229
Jean Paul Riopelle
Montreal 1923 – L'Isle-aux-Grues 2002
Untitled
Pl. 16 from the album *Lied à Émile Nelligan*
1977–79
Lithograph, 59/75
56.1 x 76.3 cm
The Montreal Museum of Fine Arts,
gift of Dr. Serge Boucher
Inv. 2005.174.1

230
Jean Paul Riopelle
Montreal 1923 – L'Isle-aux-Grues 2002
Untitled
Pl. 13 from the album *Lied à Émile Nelligan*
1977–79
Lithograph, 59/75
56.1 x 76.3 cm
The Montreal Museum of Fine Arts,
gift of Dr. Serge Boucher
Inv. 2005.174.4

231
Jean Paul Riopelle
Montreal 1923 – L'Isle-aux-Grues 2002
Untitled
Pl. 11 from the album *Lied à Émile Nelligan*
1977–79
Lithograph, 59/75
56.1 x 76.3 cm
The Montreal Museum of Fine Arts,
gift of Dr. Serge Boucher
Inv. 2005.174.7

232
Jean Paul Riopelle
Montreal 1923 – L'Isle-aux-Grues 2002
Untitled
Pl. 5 from the album *Lied à Émile Nelligan*
1977–79
Lithograph, 59/75
56.1 x 76.3 cm
The Montreal Museum of Fine Arts,
gift of Dr. Serge Boucher
Inv. 2005.174.12

233
Jean Paul Riopelle
Montreal 1923 – L'Isle-aux-Grues 2002
Untitled
Pl. 12 from the album *Lied à Émile Nelligan*
1977–79
Lithograph, 59/75
56.1 x 76.3 cm
The Montreal Museum of Fine Arts,
gift of Dr. Serge Boucher
Inv. 2005.174.5

234
**Carved and painted wooden helmet
embellished with hair (probably
Northwest Coast, Alaska, Tlingit)**
Ill. in Robert Bruce Inverarity, *Art of the
Northwest Coast Indians*
(Berkeley: University of California Press,
Berkeley, 1950), fig. 99
Museum of Anthropology at the University
of California, Berkeley

235
Northwest Coast, Alaska, Tlingit
Rattle
19th c.
Copper, painted wood, abalone shell, hair
27.3 x 14.5 cm
The Montreal Museum of Fine Arts,
purchase, gift of Dr. J. Douglas Morgan
Inv. 1950.51.Ab.13

236
Northwest Coast, Alaska, Tlingit
Dagger
About 1850
Copper, abalone shell, horn, leather
57.3 x 11 cm
The Montreal Museum of Fine Arts,
purchase, gift of F. Cleveland Morgan
Inv. 1956.Ab.1

237
Jean Paul Riopelle
Montreal 1923 – L'Isle-aux-Grues 2002
Untitled
Pl. 9 from the album *Lied à Émile Nelligan*
1977–79
Lithograph, 59/75
56.1 x 76.3 cm
The Montreal Museum of Fine Arts,
gift of Dr. Serge Boucher
Inv. 2005.174.8

238
**Dance mask representing a bear's face
(Northwest Coast of Alaska, Tlingit)**
Ill. in Robert Bruce Inverarity, *Art of the
Northwest Coast Indians*
(Berkeley: University of California Press,
1950), fig. 77
The Montreal Museum of Fine Arts Library

239
Jean Paul Riopelle
Montreal 1923 – L'Isle-aux-Grues 2002
Untitled
Pl. 1 from the album *Lied à Émile Nelligan*
1977–79
Lithograph, 59/75
56.1 x 76.3 cm
The Montreal Museum of Fine Arts,
gift of Dr. Serge Boucher
Inv. 2005.174.16

240
British Columbia, Northwest Coast,
Nuxalk, Kwakwaka'wakw
Piledriver head
About 400–1800
Stone
40 x 24.1 x 8.3 cm
Philadelphia Museum of Art, the Louise
and Walter Arensberg Collection, 1950

241
Jean Paul Riopelle
Montreal 1923 – L'Isle-aux-Grues 2002
Sorciers
1979
Lithograph, 16/75
48.6 x 58.4 cm
The Montreal Museum of Fine Arts,
gift of Yvon M. Tardif, M.D.
Inv. 2002.164

242
Jean Paul Riopelle
Montreal 1923 – L'Isle-aux-Grues 2002
Masques
1979
Lithograph, 13/75
48.5 x 58.2 cm
The Montreal Museum of Fine Arts,
gift of Yvon M. Tardif, M.D.
Inv. 2002.166

243
British Columbia, Kwakwaka'wakw,
Kwagu'l
Mask
Before 1900
Wood, metal, root, bear skin, graphite
mineral and cinnabar mineral
35.5 x 30.5 x 18 cm
Museum of Anthropology, Vancouver
Inv. A3637

244
Willie Seaweed (Kwakwaka'wakw,
Mamalilikala)
Blunden Harbour, British Columbia,
1873 – Blunden Harbour 1967
Xwexwe mask
Before 1952
Wood, paint, cotton fibre
32.5 x 23.7 x 15 cm
Museum of Anthropology, Vancouver
Inv. A4165

245
**Champlain Charest, Réjane Saint
Pierre Charest, Riopelle and an Air
France stewardess**
Early 1970s, print 2020
Black and white photograph
Archives Yseult Riopelle

246
Jean Paul Riopelle
Montreal 1923 – L'Isle-aux-Grues 2002
La Bolduc
1964
Oil on canvas
295.5 x 295.5 cm
Salle Wilfrid Pelletier, Place des Arts,
Montreal

247
Jean Paul Riopelle
Montreal 1923 – L'Isle-aux-Grues 2002
Untitled
About 1958
Oil on canvas
200 x 200 cm
Université de Montréal

248
Jean Paul Riopelle
Montreal 1923 – L'Isle-aux-Grues 2002
Le brûlé (triptych)
1974
Oil on canvas
81 x 173 cm
Collection of the Charest family

249
Riopelle at work in the studio at
Île-aux-Oies
1990
Colour photograph
Collection of Huguette Vachon

250
Inside the studio at Île-aux-Oies
1990
Colour photograph
Archives Yseult Riopelle

251
Riopelle and the hunting guide Gilles
Gagné
1990
Colour photograph
Archives Yseult Riopelle

252
Paul Rebeyrolle, unknown, Stanley
Cosgrove (?), Riopelle, unknown,
Champlain Charest, Jacques Lamy and
René Gagnon
About 1974–75, print 2020
Colour photograph
Collection of the Charest family

253
Champlain Charest and Riopelle
1970s
Colour photograph
Collection of the Charest family

254
Champlain Charest at Île-aux-Oies
Early 2000s
Colour photograph
Collection of the Charest family

255
Claude Duthuit photograph of Paul
Rebeyrolle, René Gagnon, Riopelle,
Stanley Cosgrove (?) and Champlain
Charest
About 1974–75
Colour photograph
The Montreal Museum of Fine Arts
Library

256
Film still showing Riopelle (about 1981)
at Île-aux-Oies from *Riopelle* (1982)
Directed by Marianne Feaver
and Pierre Letarte
National Film Board of Canada, Montreal

257
Champlain Charest hunting
Late 1980s–early 1990s
Colour photograph
Collection of the Charest family

258
Film still showing Champlain Charest
and his float plane (1970s) from *Marie
Saint Pierre se révèle* (2016)
Directed by Janice Zolf
National Film Board of Canada, Montreal

259
Riopelle and Champlain Charest
1970s
Colour photograph
Collection of the Charest family

260
Vincent Corriveau and Riopelle
1970s
Colour photograph
Collection of the Charest family

261
Jean Paul Riopelle
Montreal 1923 – L'Isle-aux-Grues 2002
Untitled
1981–83
10 lithographs with highlights
116.6 x 75 cm (each)
Art Gallery of Hamilton

262
Jean Paul Riopelle
Montreal 1923 – L'Isle-aux-Grues 2002
Piroche (quadriptych)
1976
Oil on canvas
203.3 x 549 cm
Collection Université de Sherbrooke
Inv. 77-0024

263
Jean Paul Riopelle
Montreal 1923 – L'Isle-aux-Grues 2002
Oies
1980–83
Mixed media on lithographs mounted
on canvas
137 x 148 cm
Collection of Huguette Vachon

264
Jean Paul Riopelle
Montreal 1923 – L'Isle-aux-Grues 2002
La Loi c'est l'oye
1972–83
Lithographs with highlights, mixed media
on paper (trial proofs for the album
"Cap Tourmente," 1983, and "Suite,"
1972) mounted on canvas
200 x 610 cm (11 panels assembled)
Beaverbrook Art Gallery, Fredericton,
gift of David and Audrey Loeb Ross
Inv. CONS2016.730

265
Jean Paul Riopelle
Montreal 1923 – L'Isle-aux-Grues 2002
Mi-Carême (recto) / *Merry go round*
(verso)
1990
Mixed media on panel
203 x 131.7 cm
The Montreal Museum of Fine Arts,
gift of Jean Paul Riopelle
Inv. 2001.160.1-2

266
Jean Paul Riopelle
Montreal 1923 – L'Isle-aux-Grues 2002
*Matinée au cap Tourmente –
Les Faisans dans la volière* (recto) /
L'Oie hélico (verso)
1990
Mixed media on panel
124.5 x 246.5 cm
The Montreal Museum of Fine Arts,
purchase, with a special grant from the
Government of Quebec
Inv. 2001.165.1-2

267
Jean Paul Riopelle
Montreal 1923 – L'Isle-aux-Grues 2002
Untitled (recto/verso)
1990
Mixed media on wood
202 x 81 cm
Art Gallery of Hamilton, gift of Irwing
Zucker, 1996

268
Jean Paul Riopelle
Montreal 1923 – L'Isle-aux-Grues 2002
Hommage à Duchamp (recto) /
Hommage à Maurice Richard (verso)
1990
Acrylic, oil, fluorescent paint, silver
metallic paint, gold metallic paint with
metal sequins on plywood
203.2 x 91.4 cm
Musée d'art contemporain de Montréal,
don de monsieur Maurice Richard
Inv. D 94 35 P 1

269
Jean Paul Riopelle
Montreal 1923 – L'Isle-aux-Grues 2002
Maple
1977
Oil on canvas
73 x 54 cm
Private collection, Sainte-Thérèse,
Quebec

270
Shawn Hunt
Born in Vancouver in 1975
Transformation Mask
2017
Mixed media
Various dimensions
Collection of the artist, courtesy of
Equinox Gallery, Vancouver

270
Shawn Hunt
in 1975
Transformation Mask
2017
Mixed media

COPYRIGHT
AND PHOTO CREDITS

All works by Jean Paul Riopelle: © Estate of Jean Paul Riopelle / SOCAN 2020

Courtesy Estate of Fred Bruemmer

© Estate of Beau Dick

Noah Arpatuq Echalook and Mattiusi Iyaituk: Fédération des coopératives du Nouveau-Québec

© Éliane Excoffier

© Bruno Massenet

© Succession H. Matisse / SOCAN (2020)

Pudlo Pudlat © Reproduced with the permission of Dorset Fine Arts

© Estate of Kay Sage / SOCAN (2020)

Archives catalogue raisonné Jean Paul Riopelle: 3, 5, 6, 19, 20, 56, 57, 60, 62, 63, 64, 65, 66, 74, 76, 77, 80, 84, 86, 87, 90, 91, 97, 103, 105, 107, 108, 109, 120, 121, 123, 124, 126, 137, 138, 143, 145, 146, 147, 148, 149, 150, 151, 152, 155, 156, 157, 160, 176, 181, 184, 185, 189, 197, 199, 202, 203, 206, 207, 211, 216, 217, 218, 219, 221, 223, 224, 246, 247, 248, 263, 267, 269

Archives catalogue raisonné Jean Paul Riopelle. Photo Vancouver Art Gallery, Trevor Mills: 61

Archives Yseult Riopelle: 8, 17, 21, 23, 24, 79, 100, 101, 153, 154, 170, 187, 188, 245, 250, 251, 252, 253

Photo Denise Colomb – Archives Yseult Riopelle: 1

Photo Dominique Darbois – Archives Yseult Riopelle: 205, 208, 225

Photo Claude Duthuit – Archives Yseult Riopelle: 10, 14, 161, 162

Photo Jacqueline Hyde – Archives Yseult Riopelle: 175

Photo probably by Jean Lespérance – Archives Yseult Riopelle: 81

Photo Rosie Rey – Archives Yseult Riopelle: 195, 196, 198, 204, 209, 210, 222, 226

Photo Sylvie Riopelle – Archives Yseult Riopelle: 82

Image courtesy Albright-Knox Art Gallery: 59

© Alianait Entertainment Group: 112

Applicat-Prazan, Paris: 43

Archive Photos / Getty Images: 53

Bibliothèque Kandinsky – MNAM – CCI – Centre Pompidou, Paris: 2, 18, 27, 29, 30, 31

Alison Bremner: 193

Brooklyn Museum: 58

Canadian Museum of History: 28, 33, 35, 117

Choses Vues, Paris / Rights reserved: 47

CNAP: 11

F.C.N.Q.: 134

© Photo Galerie Maeght, Paris: 111, 125, 136, 140, 180

Richard P. Goodbody, Inc. New York: 44

Anita Henry: 159

Heritage Image Partnership Ltd / Alamy Stock Photos: 131

Institut culturel Avataq. Photo Robert Fréchette: 132

François Lafrance: 262

Guy L'Heureux: 75

© Library and Archives Canada. Reproduced with the permission of Library and Archives Canada / e011435420: 114

© Library and Archives Canada. Reproduced with the permission of Library and Archives Canada/Basil Zarov fonds/e011205146: 15, 83, 93, 94, 172, 173, 174

Lianed Marcoleta, courtesy of the Winnipeg Art Gallery: 115

© McCord Museum: 68

The Montreal Museum of Fine Arts: 71, 110; Jean-François Brière: 102, 171; Denis Farley: 4, 85, 98, 139, 144, 177, 179, 183; Christine Guest: 12, 67, 69, 70, 88, 104, 106, 119, 178, 186, 220, 227, 229, 230, 231, 232, 233, 235, 236, 237, 239, 241, 242; Brian Merrett: 265, 266

Musée d'art contemporain de Montréal: 268

Digital Image © The Museum of Modern Art / Licensed by SCALA / Art Resource, New York: 78

Musée national des beaux-arts du Québec, Idra Labrie: 13, 163; Denis Legendre: 73, 135

© Musée du quai Branly-Jacques Chirac / Dist. RMN-Grand Palais / Art Resource, New York: 34, 49, 55

Produced and distributed by the National Film Board of Canada: 191, 256, 258

Photo National Gallery of Canada: 116

NMAI Services: 48

Kent Pell: 122, 158, 182

Philadelphia Museum of Art: The Louise and Walter Arensberg Collection, 1950: 240

Image courtesy of the Royal BC Museum and Archives: 201

c/o Kay Sage Catalogue Raisonné, New York: 45

Pamela Saunders: 200, 270

Roger Smith: 264

Courtesy of University of British Columbia Museum of Anthropology. Photo Kyla Bailey: 212, 213, 214, 243, 244

Cover: 177